LIVES OF THE WELSH SAINTS

LIVES OF
THE WELSH SAINTS

by

G. H. DOBLE

edited by

D. SIMON EVANS

CARDIFF
UNIVERSITY OF WALES PRESS
1971

© University of Wales, 1984

First edition 1971
Paperback edition 1984

British Library Cataloguing in Publication Data

Doble, G.H.
  Lives of the Welsh saints
  1. Saints, Welsh
  I. Title   II. Evans, D. Simon
  274.29   BX 4659.G7

  ISBN 0-7083-0870-8

Printed in Wales by
D. Brown and Sons Ltd.,
Cowbridge and Bridgend, Glamorgan

PREFACE

BY THE ARCHBISHOP OF WALES

It gives me much pleasure to write a short preface to this edition of Canon Doble's Lives of Five Welsh Saints. These appeared originally in different publications and for a long time have been very difficult to find. It seemed to me that such important and pioneering work in an obscure period of our history should be readily available to students and I was delighted when the University of Wales agreed with this view and undertook to put the five lives together in one volume. Canon Doble lived from 1880 to 1945 and for much of that period was a country priest in Cornwall. His particular interest was in the study of dedications of churches, place-names, and legends of saints, as providing important evidence of the life and work of Celtic saints, particularly in his native Cornwall. No fewer than forty-eight booklets on Cornish saints exist, of original and reliable scholarship. His researches of course revealed all kinds of links with Wales and Brittany, and this new volume makes available his work on Dyfrig, Illtud, Euddogwy (Oudoceus), Paul Aurelian and Teilo. Other Welsh saints may be studied in the four volumes of *The Saints of Cornwall*, published for the Dean and Chapter of Truro Cathedral.

The University of Wales Press has entrusted the editing of Canon Doble's Welsh Saints to the competent hands of Mr. D. Simon Evans, Head of the Department of Celtic Studies at Liverpool University, who has also written an introduction. As editor he has kept alterations in Canon Doble's text to a minimum, adding once or twice notes of his own, and references, where necessary, to works which have appeared since Doble's day.

Llys Esgob,
Llandaff, 1970.

CONTENTS

EDITORIAL NOTE

I am indebted to the Archbishop of Wales, Dr. Glyn Simon, who not only agreed to write a preface to this volume but also offered helpful criticisms of my introduction. This introduction was read also by my colleague, Dr. T. G. E. Powell of the University of Liverpool, whose advice and guidance on many matters has been eagerly sought during numerous informal discussions. The Rev. R. M. Catling of Beckenham, Kent, readily helped me with information I required regarding Doble's works. The copies of his works used for this edition were kindly lent by the Libraries of the University of Liverpool and of St. David's University College, Lampeter. I owe a special debt of gratitude to Mr. R. C. Rider and the staff of St. David's College Library for their constant help and consideration during the many hours I worked in their library. Further I must mention my son, Mr. Dafydd Huw Evans, who gave me considerable help with proof-reading, and Professor E. G. Bowen, Aberystwyth, who very kindly allowed me to read (with profit) in advance of publication his new and valuable book on the Celtic saints. Finally, there is my friend Dr. R. Brinley Jones of the University of Wales Press, who with his most pleasing blend of firmness and sympathy has made my task lighter (and his more arduous) than it would otherwise have been.

The late Canon Doble was a dedicated scholar, as anyone acquainted with his work on the saints well knows, and it has been a pleasure and a privilege to prepare this edition of his 'Welsh Saints'. His work is reproduced here with few changes and emendations. 'Dubricius' and 'Iltut' are allowed to remain, and have not been transformed into 'Dyfrig' and 'Illtud'. I have also left most other things unchanged, including his quotations where he quite often presents a very loose translation or even a paraphrase of the Latin original. Additions to his notes are preceded by an asterisk and closed by a square bracket.

D. Simon Evans

NOTE TO THE PAPERBACK EDITION

The years which have elapsed since Doble's *Lives of the Welsh Saints* first appeared as a single volume (in 1971) have witnessed further research and publication in the various fields with which he had been concerned. However, it has been possible in this second edition to introduce only a few minor changes and additions in the body of the work, and it must suffice to refer briefly here to some of the more relevant contributions which have appeared in the meantime. The following may be noted: Charles Thomas, *Britain and Ireland in Early Christian Times A.D. 400-800* (London, 1971); Melville Richards, 'Persons and Places of the Early Welsh Church' (WHR v. 1971, 333-49); Kathleen Hughes, *Early Christian Ireland: Introduction to the Sources* (1972); G.R.J. Jones, 'Post-Roman Wales' (*The Agrarian History of England and Wales* i. pt. 2, ed. H.P.R. Finberg, 1972, 283-382); Wendy Davies, '*Liber Landavensis*: Construction and Credibility' (*English Historical Review* lxxxviii. 1973, 335-51); Kathleen Hughes, 'The Welsh Latin Chronicles *Annales Cambriae* and Related Texts' (*Proceedings of the British Academy* lix. 1973, 3-28); Melville Richards, 'The "Lichfield" Gospels (Book of "Saint Chad")' (NLWJ xviii. 1973/4, 135-45); J.W. James, 'The Book of Llan Dav and Canon G.H. Doble' (Ib. xviii. 1973/4, 1-36); M. Winterbottom, 'The Preface of Gildas' *de Excidio*' (*Trans. Cymmr.* 1974/75, 277-87); Wendy Davies, 'Breint Teilo' (BBCS xxvi. 1975, 123-37); David N. Dumville, '"Nennius" and the *Historia Brittonum*' (*Studia Celtica* x/xi. 1975/6, 78-95); Molly Miller, 'Date-guessing and Pedigrees' (Ib. 96-109); D.P. Kirby, 'British Dynastic History in the Pre-Viking Period' (BBCS xxvii. 1976, 81-114); Charles Thomas, 'Imported Late Roman Mediterranean Pottery in Ireland and Western Britain: Chronology and Implications' (*Proceedings of the Royal Irish Academy* lxxvi. 1976, 245-55); *Inventory of Ancient Monuments in Wales and Monmouthshire Glamorgan* i. pts. 1 and 3 (1976); David Dumville, 'Sub-Roman Britain, History and Legend' (*History* lxii. 1977, 173-92); Molly Miller, 'Date-guessing and Dyfed' (*Studia Celtica* xii/xiii. 1977/8, 33-61); J.D. O'Sullivan, *The De Excidio of Gildas, Its Authenticity and Date* (Leiden, 1978); Wendy Davies, *The Llandaff Charters* (Aberystwyth, 1979); John Morris (ed. and trans.) *Nennius' British History and the Welsh Annals* (Phillimore, 1980); Wendy Davies, 'Property Rights and Property Claims in Welsh *Vitae* of the Eleventh Century' (*Hagiographie, cultures et societés*, ed. E. Patlagean and P. Riché, Paris, 1981, 515-33); Id., *Wales in the Early Middle Ages* (Leicester, 1982); Charles Thomas, 'The Irish Settlements in post-Roman Western Britain: a Survey of the Evidence' (*Journal of the Royal Institution of Cornwall* vi. 1972, 251-74); Myles Dillon, 'The Irish Settlements of Wales' (*Celtica* xii. 1977, 1-11). Dr. David Dumville is preparing a definitive edition of *Historia Brittonum*.

The University of Wales Press Board and the Editor of this volume wish to thank the Dean and Chapter of Truro Cathedral (who are reprinting Doble's works on the Cornish saints) for their kind permission to publish the works reprinted here.

OUR EARLY WELSH SAINTS AND HISTORY

D. Simon Evans

A N investigation into the lives and works of the Welsh (and
Celtic) saints takes us back to what may justifiably be
described as the most exciting and momentous period in the
history of our peoples within the Christian era. We return to
the fifth and sixth centuries, to the time when the seeds were
sown for the later growth and development of the different
cultures in this island. From the turmoil and convulsions of
these times there emerged new peoples, and new forms of life
and thought.

The beginning of the fifth century marks the end of the
so-called Roman period.[1] At that time, Britain, south of

---

[1] Thanks to the researches of many scholars, we now possess a clearer and
more detailed picture of Roman Britain. Indeed it is more fully known than
the period discussed here. The following works may be cited : F. Haver-
field, *The Romanization of Roman Britain* (ed. G. Macdonald, 4th ed.,
Oxford, 1923); F. Haverfield and G. Macdonald, *The Roman Occupation of
Britain* (Oxford, 1924); R. G. Collingwood, *The Archaeology of Roman Britain*
(London, 1930, new ed. 1968), *Roman Britain* (2nd ed., Oxford, 1934); R. G.
Collingwood and J. N. L. Myres, *Roman Britain and the English Settlements*
(2nd ed., Oxford, 1937); M. P. Charlesworth, *The Lost Province or the
Worth of Britain* (Cardiff, 1949); E. Birley, *Roman Britain and the Roman
Army* (Kendal, 1953); D. A. White, *Litus Saxonicum. The British Saxon
Shore in Scholarship and History* (University of Wisconsin, Madison, 1961);
I. A. Richmond (ed.), *Roman and Native in North Britain* (Edinburgh, 1958),
Roman Britain (2nd ed., London, 1963); J. M. C. Toynbee, *Art in Britain
under the Romans* (Oxford, 1964); A. R. Birley, *Life in Roman Britain* (London,
1964); A. L. F. Rivet, *Town and Country in Roman Britain* (2nd ed., London,
1964); A. H. M. Jones, *The Later Roman Empire*, 3 vols. (Oxford, 1964); P.
Salway, *The Frontier People of Roman Britain* (Cambridge, 1965); M. G. Jarret
and B. Dobson (ed.), *Britain and Rome* (Kendal, 1965); G. Webster and D. R.
Dudley, *The Roman Conquest of Britain* (London, 1965); R. G. Collingwood
and R. P. Wright, *The Roman Inscriptions of Britain* (Oxford, 1965);
C. Thomas (ed.), *Rural Settlement in Roman Britain* (Council for British
Archaeology. Research Report, No. 7, 1966); J. S. Wacher (ed.), *The
Civitas Capitals of Roman Britain* (Leicester, 1966); M. J. T. Lewis, *Temples
in Roman Britain* (Cambridge, 1966); S. Frere, *Britannia. A History of
Roman Britain* (London, 1967); J. Liversidge, *Britain in the Roman Empire*
(London, 1968); also Ordnance Survey, *Map of Roman Britain* (3rd ed.,
Chessington, 1956). Cf. further W. Bonser, *A Romano-British Bibliography
(55 B.C.-A.D.449)*, 2 vols. (Oxford, 1964).

1

Hadrian's Wall, was still a part of the Roman Empire.[2] The two main languages in use here were British, the native language of the Britons, and Latin, the official language of the Empire, while in parts of the west some Irish also must have been spoken. We know that Christianity had already been introduced into this remote province of the Empire, brought here by 'nameless saints'[3]; what we do not know for certain is the extent and firmness of its grip at the end of the Roman period, and later in sub-Roman times[4]. No doubt there had been instituted an episcopal system of some kind. We learn that three bishops (?or metropolitans) from Britain were present at the Council of Arles in 314[5]: these came from York, London, and Colchester (or perhaps Lincoln), and were accompanied by a presbyter and deacon. British bishops also attended the Councils of Sardica in 343 and of Rimini in 359.[6] There is evidence that the church in Britain (as in Gaul) at this time supported the Nicene faith in the controversy over Arianism.[7] There was, of course, contact and communication between Britain and Gaul.[8] Victricius of

---

[2] Originally one province, but divided by Severus into two, and later by Diocletian into four : *Britannia Prima, Britannia Secunda, Maxima Caesariensis* and *Flavia Caesariensis*. A fifth province, *Valentia*, was formed towards the end of the Roman period. But these divisions are not easy to identify.

[3] Cf. CEB 69, also ib. 77, where it is concluded that there were probably Christian congregations in Britain by about 180-200 A.D.

[4] On the subject of Christianity in Britain at an early period, see H. Zimmer, *The Celtic Church in Britain and Ireland*, trans. A. Meyer (London, 1902), 1-6; H. Williams, CEB 54-233; D. L. Gougaud, CCL 20-26; J. E. Lloyd, HW i. 102-10; N. K. Chadwick, ASECC 12-13; F. Haverfield, 'Early British Christianity' (*English Historical Review* xi. 417-30); 'Early Northumbrian Christianity and the Altars to the *Di Veteres*' (*Archaeologia Aeliana* 3rd series, xv. 22-43); J. M. C. Toynbee, 'Christianity in Roman Britain' (*Journal of the Brit. Archaeol. Assoc.* 3rd series, xvi. 1-24); W. H. C. Frend, 'Religion in Roman Britain in the Fourth Century A.D.' (ib. xviii. 1-18); CB 37-49; J. Wall, 'Christian Evidences in the Roman Period; the Northern Counties' (*Arch. Aeliana*, xliii. 201-25, xliv. 147-64).

[5] See CEB 141-2; also Mann, *Antiquity* xxxv. 316-20, Hanson, SPOC 31-32.

[6] Sulpicius Severus, *Historia Sacra* ii. c. 41 (*c.* 400 A.D.); translated by A. Roberts (Oxford, 1894).

[7] Cf. Haddan and Stubbs, *Councils* i. 7-9; H. Williams, CEB 155-66; L. Gougaud, CCL 22; A. W. Wade-Evans, *Welsh Christian Origins* (The Alden Press, Oxford, 1934), 20-22; N. K. Chadwick, *Yorkshire Celtic Studies* iii. 25-26, SEBC 201-2.

[8] N. K. Chadwick, SEBH 189-263. We must remember that this contact was never completely severed, despite the incursions and turmoils of the fifth and sixth centuries.

Rouen[9] paid a visit to Britain about 396. Germanus of Auxerre[10] came here in 429, and possibly later sometime in the 440s[11]. Patrick,[12] the apostle of the Irish, came from western Britain, and may well have received some of his training on the Continent. From Britain also possibly came Faustus,[13] abbot of Lerins in 433 and bishop of Riez in 462. He is the author of the well-known works, *De Gratia* and *De Spiritu Sancto* (condemned in 529 by the Council of Orange), clearly a man of daring and independent mind, a quality which seems to tally with the supposition that he was a son of Vortigern. Although Britain must have been affected by heretical tendencies, it appears that the leading men in this country mostly subscribed to 'orthodoxy' in teaching and in the system of ecclesiastical government. The British usurper, Maximus, who moved his troops to the Continent *c.* 383, has been described as a champion of orthodoxy.[14] Even as late as the fifth century the position in Britain and Ireland was probably similar to that on the Continent, notwithstanding the fact that direct Roman rule ceased early in the century. Indeed, we learn from the *Annales Cambriae* that the British church adopted the alteration in the mode of calculating Easter made in 455.[15] As for the impact of Christianity on Britain during the Roman period, it appears

[9] In a sermon (*De Laude Sanctorum*, PL xx. 443-4) preached about 396 he refers to a journey recently made to Britain. Cf. E. Vacandard, *St. Victrice évêque de Rouen* (Paris, 1909), 126-7; P. Grosjean, 'Notes d'hagiographie celtique' (AB lxiii. 94-100); J. Morris, 'The Dates of the Celtic Saints' (JTS xvii. 352-3).

[10] His mission was probably concerned with political as well as theological matters, and he may well have helped the Britons in their struggles against their enemies. We are here dealing with times when it may not always have been easy to distinguish between saint and soldier. He may have encountered the weak and treacherous Vortigern, whose political progress may not be unrelated to the sporadic outbreaks of Pelagianism. In the *lives* of British saints he is not infrequently referred to as a teacher and promoter of monasticism. Cf. N. K. Chadwick, PLECG 240-74; J. Evans, *Archaeologia Cantiana* lxxx. 175-85.

[11] In 444, according to Professor Thompson, AB lxxv. 135-8 : according to P. Grosjean (ib. 174-85), Germanus died 31 July, 445.

[12] Cf. D. A. Binchy, 'Patrick and his Biographers' (*Studia Hibernica* ii. 1-173); R. P. C. Hanson, *Saint Patrick: his Origins and Career* (Oxford, 1968).

[13] He may have come from Brittany. Cf. further N. K. Chadwick, PLECG 199-207.

[14] Cf. CEB 173-4.

[15] But cf. Hanson, SPOC 68-69.

that its influence had been strongest in the towns,[16] first apparently among the poorer inhabitants, but later among the higher strata of society also. Its effect on the villa community, and especially on the more native rural establishments of the Britons, must have been considerably slighter.[17]

Such, then, in general was the position around the year 400. If we look at the country some two hundred or two hundred and fifty years later, we encounter a totally different situation. By then Britain had long ceased to be a Roman province. Latin was no longer the official language. A completely new speech had been introduced, brought here from the Continent by Anglo-Saxon invaders and colonizers, who now held most of the country which later came to be known as England. These new occupants were as yet mostly pagan, little affected by the Christian religion. In the north, west and south-west of the country, the native Britons remained in possession. Here small kingdoms had been formed under energetic leaders or *tyranni*, who had, as it appears, restored their native language to a position of honour and dignity. But that language, like so much else, had undergone so radical and drastic a change since Roman times, that it can no longer be called British.

---

[16] For Gaul cf. ASECC 9, "The Gaulish Church was essentially an urban Church." W. H. C. Frend (op. cit. pp. 7-8) is of the opinion that "fourth century Christianity remained an official and somewhat extraneous worship which had still to make its impact on those who lived beyond the walls of town, fort, or villa." But Christianity may have penetrated into some at least of the remoter areas of Britain, even at an early period. We have the testimony of Tertullian, writing soon after 200 (in the *Lib. adversus Judaeos* c. 7, Migne, PL ii. 610) that parts of Britain not accessible to the Romans (*Britannorum inaccessa Romanis loca vero subdita*) had been christianized. However our evidence is generally far too meagre to warrant firm conclusions.

[17] Despite the advance and progress of disruptive forces at this time, there is in Britain, as in Gaul, clear evidence of intellectual and spiritual vitality and alertness among the Christian community. The active speculative thought of the heresiarch Pelagius could not have sprung from nothing : there is no evidence that he left Britain before he reached manhood (c. 380). Cf. J. B. Bury, 'The Origins of Pelagius' (*Hermathena* xiii. 26-35; A. Souter, *Pelagius' Expositions of Thirteen Epistles of St. Paul* (Cambridge, 1922); G. de Plinval, *Pélage, ses écrits, sa vie et sa réforme* (Lausanne, 1943); M. P. Charlesworth, *The Lost Province* 73; T. Ferguson, *Pelagius* (Cambridge, 1956); P. Grosjean, 'Notes d'hagiographie celtique' (AB lxxv. 206-11); J. N. L. Myres, 'Pelagius and the End of Roman Rule in Britain' (JRS l. 21-36); J. Morris, 'Pelagian Literature' (JTS new series, xvi. 26-60); R. P. C. Hanson, SPOC 35-46. The missions of Germanus were connected, at least in part, with the impact of his heresy on Britain : men like Severian, his son Agricola and other

Looked at thus from both ends, it is clear that here was a time of thorough transformation in all facets of life. And somewhere in this transformation must we look for our Welsh (and Celtic) saints, who contributed in no small measure to the new life and culture that emerged. We can, indeed we must, emphasize that this was a period of drastic change: our evidence warrants certainty regarding this. We can take a general view of the picture as it is presented to us, look at it from afar as it were, and discern with some clarity the main outlines. But when we come to examine this picture in closer detail, we find so much that is clouded in doubt and mystery. Here is a period that "lies outside the ordinary range of historians",[18] where precise and detailed knowledge, especially such as relates to the thoughts and actions of the individual, is almost impossible to come by. Small wonder perhaps, when we consider that our forbears had too much on their hands to be concerned with furnishing information for posterity.

It behoves us, therefore, first to review our sources[19] and the nature of the evidence, which may guide us as we seek to penetrate through the haze and hazards of this period. First, there are the literary sources.[20] St. Patrick has left us his

'enemies of grace' must have been proving troublesome. Cf. H. Williams, CEB 210; N. K. Chadwick, *Yorkshire Celtic Studies*, iii. 29-30; Pennar Davies, *Rhwng Chwedl a Chredo* (Caerdydd, 1966), 55-57. The heresy and the controversy it aroused seem to be relevant to the work and mission of the early Welsh saints, in as much as free will must be related to the conscious effort involved in the ascetic's life of self-discipline and self-restraint. We must also mention the work *De Vita Christiana* 'On the Christian Life', which was probably written in Britain and serves to illustrate the kind of piety that obtained here. It is addressed to a British woman, and may have been composed around 410 by 'Fastidius'; another work, *De Viduitate Servanda* 'On the Preserving of Widowhood', may be by the same author. See Migne, PL xl. 1031-46; R. S. T. Haslehurst, *The Works of Fastidius* (London, 1927). Cf. also R. F. Evans, 'Pelagius, Fastidius and the Pseudo-Augustinian *De Vita Christiana*' (JTS new series, xiii. 72-98); R. P. C. Hanson, SPOC 40-44. Later we have the works of Faustus, who may have hailed from Britain (or Brittany), v. supra.

We ought also to mention that towards the end of the fourth century there seem to be indications of a pagan revival. A great deal of paganism probably still persisted in both town and country at the end of the Roman period; see p. 43, n. 212.

[18] Haverfield and Macdonald, *The Roman Occupation of Britain* 261. Cf. J. Morris, 'The Dates of the Celtic Saints' (JTS new series, xvii. 342 ff.).

[19] I am in the main concerned here with such sources as relate to the history of the Britons and (later) of the Welsh.

[20] For sources relating to the history of the British Church, cf. A. W. Haddan

Letter to the Soldiers of Coroticus and his *Confession.*[21] The
De Excidio et Conquestu Britanniae[22] has been attributed to Gildas,
a British monk of the first half of the sixth century. This work, in
many ways more prophetic than historical, falls into two very
unequal parts. The one (*cc.* 2-26) offers a sketch of British
history during and after the Roman occupation. The other
(cc. 1, 27-110) is longer, and consists of a diatribe against the
people of the island and their temporal and spiritual rulers.[23]
The five rulers[24] castigated are all from the west, a circumstance
which arouses in us a suspicion that the author was blinded by an
aversion to the western or British areas generally. Two Welsh
penitentials,[25] one attributed to Gildas, the other to David, may
be assigned to the sixth century. The writings of Columbanus[26]
date from *c.* 590-615. In 731 that indefatigable English historian,
Bede, completed his great work on the history of the English
Church, namely the *Historia Ecclesiastica Gentis Anglorum*[27],
a valuable record by a scholar with a passion for accuracy, who,
nevertheless, cannot conceal an anti-Welsh bias! To the
beginning of the ninth century (a time of intense intellectual

and W. Stubbs, *Councils and Ecclesiastical Documents relating to Great Britain
and Ireland* i. (Oxford, 1869, reprinted 1965). Note also J. F. Kenney,
Sources for the Early History of Ireland (New York, 1929, rev. ed. L. Bieler,
1966). Cf. J. R. Morris, CB 55-73.

[21] Cf. SEBH 216-9. Edited by L. Bieler, *Libri Epistolarum Sancti Patricii
Episcopi* (Dublin, 1952), and translated by him (with a commentary) in
The Works of St Patrick (London, 1953). See also C. Mohrmann, *The Latin
of St Patrick* (Dublin, 1961); J. Ryan (ed.), *St Patrick* (Dublin, 1964);
R. P. C. Hanson, 'Assessment of the Sources' (SPOC 72-105).

[22] Ed. Th. Mommsen, *Mon. Hist. Germ., Chronica Minora* iii (1896); H.
Williams, *Gildae de Excidio Britanniae*, 2 vols. (Cymmrodorion Record
Series, No. 3, London, 1899, 1901). On St Gildas, see the article by
Mrs. N. K. Chadwick in *Scottish Gaelic Studies* vii. 122 ff.; also C. E.
Stevens, 'Gildas and the Civitates of Britain' (*English Hist. Review* lii.
193-203); 'Gildas Sapiens' (ib. lvi. 353-73). Cf. now ed. & trans. by M.
Winterbottom (1978).

[23] Cf. P. Grosjean in *Archivum Latinitatis Medii Aevi* xxv.155-87, and in *Celtica*
iii. 78-79; W. H. Davies, CB 138-42, 146-7 (refs.); F. Kerlouégan, ib. 151-
76.

[24] Cf. A. W. Wade-Evans, *Welsh Christian Origins* (The Alden Press, Oxford,
1934), 258-66.

[25] See *Gildas* ii. 272-88, and cf. L. Bieler, *The Irish Penitentials* (Dublin, 1963).

[26] G. S. M. Walker, *Sancti Columbani Opera* (Dublin, 1957).

[27] C. Plummer, *Venerabilis Baedae Opera Historica* (Oxford, 1896, reprinted
1961); A. Hamilton Thompson, *Bede, his Life, Times and Writings* (Oxford,
1935, reprinted New York, 1966). Translations are provided by Leo Sherley-
Price in the Penguin Classics L 42 (Harmondsworth, reprint, 1965), and by
J. Stevens (revised by J. A. Giles) in Everyman's Library, No. 479 (London,
1965).

activity throughout the Celtic lands) belongs that somewhat chaotic collection of documents, associated (at least in its final form) with the name of Nennius, and entitled *Historia Brittonum*[28]. Some of the material here, notably the section known as the 'Northern History and Saxon Genealogies' (cc. 57-65),[29] derives from an earlier period, in part probably from the seventh century. The *Anglo-Saxon Chronicle*[30], first compiled in the reign of King Alfred (871-99), but incorporating earlier material, gives the history of the Anglo-Saxons in a series of annals down to the Conquest (and later in some manuscripts). Early in the second half of the tenth century there was completed another chronicle, known as the *Annales Cambriae*[31], in which certain events in the history chiefly of the Britons, Welsh, Irish and English from 453/5 are recorded. These were probably originally compiled in the ninth century, but it has been argued

[28] Ed. Th. Mommsen, *Monumenta Germaniae Historica, Auctores Antiquissimi* xiii=*Chronica Minora Saec.* iv-viii, vol. 3 (Berlin, 1898, reprinted 1961). Also see H. Zimmer, *Nennius Vindicatus* (Berlin, 1893); F. Liebermann, 'Nennius the Author of the *Historia Brittonum*', in *Essays in Medieval History presented to Thomas Frederick Tout,* ed. Little and Powicke (Manchester, 1925), 25 ff.; F. Lot, *Nennius et l'Historia Brittonum* (Paris, 1934); A. W. Wade-Evans, *Nennius's History of the Britons* (London, 1938); H. M. Chadwick, *The Origin of the English Nation*, 38-53. Cf. also ZCP i. 157-68, xx. 97-137, 185-91; RC xv. 174-97, xvii. 1-5, xlix. 150-65, li. 1-31; AC sixth series, xvii. 87-122, 321-45, xviii. 199-262; *Cymmr.* ix. 141-51; BBCS vii. 380-9, xi. 43-48; LHEB 48; EWGT 5-8; SEBC 23-26, 37-46. It may have been compiled at Bangor Fawr in Arfon; cf. ib. 92.

[29] Cf. N. K. Chadwick in SEBC 58-73; K. H. Jackson in *Celt and Saxon* (Cambridge, 1963), 20-63.

[30] C. Plummer, *The Anglo-Saxon Chronicle: Two of the Saxon Chronicles Parallel,* based on an edition by J. Earle (2 vols. Oxford, 1892 and 1900), reprinted with bibliographical note by Dorothy Whitelock, 1952; G. N. Garmonsway, *The Anglo-Saxon Chronicle* (Everyman's Library, 1953, corrected edn. 1960)—a translation; D. Whitelock, with D. C. Douglas and S. I. Tucker, *The Anglo-Saxon Chronicle* (London, 1961).

[31] Ed. H. Petrie in *Monumenta Historica Britannica* i (London, 1848). The printed text was edited for the Rolls Series by J. W. ab Ithel (London 1860), a text (accompanied by variant readings) based on B.M. MS. Harleian 3859. The Harleian version was published by M. Egerton Phillimore in *Cymmr.* ix. 152-69, and readings from the two other mss for the period 1035-1093 are listed by J. E. Lloyd in *Trans. Cymmr.* 1899-1900, 166-79. See also H. Williams, CEB 404-16; J. Loth, *Les Mabinogion* ii. (Paris, 1913); E. W. B. Nicholson, 'The "Annales Cambriae" and their so-called "Exordium"' (ZCP viii. 121-50); J. Carney, *Studies in Irish Literature and History* (Dublin, 1955), 339-49, 371-3; N. K. Chadwick in SEBC 46-73; AS ECC 14; N. Tolstoy, *Trans. Cymmr.* (1964), 298-304. An English translation is rendered in A. W. Wade-Evans, *Nennius's History of the Britons* (London, 1938).

that use was made of a Cumbrian or Strathclyde document dating from the seventh.

Some information is contained in various other works to which we may refer, such as the Irish annals,[32] the *Catalogue of Irish Saints* (*Catalogus Sanctorum Hiberniae*)[33] compiled in the ninth or tenth century, and the *Cartulary of Landévennec*[34] written before 884 A.D. Letters from this period may also be consulted.[35] For example, we have the correspondence between Columbanus and Pope Gregory the Great (*c.* 595-600), where the problem of the Celtic Easter is first encountered.

A number of early pre-Norman *lives* of saints have survived.[36] Of these the earliest is the *Life* of the Welsh saint Samson of Dol,[37] written possibly sometime during the first half of the seventh century (?610-615). The author, or rather the compiler, of this *life* was a monk from Dol in Brittany. From Brittany also came the other early *lives* of Welsh saints, who, like Samson, worked in Brittany. The *Life* of Maclovius (St. Malo), a Welsh monk of the sixth century, was compiled *c.* 869 or 870 by a Breton named Bili.[38] Another Breton, Wrdisten, abbot of Landévennec, wrote the *Life* of St. Winwaloe (St. Guénolé) *c.* 880.[39] Next we have the *Life* of Paul Aurelian (St. Pol de Léon)

---

[32] The *Annals of Ulster*, *Annals of Tigernach*, *Annals of Innisfallen*, *Annals of Clonmacnoise*, *Annals of the Kingdom of Ireland by the Four Masters*, *Annals from the Book of Leinster*, also the *Chronicum Scotorum*. Cf. N. K. Chadwick, *Celtic Britain* (London, 1963), 169; Hanson, SPOC, 230; J. Morris, JTS new series, xviii. 343-5.

[33] See text and commentary by P. Grosjean, AB lxxiii. 197-213, 289-322.

[34] L. Maître et Paul de Berthou (ed.), *Cartulaire de Landévennec* (Paris, 1886).

[35] Letter-writing appears to have been quite common in Gaul in the late fourth and fifth century. But not only in Gaul : Britons abroad were writing letters to their families at home. Cf. O. M. Dalton, *The Letters of Sidonius*, 2 vols. (Oxford, 1915), G. S. M. Walker, *Sancti Columbani Opera* (1957); R. S. T. Haslehurst, *The Works of Fastidius* (London, 1927); and cf. N. K. Chadwick, PLECG 14-15; H. Williams, CEB 363-5.

[36] No doubt others (now lost) were written, some possibly as early as the seventh century, and some of their material may well have been incorporated in later *vitae*. Cf. N. K. Chadwick, ASECC 154-6; also B. Colgrave, 'The Earlier Saints' Lives written in England' (*Proceedings of the British Academy* xliv. 35-60).

[37] *Acta Sanctorum*, 6 July, 573 ff.; Dom. Plaine, AB vi. 77-150; R. Fawtier. *La Vie de saint Samson* (Paris 1912); T. Taylor, *The Life of St. Samson of Dol* (London, 1925). Cf. also J. Loth, RC xxxv. 269-300, xxxix. 301-33, xl. 1-50; F. C. Burkitt, 'St. Samson of Dol' (JTS xxvii (1926), 42-57; G. H. Doble, *St. Samson in Cornwall* (1935).

[38] F. Lot, *Mélanges d'histoire bretonne, vie-xie siècle* (Paris, 1907), 287-329.

[39] C. de Smedt, AB vii. 167-264. Cf. R. Latouche, *Mélanges d'histoire de*

by Wrmonoc in 884.[40] The *Life* of Gildas by Vitalis, written in Ruys in Brittany, also probably belongs to the ninth century : later we have a *life* of him composed by Caradog of Llancarfan, probably in the 1130s[41]. The *Life* of St. Brioc (*c.* 440-530)[42] was composed in the eleventh century. Another *life* apparently of Breton origin is that of Melanius.[43]

We must also mention certain other works and compilations of 'foreign' provenance, more especially Gallo-Roman works[44] from this period. Here we find not a few references relevant to our investigation, although in general the events of this period in Britain were little noticed by foreign chroniclers. From Sulpicius Severus,[45] the biographer of St. Martin of Tours, we learn much about certain aspects of life and thought in Gaul in the latter part of the fourth century. Further we may consult the poems of Claudian(395-400),[46] and the works of Orosius (417)[47] and of Sozomen (440).[48] Prosper Tiro of Aquitaine[49] in the first half of the fifth century has in his chronicles references to

Cornouaille (*Bibl. de l'École des Hautes Études*, cxcii, 1911), 1-39, and Appendice iii, pp. 97 ff.; R. Largillière, *Mélanges d'hagiographie bretonne* (Brest, 1925), 5, 15; G. H. Doble, SC ii. 59-108; J. R. Du Cleuziou, *Société d'Emulation des Côtes-du-Nord, Bulletins et Mémoires* lxxxviii. 29 ff., xciii. 7 ff.

40 Dom. Plaine, AB i. 208-58, cf. also ii. 191-4; Ch. Cuissard, RC v. 413-60. Also G. H. Doble, SC i. 10-60.

41 Th. Mommsen, *Mon. Germaniae Historica, Auctor. Antiquissimi* xiii. 107-10; H. Williams, *Gildas* (Cymmrodorion Record Series iii, 1899), ii. 317-413. Cf. SEBC 230.

42 Dom. Plaine, AB ii. 161-90, xxiii. 264 f.; Doble, CS iv. 67-104.

43 *Acta Sanctorum* (Bollandus, J.) Jan., tom. l. 327. For other *lives* cf. Tudual (ed. de la Borderie, Paris, 1887), Méen (ed. AB iii. 141 ff.), Magloire (ed. Mabillon), Conval (ed. André Oheix, Paris, 1911).

44 See N. K. Chadwick, PLECG.

45 His works have been edited by C. Helm, *Sulpicii Severi Libri qui Supersunt* (Vienna, 1866). See Migne, PL xx. 159 ff (*De Vita Martini*), ib. 146 ff. (*Historia Sacra*), ib. 175-84 (*Epistolae Tres*), ib. 185 ff. (*Dialogi*). See also N. K. Chadwick, PLECG 89-121.

46 Trans. M. Platnauer (Loeb Classical Library), 1922.

47 His seven books of history against the Pagans, *Historiae adversus Paganos* vii, ed. C. Zangemeister (Leipzig, 1889); Migne, PL xxxi.—Trans. Irving Woodworth Raymond, 1936, R. J. Deferrari, Washington (Catholic Un. of America), 1964.

48 His ecclesiastical history, *Historia Ecclesiastica* ix, ed. J. Bidez and G. C. Hansen (Berlin, 1960, Series *Griech. christl. Schrift.*). Select Library of Nicene and Post-Nicene Fathers, vol. ii, 1891.

49 Th. Mommsen, *Prosperi Tironis Epitoma Chronicon* in *Chronica Minora* i. (Berlin, 1892), 341 ff.; PL l. 535 ff. There are also his *Contra Collatorem* (PL li. 271 ff.), and his long poem *De Ingratis* written to oppose the semi-Pelagians.

Britain. To the third quarter of the fifth century belong the correspondence and verses of Sidonius Apollinaris.[50] Then we have Constantius's *Life* of St. Germanus,[51] which may have been written *c.* 480 or soon afterwards. Zosimus[52] wrote towards the end of the fifth century. Procopius of Caesarea (*c.* 550) in his history of Justinian's wars against the Goths in Italy interjected a chapter on Britain.[53] Valuable information is forthcoming from the inventory of officers and forces of the Empire at the beginning of the fifth century, a kind of government handbook known as the *Notitia Dignitatum*.[54] About 700 A.D. there was written at Ravenna a geography of the Roman Empire, known as the Ravenna Cosmography. The British section[55] appears to be derived from a fourth century source, and its relevance for our period is therefore slight.

The works enumerated above we may designate as 'historical'. They purport to record events from our period, while a few date from the period itself. Most of them, however, are later, but seem to have drawn at least some of their information from earlier works no longer extant. It need hardly be emphasized that they are not the productions of unbiased, critical historians : the information they offer is frequently patently inaccurate, especially in matters of detail, and great scrutiny and caution is required in sifting the evidence in them.

We may next refer to some other literary sources which

[50] *Epistula et Carmina*, ed. C. Luetjohaun, *Mon. Germ. Hist. Auct. Ant.* viii (Berlin, 1877, reprinted 1961)—Trans. O. M. Dalton, v. supra. The poems are translated by W. B. Anderson (Loeb Classical Library), 1936. See also C. E. Stevens, *Sidonius Apollinaris and his Age* (Oxford, 1933); N. K. Chadwick, PLECG 296-327.

[51] Two versions are extant. The shorter of these, and the better, is edited by W. Levison, *Mon. Germ. Hist.* : *Script. Rer. Merov.* vii (Berlin, 1920), 225 ff.—Trans. F. R. Hoare, *The Western Fathers* (London, 1954).

[52] *Historia Nova*, ed. Mendelssohn (Leipzig, 1887, reprinted Hildesheim, 1963). Trans. J. Davin, 1814. Cf. E. A. Thompson, 'Zosimus on the End of Roman Britain' (*Antiquity* xxx. 163-7).

[53] *De Bello Goethico* iv. c. 20. Trans. H. B. Dewing (Loeb Classical Library). Procopius, vol. v, p. 252 ff.

[54] Ed. O. Seeck (Berlin, 1876, reprint Frankfurt, 1962). See E. Birley, 'The Beaumont Inscription, the Notitia Dignitatum and the Garrison of Hadrian's Wall' (*Trans. of the Cumberland and Westmorland Ant. and Arch. Soc.* xxxix. 190 ff.), and C. E. Stevens, 'The British Sections of the "Notitia Dignitatum" ' (*Archaeological Journal* xcvii. 123-54); more recently A. H. M. Jones, *The Later Roman Empire* iii. 347-80.

[55] I. A. Richmond and O. G. S. Crawford, *The British Section of the Ravenna Cosmography* (Oxford, 1949).

demand even more intensive and searching scrutiny, but which, as is now generally conceded, also embody material for the historian to investigate. The mind and culture of the Britons and Welsh at an early stage[56] is reflected in the poetry of the Cynfeirdd, notably Aneirin[57] and Taliesin,[58] who lived in the latter part of the sixth century and who belonged to the old kingdoms of the North. There are also the Myrddin[59] and Llywarch Hen[60] cycles, which derive ultimately from about the same period. There are valuable clues in the Welsh genealogies.[61] The triads, more especially the Triads of the Isle of Britain, *Trioedd Ynys Prydein*, contain references which are of significance for our period, as Mrs. Rachel Bromwich demonstrates in a detailed and masterly work of scholarship.[62] We have the laws,[63] the sagas[64] and the early Welsh traditions regarding Arthur.[65] Nor can we discount as utterly spurious and worthless the *Historia Regum Britanniae* of the enigmatic Geoffrey of Monmouth.[66] In his work we may yet be able to recover some of the truth he has distorted.

[56] See R. Bromwich, 'The Character of the Early Welsh Tradition' in SEBH 83-136.

[57] I. Williams, *Canu Aneirin* (Caerdydd, 1938), and *Transactions of the Anglesey Antiquarian Society and Field Club* (1935), 25 ff; K. H. Jackson, *Antiquity* xiii. 25-34; *The Gododdin* (Edinburgh, 1969); C.A.Gresham, *Antiquity* xvi. 237-57.

[58] I. Williams, *Canu Taliesin* (Caerdydd, 1960), *The Poems of Taliesin*, ed. J. E. C. Williams (Dublin, 1968). Cf. also SEBC 76-79.

[59] A. O. H. Jarman, *The Legend of Merlin* (Cardiff, 1959).

[60] I. Williams, *The Poems of Llywarch Hen* (The Sir John Rhys Memorial Lecture, British Academy, 1932), *Canu Llywarch Hen* (Caerdydd, 1935), *Lectures on Early Welsh Poetry* (Dublin, 1944); G. Jones and T. J. Morgan, *The Saga of Llywarch the Old* (London ,1955); N. K. Chadwick, SEBC 86-90.

[61] F. Jones, 'An Approach to Welsh Genealogy' (*Trans. Cymmr.* 1948, 303-466); P. C. Bartrum, *Early Welsh Genealogical Tracts* (Cardiff, 1966). Cf. D. S. Evans, *A Grammar of Middle Welsh* (Dublin, 1964), xlii.

[62] R. Bromwich, *Trioedd Ynys Prydein* (Cardiff, 1961).

[63] Cf. H. D. Emanuel (ed.), *The Latin Texts of the Welsh Laws* (Cardiff, 1967); see pp. 523-30 for a detailed bibliography.

[64] Cf. T. Parry, *A History of Welsh Literature*, trans. H. I. Bell (Oxford, 1962), 69-84; G. Jones and T. Jones (trans.), *The Mabinogion* (Everyman's Library No. 97. London, 1949).

[65] See, for example, R. S. Loomis (ed.), *Arthurian Literature in the Middle Ages* (Oxford, 1959).

[66] See A. Griscom, *The Historia Regum Britanniae of Geoffrey of Monmouth* (London, New York, 1929); J. S. P. Tatlock, *The Legendary History of Britain* (Berkeley, Cal., 1950); J. Hammer, *Geoffrey of Monmouth, Historia Regum Britanniae* (Cambridge, Mass., 1951). Cf. S. Piggott, 'The Sources of Geoffrey of Monmouth' (*Antiquity* xv. 269-86, 305-19); also R. W. Hanning, *The Vision of History in Early Britain* (Columbia U.P., 1966), which discusses the historical ideas of Gildas, Nennius and Geoffrey.

In the twelfth century there were composed numerous *lives* of Welsh saints.[67] Towards the end of the eleventh century Rhigyfarch, son of bishop Sulien, wrote his *Life* of St. David.[68] About the same time (probably a little later) the *Life* of St. Cadog[69] was compiled by Lifris of Llancarfan, son of bishop Herewald. Norman clerks produced most of these *lives*, which thus testify to their interest in the pseudo-historical traditions of the Welsh. To the twelfth century belongs that fascinating compilation known as the *Liber Landavensis*[70] 'The Book of Llandaff', a work in the main originally inspired by the industry and devotion of Urban, bishop of Llandaff, and produced in order to assert the rights and privileges of the newly constituted see of Llandaff, often over territories claimed by Hereford, but more especially by St. David's. It also reflects the concern felt at the increasing interference and appropriation of property by the lay Norman conquerors.[71] Here we find the *lives* of saints like Dubricius, Teilo, Oudoceus,[72] who had become associated with Llandaff. It also contains the *Life* of St. Samson. One of the earliest and most comprehensive collection of saints' *lives* is found in the British Museum manuscript, Cotton Vespasian A

---

[67] Cf. S. Baring-Gould and J. Fisher, *The Lives of the British Saints* 4 vols. (Cymmrodorion Society, 1907-13); A. W. Wade-Evans, *Vitae Sanctorum Britanniae et Genealogiae* (Cardiff, 1944).

[68] A. W. Wade-Evans, *Life of St. David* (London, 1923); D. S. Evans, *Buched Dewi* (2nd ed. Caerdydd, 1965); N. K. Chadwick, 'Intellectual Life in West Wales in the Last Days of the Celtic Church' (SEBC 121-82); J. E. C. Williams, 'Buchedd Dewi' (*Llên Cymru*, v. 105-18); J. W. James, *Rhigyfarch's Life of St. David* (Cardiff, 1967).

[69] VSBG 24-141. See H. D. Emanuel, 'An Analysis of the Composition of the "Vita Cadoci"' (NLWJ vii. 217-27), 'Beneventa Civitas' (*Journ. Hist. Soc. of the Church in Wales* iii. 54-63); C. Brooke, 'St. Peter of Gloucester and St. Cadoc of Llancarfan' (*Celt and Saxon* Cambridge, 1963, pp. 283-322). Also Doble, SC iv. 55-66.

[70] For a description of the manuscript and its contents, see E. D. Jones, 'The Book of Llandaff' (NLWJ iv. 123-57). Also Dr. J. Conway Davies, *Episcopal Acts relating to Welsh Dioceses, 1066-1272* (Cardiff, 1946) i. 147-90. See further Professor Christopher Brooke's analysis in SEBC 201-42, where a good case is presented for attributing its compilation to Caradog of Llancarfan; and cf. J. W. James, JHSCW viii. 5-14, ix. 5-22, *Trans. Cymmr.* (1963), 82-95.

[71] Urban also lays claim to his *ecclesiae propriae*, including such as were outside the boundaries fixed for his diocese. Cf. J. Conway Davies, op. cit.; also *Llên Cymru* vii. 156. Note Mr. Ceri Lewis's important articles in *Llên Cymru* vii. 46-62, 125-71, *Morgannwg* iv. 50-65.

[72] BLD 68-86, 97-129, 130-60.

xiv,[73] a manuscript somewhat haphazardly compiled around 1200 A.D. by the monks of Brecon or Monmouth priory.[74] This collection contains the *lives* of most of the important Welsh saints, including Gwynllyw, Cadog, Illtud, Teilo, David, Dubricius, Brynach, Padarn, Clydog, Cybi, Tatheus, Carannog. The *Life* of St. Winifred is found in the British Museum MS. Claudius A v (xii-xiii centuries), the Welsh *Life* of St. Beuno in Jesus College MS. 119 (xiv century)[75], the *Life* of Collen in Hafod MS. 19 (1536) and in Llansteffan MS. 34 (end of xvi century), which also contains the *Life* of ? Llawddog.[76] Finally, we must mention *lives* of other saints (mostly Irish) such as Aidan,[77] Brendan,[78] Finnian,[79] Congall[80] and Kentigern,[81] all of which are of some relevance to our study.

It is hardly necessary to dwell here on the value and significance of these *lives*. We may regard them as religious romances or novels, and as is generally agreed, they were written to enhance the cause of a church or *parochia*, whose freedom and independence was not infrequently threatened at this time. In no sense are they 'historical'; indeed they have more to offer the student of social anthropology and primitive religion.

---

[73] Some of the *Lives* are printed by W. T. Rees in *Lives of the Cambro-British Saints* (London, 1853), an edition teeming with errors; see *Cymmr*. xiii. 76-96. They are printed also in VSBG (for a description of the manuscript, see pp. viii-xi). See S. M. Harris, *Journal of the Historical Society of the Church in Wales* iii. 3-53, for a study and edition of the kalendar in the manuscript.

[74] Cf. 'Vespasian A xiv' (AC ci. 91-104), presidential address by the Lord Bishop of Swansea and Brecon. The manuscript is discussed by Kathleen Hughes in SEBC 183-200 : "Until further evidence is produced it seems likely that Mr. Harris is right in claiming the Monmouth monks as the actual compilers of the manuscript." (ib. 197).

[75] Both printed in VSBG : Beuno, pp. 16-22; Winifred, pp. 288-308.

[76] See S. Baring-Gould and J. Fisher, LBS iv. 375, 426.

[77] VSH ii. 141-63, 295-311.

[78] VSH i. 98-151.

[79] Cols.189-210'of *Acta Sanct.Hib.ex Cod.Salmanticensi* (Edinburgh,1888—more recently W. W. Heist, 1965); also W. Stokes, *Lives of Saints from the Book of Lismore* (Oxford, 1890), 222-30. Cf. K. Hughes, *English Hist. Rev.* lxix 351-72.

[80] VSH ii. 3-21.

[81] See K. H. Jackson, SEBC 273-357. Edited from B. M. MS. Cotton Titus A xix, by A. P. Forbes in *The Lives of S. Ninian and S. Kentigern* (Edinburgh, 1874), 243-52.

Much of what they contain is pure imagination, mingled and blended with myth, folklore and legend.[82] But, as Doble reminds us, "Legend is history, in the sense that the legends and traditions of a people are part of its history." These *lives*, all too often cumbered with vague and irritating generalities and vitiated by a spirit of encomium, must, however, at times echo historical events and movements. They contain useful clues for further enquiry, and investigation by a competent scholar might well elicit from them valid and valuable information. Here we must, of course, mention the important work done on the *lives* of the Welsh and Cornish saints by scholars like the Rev. A. W. Wade-Evans[83] and Canon G. H. Doble.[84]

Finally, there are cartularies, liturgical books, martyrologies and other hagiographical material, all of which must be investigated.

Such then, in brief, are our literary sources. As we have noted, they are not all of equal value and importance, and even when it is all added up, the sum total of their evidence amounts to very little. On so many questions the written record is mute. Consequently we must have recourse to other kinds of sources. And other sources are now available, thanks to the marked progress made in various fields, more especially during the present century. It is not always easy, however, to take full advantage of such progress, as these disciplines cannot all be tethered within the competence of a single scholar. Certainly one of the most important of these disciplines is that of the archaeologist.[85] The value of his contribution is undeniable, and we can refer to the studies of scholars such as Mortimer

---

[82] For a general account of hagiography, see René Aigrain, *L'Hagiographie: ses sources, ses méthodes, son histoire* (Paris, 1953); H. Delehaye, *The Legends of the Saints*, trans. D. Attwater (London, 1962).

[83] Note for example his *Life of St. David* (v. supra), and his *Vitae Sanctorum Britanniae et Genealogiae* (VSBG).

[84] Especially the 'Cornish Saints' series, Nos. 1-48. Thirty-eight of these have been reprinted in the four volumes of *The Saints of Cornwall* (Truro, 1960, 1962, 1964, 1965), edited by D. Attwater. Two more volumes remain to be published. Also his 'Welsh Saints' series, reprinted here.

[85] For the history of Welsh archaeology, see R. E. M. Wheeler, *Wales and Archaeology* (The Sir Rhys Memorial Lecture, British Museum, 1929); V. E. Nash-Williams (ed.), *A Hundred Years of Welsh Archaeology* (Cardiff, 1946), 105-28; G. E. Daniel, *Who are the Welsh?* (The Sir John Rhys Memorial Lecture, British Museum, 1954); also I. Ll. Foster and Glyn Daniel (ed.), *Prehistoric and Early Wales* (London, 1965), 1-15.

Wheeler,[86] Cyril Fox,[87] E. T. Leeds,[88] V. E. Nash-Willams,[89] C. A. Ralegh Radford,[90] Leslie Alcock, H. N. Savory, and others.[91] The archaeological material for this period on the British side is sadly lacking in variety. It consists mainly (but not exclusively) of stone monuments (inscribed and sculptured), which furnish valuable evidence, especially for a study of the introduction of Christianity into western areas. The most inclusive corpus of Celtic inscriptions published this century is the *Corpus Inscriptionum Insularum Celticarum* by R. A. S. Macalister (Dublin, 2 vols, 1945, 1949). In this work all the Celtic inscriptions of the British Isles down to about 1200 A.D. and later are included. Excavations such as those being currently carried out at Cadbury Castle in Somerset promise to uncover valuable information. Another discipline is that of historical geography,[92] where the geographer brings his evidence to the historian's aid, as Professor E.G. Bowen has done in his important studies on the settlements of the Celtic saints and their distribution patterns.[93] We may also mention the researches of other

[86] 'Roman and Native in Wales : an Imperial Frontier Problem' (*Trans. Cymmr.* 1920-21, 40-96), 'Segontium and the Roman Occupation of Wales' (ib. xxxiii. 1-186), *Prehistoric and Roman Wales* (Oxford, 1925), *London in Roman Times* (1930), *Rome beyond the Imperial Frontier* (London, 1955), *The Hill Forts of Northern France*, with K. M. Richardson (London, 1957).

[87] *The Archaeology of the Cambridge Region* (Cambridge, 1923), *The Boundary Line of Cymru* (The Sir John Rhys Memorial Lecture, British Museum, 1941), *The Personality of Britain* (4th ed. Cardiff, 1959), *Offa's Dyke* (Oxford, 1955). See further CE 503-12.

[88] *The Archaeology of the Anglo-Saxon Settlements* (1913), *Celtic Ornament in the British Isles down to A.D.700* (Oxford, 1933).

[89] *The Roman Legionary Fortress at Caerlleon, Monmouthshire* (2nd ed. Cardiff, 1946), 'Topographical List of Roman Remains found in South Wales' (BBCS iv. 246-71), 'Some Dated Monuments of the "Dark Ages" in Wales' (AC xciii. 31-56), 'The Medieval Settlement at Llantwit Major, Glamorganshire' (BBCS xiv. 313-33). Also *The Early Christian Monuments of Wales* (ECMW), and *The Roman Frontier in Wales* (Cardiff, 1954).

[90] E.g. 'The Early Christian Monuments of Scotland' (*Antiquity* xvi. 1942), 'The Celtic Monastery in Britain' (AC cxi. 1-24), 'The Cultural Relations of the Early Celtic World' (*Proceedings of the International Congress of Celtic Studies*. Cardiff, 1963, pp. 3-27).

[91] See PEW 208-11 for a bibliography of the more recent contributions relating more especially to Wales; also A. Fox, *South West England* (London, 1964), ch. ix. Cf. also WHR iii. 249.

[92] For England cf. S. W. Wooldridge and E. Ekwall, *A Historical Geography of England before A.D. 1800* (Cambridge, 1936.).

[93] Note especially *The Settlements of the Celtic Saints in Wales* (SCSW), and *Saints, Seaways and Settlements in the Celtic Lands* (SSSCL). Also articles: 'The Travels of the Celtic Saints' (*Antiquity* xviii. 16-28), 'The Settlements of the Celtic Saints in South Wales' (ib. xix. 175-86),

scholars, such as Professor Emrys Jones[94] and Mr. G. R. J. Jones.[95] The systematic and scientific study of place-names can shed considerable light on social and cultural conditions in the past.[96] In England the Place-name Society has already produced an impressive array of county surveys: we must also mention E. Ekwall's *Concise Oxford Dictionary of English Place-names* (4th ed. Oxford, 1960);[97] and especially his *English River-names* (Oxford, 1928). Further there is that massive work of Max Förster, *Der Flussname Themse und seine Sippe* (Munich, 1942). For Wales we must mention works like J. Lloyd-Jones, *Enwau Lleoedd Sir Gaernarfon* (Caerdydd, 1928), B. G. Charles, *Non-Celtic Place-names in Wales* (London, 1938), R. J. Thomas, *Enwau Afonydd a Nentydd Cymru* i (Caerdydd, 1938), Ellis Davies, *Flintshire Place-names* (Cardiff, 1959), Gwynedd O. Pierce, *The Place-names of Dinas Powys Hundred* (Cardiff, 1968), and the projected study of Professor Melville Richards promises to furnish us with very full and detailed knowledge in the domain of Welsh toponomy generally. We are reminded of the comment of that great Celtic scholar, M. Joseph Loth[98] (more than once referred to by Doble in his works): "In Wales,

'The Saints of Gwynedd' (*Trans. Caern. Hist. Soc.* ix. 1-15), 'The Celtic Saints in Cardiganshire' (*Ceredigion* i. 3-17), 'The Cult of Dewi Sant at Llanddewibrefi' (ib. ii. 61-65), 'The Churches of Mount and Verwig' (ib. ii. 202-5). Cf. also *Wales : a Physical, Historical and Regional Geography* (reprint. London, 1965), *Daearyddiaeth Cymru fel Cefndir i'w Hanes* (Llundain, B.B.C., 1964).

[94] E.g. 'Settlement Patterns in the Middle Teifi Valley' (*Geography*, No. 150, vol. xxx, pt. 4 (1945), p. 109), 'Some Aspects of the Study of Settlement in Britain' (*The Advancement of Science*, No. 29, vol. iii (1951), p. 12).

[95] 'Basic Patterns of Rural Settlement in North Wales' (*Inst. of British Geographers Transactions*, No. 19, 1953), 'Medieval Settlement in Anglesey' (*Trans. Anglesey Antiq. Soc. and Field Club*, 1955, 27-96), 'The Site of Llys Aberffraw' (ib. 1957), 'The Tribal System in Wales : A Re-assessment in the Light of Settlement Studies' (WHR i. 111-32), 'The Pattern of Settlement in the Welsh Border' (*Agricultural History Review* viii. 66-81), 'Settlement Patterns in Anglo-Saxon England' (*Antiquity* xxxv. 221-32), 'Early Settlement in Arfon; the Setting of Tre'r Ceiri' (*Trans. Caern. Hist. Soc.* 1963, 11-17), 'The Distribution of Bond Settlements in North-West Wales' (WHR ii. 19-36). Cf. BBCS xx. 142.

[96] Cf. F. M. Stenton, 'The Historical Bearing of Place-Name Studies' (*Trans. Royal Hist. Soc.* xxi-xxv, 1939-43); F. T. Wainright, *Archaeology and Place-names in the Period A.D. 400-1100* (London, 1962).

[97] Cf. also A. H. Smith, *English Place-name Elements*, 2 vols. (Cambridge, 1956); P. H. Reaney, *The Origin of English Place-names* (London, 1960); K. Cameron, *English Place-names* (London, 1961).

[98] See J. Loth, *Les Noms des saints bretons* (Paris, 1910).

Cornwall and Brittany, it is not the 'Lives' of the saints that tell us most about the existence of the saints and the national organisation of religion, but the names of places". The linguistic scholar has a significant contribution to make, as has been shown, for example, by Professor Kenneth Jackson in his *Language and History in Early Britain*. The study of folklore and oral tradition, as enshrined in the work of poets, genealogists and story-tellers, is another avenue which we may explore in our search for light on an obscure past.[99]

With the evidence at our disposal from both literary and other sources,[100] what can we learn about the movements and changes of these two centuries? A knowledge of these movements could help us to understand and assess the contribution of the Welsh saints. The most suitable starting-point for such an investigation appears to be the general division of Britain into two main zones, a division based on physiography and offered primarily by geographers, geologists and archaeologists. The two zones, designated as highland and lowland, differ in the general character of the landscape, of the soil, of climate, etc., and also in certain basic aspects of life and culture, both material and spiritual.[101] The highland zone consists of three parts; the whole of Scotland and a large part of northern England within a line drawn from Lancaster round the edge of the Pennines by way of Manchester, Derby and Sheffield, to reach the sea near the mouth of the Tees, Wales (except for the south-east) and the marches, and the Devon-Cornwall peninsula in south-west

[99] Cf. p.11. Here we may also mention the study of well-cults, for which there is ample material of various kinds. One of the subjects that can be of value in this kind of investigation is the distribution pattern of wells dedicated to saints. Cf. the highly interesting and valuable study of Francis Jones in *The Holy Wells of Wales* (Cardiff, 1954).

[100] The sources described above offer little evidence regarding beliefs, ideas and doctrines. Little (if any) information can we recover about individuals, especially about the events of a person's life. Fixing chronology is difficult, if not impossible. On the whole, we must be content with fairly general, but nevertheless reliable, information regarding tendencies and movements, and we certainly learn more about the material and physical than about the intellectual and spiritual aspects of life and culture.

[101] See Sir Cyril Fox, *The Personality of Britain*, for a classic exposition of this division. Cf. also Collingwood and Myers, RBES 1-4; and more recently Bowen (SSSCL 29-30), who calls attention to a division of Britain into *three* major culture areas posited by A. Downes. One of these, namely the Outer area, broadly corresponds to Fox's highland zone.

England. The lowland zone is by contrast undivided: it comprises the midlands, and the south and east of England as far north as north Yorkshire. While such a division should in no wise be regarded as absolute, it does serve as a valuable basis for understanding some of the more important trends in the history of Britain at all periods. The lowland zone generally first feels the impact of new movements and influences: here communications have always been comparatively easy. It is the richer part where most of the people live. The highland zone is poorer, is less attractive to invaders or immigrants, and is the more stubborn to resist change. The new is not excluded, but seldom does it completely supersede the old. What usually happens is assimilation and compromise, a blend of old and new, resulting in a permanence and continuity of culture, and a feeling for tradition and ancestry which has always been a marked feature of the life of these parts. In a gradual process of change the old has always a chance of survival, but usually in a modified form.

Now let us look a little closer at Britain at the beginning of our period.[102] It is estimated that Roman Britain had a population of about one million.[103] Large areas were, of course, uninhabited, while others were very sparsely populated. Most of the people lived in the south-east, but there were also well-populated areas in the Thames valley and in that part of the country broadly coextensive with modern Gloucestershire.

In the lowland zone Roman law and administration had been dominant for over three centuries. Here Roman life and culture had exerted a deep influence, and as has been observed, the Christian religion had been introduced. It is here that we find the Romano-British towns and urban centres (the *coloniae* and *municipia*, and also the *vici*),[104] and the flourishing romanized establishments or villas of the countryside.[105] Latin was, of

---

[102] Such appraisal must appear to be, for the most part, crude and uncritical. This is inevitable in a brief and concise statement of the evidence acquired from the different sources.

[103] RBES 180.

[104] Cf. A. R. Birley, 'Town Life' in *Life in Roman Britain* (London, 1964), 57-77; G. C. Boon, *Roman Silchester* (Max Parrish, 1957).

[105] Cf. Birley, op. cit. 78-99; A. L. F. Rivet, *Town and Country in Roman Britain* (2nd ed. London, 1964), 105-10; J. S. Wacher (ed.), *The Civitas Capitals of Roman Britain* (Leicester, 1966); C. E. Stevens in *Council for Brit. Arch. Res. Report* 7, 1966, 108-28; A. L. F. Rivet (ed.), *The Roman Villa in Britain* (London, 1968).

course, the official language; it was the language of writing, of education, of large-scale trade and commerce, and must have been commonly used in town and villa.[106] But it is now generally accepted that British also must have been much in use, and was far from being completely superseded. It must have survived in the towns, mainly among the lower classes, and especially in the countryside where most of the people lived. We are probably right in supposing that it continued as the language of the more native elements in the population, the small tenants or *coloni*, as well as the small farmers in their native-type farmsteads, who formed the bulk of the population.[107]

What of the highland zone about this time? Here we find a situation markedly different. These parts were on the whole more sparsely peopled, and large areas such as the main plateau of the Pennines, the Lake District and parts of Wales, were almost entirely uninhabited, although there seems to be evidence that during the Roman period there was a general increase of population. Except for the Pennine-Scottish region where conquest was never complete, the highland zone also had been subjugated by the Romans : they had exploited the mineral resources and the manpower of these areas. Yet, the *pax Romana* was not so securely established here as in the lowland zone; the graces and refinements of Latin civilization are much less in evidence. We search in vain for Roman towns and cities, and the paucity of Roman villas [108] is further evidence that here was little settled Roman life. Government in the main consisted of military rule. The three legions in Britain had their base fortresses at points where the lowland zone penetrates deeply into the highland, at York in the north, and at Chester and Caerlleon in the west. Enemies had to be reckoned with. In the

---

[106] A form more akin to Classical Latin than the ordinary speech of that time; this may be taken as an indication that in Britain it was often an acquired language and in use mainly among a bilingual upper class.

[107] Cf. Birley (op. cit. 161): "A significant commentary on the extent to which Latin was used is provided by *graffiti*—words or records scratched on tiles or pieces of pottery. Nearly half of these have been found in the towns, another two-fifths at military sites, and only a tiny proportion—less than a fifth— in the countryside, most of which are, in any case, cases where a man's name has been scratched on a dish or cup." See further LHEB 96-106.

[108] On economic and social aspects relating to 'native' farms and the countryside in general, cf. I. A. Richmond, *Roman Britain* (London, 1963), 99-109.

north there were the Picts and the Scots (or Irish); in the west also[109] the Irish were proving troublesome. In general, the inhabitants of these parts cannot have been as docile as were the more romanized Britons of the lowland zone. Small military stations had been established, such as Segontium (Caernarfon), Caersws, Y Gaer (near Brecon), Llanio (Cardiganshire), etc. in Wales, and these were all linked by a network of interconnecting roads. Latin was probably the language of these stations, but outside of them the connection between the native population and Latin culture must have been on the whole tenuous. The probability is that they knew little Latin.[110] Later, however, we find that the influence of Roman culture penetrated into these parts also, and, indeed, its effects on them have been more permanent.

Our knowledge of conditions in that part of the highland zone now known as Wales is both scanty and shaky. During the Roman period the population probably increased; there may also have been some official transfer of people to certain areas, although large areas must have remained uninhabited. There is hardly any direct evidence from literary sources, and we must consequently have recourse to what may be gleaned from archaeological and other fields.[111] The various mineral resources here

---

[109] St. Patrick, whose home was somewhere in western Britain, tells us in his *Confession* that he was taken captive to Ireland along with many thousands (*cum tot milia hominum*). This must have happened early in the fifth century; cf. R. P. C. Hanson, SPOC 119-20.

[110] Cf. LHEB 105-6.

[111] Investigations in the various fields are, of course, far from complete, and firm conclusions are hardly justified. Note, for example, Miss G. Simpson's comment in *Britons and the Roman Army* (p. 162) : "Much excavation is needed before the significance of the great variety of settlement of the Roman period in Wales is fully understood." For only Anglesey and Caernarvonshire are the surveys of the RCAHM available.

On Roman rule and order in Wales, see F. Haverfield, 'Military Aspects of Roman Wales' (*Trans. Cymmr.* 1908-9, 55-187, re-issued 1910, pp. 1-135; R. E. M. Wheeler, 'Segontium and the Roman Occupation of Wales' (*Cymmr.* xxxiii), 'The Roman Fort near Brecon' (ib. xxxvii), 'Roman and Native in Wales : an Imperial Frontier Problem' (*Trans. Cymmr.* 1920-21, 40-96), *Prehistoric and Roman Wales* (Oxford, 1925), *Roman Archaeology in Wales*—a tribute to V. E. Nash-Williams (Welsh Home Service 30 January, 1957, in conjunction with the Cardiff Scientific Society); E. Davies, *Prehistoric and Roman Remains of Denbighshire* (Cardiff, 1929), *Prehistoric and Roman Remains of Flintshire* (Cardiff, 1949); P. K. Baillie Reynolds, 'The Roman Occupation of North Wales' (*Trans. Anglesey Ant. Soc. and Field Club* 1932-33, 21); V. E. Nash-Williams, 'Topographical List of Roman Remains in South Wales' (BBCS iv. 246-71), *The Roman Legionary Fortress at*

had been discovered. Lead had been mined in Flintshire, on the eastern slopes of Plumlumon, and in Machen[112] (Gwent). The copper deposits in Shropshire, Anglesey[113] and Caernarvonshire[114] had been exploited, and gold had been mined at Dolau Cothi in Carmarthenshire.[115] It appears that most, if not all, of the military stations in Wales had been evacuated by 400 A.D. In 383 Magnus Maximus, who may have held some high position in the Roman government of western Britain, had taken his forces to the Continent in pursuance of the imperial power.[116] Little (or indeed nothing) do we know of the political developments of these times, but it appears that they resulted in the emergence about this time of small kingdoms under native warlords or princes. In the emergence of such units we are probably witnessing in embryo a process which eventually produced the larger kingdoms of a later period, kingdoms such as those of Powys, Gwynedd, Dyfed, etc.

As for the earlier history of Wales, we have references at various times to different tribes inhabiting this part of Britain,

---

Caerlleon, Monmouthshire (2nd ed. Cardiff, 1946), *A Hundred Years of Welsh Archaeology* ed. (Gloucester, Centenary Volume, 1846-1946), *The Roman Frontier in Wales* (Cardiff, 1954, rev. ed. 1969); W.E.Griffiths,'Topographical List of Roman Remains in North Wales' (BBCS xii. 108-22); E. Birley, 'Roman Garrisons in Wales' (AC cii. 9-19); Grace Simpson, *Britons and the Roman Army* (London, 1964); A. H. A. Hogg, 'Native Settlement in Wales' (*Council Brit. Arch. Report* 7, 1966, pp. 28-38); G. C. Boon and C. Williams, *Plan of Caerleon: Discoveries to December 1966* (Cardiff, Nat. Mus. of Wales, 1967); I. A. Richmond, 'Roman Wales' (PEW 151-75); L. Alcock, 'Celtic Archaeology and Art' (*Celtic Studies in Wales*, Cardiff 1963, pp. 3-46). See also *Bibl. of the Hist. of Wales* (Cardiff, 1962), 78-81, BBCS xx. 138; M. G. Jarrett ib. 206-20, and more recent archaeological contributions, more especially in AC and BBCS.

For the most recent study of Roman roads, cf. I. D. Margary, *Roman Roads in Britain*, 2 vols. (London, 1955, 1957—2nd ed. 1967): note especially 'Wales and the Marches' (ii. 47-89).

[112] Cf. AC xciv. 108-10.
[113] AMCA, Appendices iii, iv. pp. lxxxvi-xc.
[114] Cf. AC c. 61-66.
[115] BBCS xiv. 79-84, xix. 71-80.
[116] He was proclaimed Emperor in 383. With his forces he left for the Continent, where he held his Imperial court at Trèves. He and his wife, Helena, appear to have been in close touch with St. Martin of Tours (Sulpicius Severus, *Dialogues* ii. 6, and the *Vita S. Martini*). After his death in 388, Helena is reported to have returned to Wales, where she became honoured as a saint, with the additional distinction of being the mother of saints (*Custennin, Peblig*). There are a number of dedications to reputed members of the family of Macsen Wledig—in Dyfed and Gwent as well as in the north-west, cf. SCSW 21-23. See further C. E. Stevens, 'Magnus Maximus in British History' (EC iii. 86-94).

although very little certain knowledge about them is available. We have to be content with small crumbs of information from Classical sources such as the works of Tacitus, Ptolemy and others.[117] There were the Silures (Iberians perhaps) in the south-east area, parts of which may have been well populated. Venta Silurum (Caerwent), where there was located the only Roman town in Wales, was possibly their *chef-lieu*.[118] They had fiercely resisted the Romans, and are described by Tacitus as *valida et pugnax Silurum gens*: but they seem eventually to have lost their identity. The Demetae were in the south-west[119]: their *chef-lieu* was Maridunum (Carmarthen). The Deceangli belonged mainly to Flintshire, and the Cornovii (with Viroconium (Wroxeter) as their *chef-lieu*) to the Severn basin in central Wales and Shropshire.[120] Somewhere in mid-Wales and to the north in Caernarvonshire and Merionethshire lived the Ordovices, who like the Silures had offered strong resistance to the Romans. Ptolemy recorded two places in their territory, *Mediolanum* and *Brannogenium*.[121] Their main interest lies in the possibility that they may have been the only people in Wales originally to speak British. We can hardly hazard precision or certainty regarding the linguistic situation in the Wales of those times, but there can be no doubt that by the end of the Roman period, and later in sub-Roman times, some Irish must have been in use especially in the south-west, and also in the north-west,[122] as well as further inland in certain parts, such as the area around Brecon. There is, of course, ample evidence of the existence of Irish settlements.[123]

---

[117] See Jarrett and Mann, 'The Tribes of Wales' (WHR iv. 161-74).
[118] Cf. V. E. Nash-Williams in *Archaeologia* lxxx. 229-88, BBCS xiv. 242-9, xv. 81-98, 159-67, *Ministry of Works Guide, Caerwent Roman City, Monmouthshire*, 1951, 'The Roman Town of Venta Silurum and its Defences' (*Carnuntia Römanische Forschungen in Niederösterreich* iii. 100-6).
[119] Cf. *De Excidio* c. 31 (*Gildas* i. 72).
[120] See I. A. Richmond, 'The Cornovii' in *Culture and Environment*, ed. I. Ll. Foster and L. Alcock (London, 1963), 251-62.
[121] *Geographia* ii. 3, 18.
[122] Note the names *Llŷn, Din-llaen, Nefyn, Desach, Soch*, also possibly *Gwynedd*; see J. Lloyd-Jones, *Enwau Lleoedd Sir Gaernarfon* (Caerdydd, 1928), 6; also I. Williams, BBCS xvii. 94-95 (*Desach*), C. Williams, ib. xxii. 37-41 (*Mallaen*).
[123] For the activities and presence of the Irish in Wales, see H. Zimmer, *Nennius Vindicatus* (Berlin, 1893), 86-88; Kuno Meyer, *Trans. Cymmr.* 1895-6, 55-86, *Cymmr.* xiv. 101-35, *Eriu* iii. 135-42; J. Rhys, 'The Goidels in

We learn from Irish sources of a tribe from Waterford, known as the Déisi, which settled in the south-west. In the *Historia Brittonum*[124] there is mention of the Irish, the sons of Liatháin (*filii Liethan*) living in Dyfed, in Gower and Cydweli. No doubt, there was some immigration or invasion from Ireland consequent on the withdrawal of Roman control. Indeed, already in the fourth century it appears that the Roman garrisons in Wales were unable to provide the necessary shield from attacks from this and other quarters.[125]

The Ogam inscriptions[126] testify to the presence of the Irish in these parts. About thirty-five of these have been discovered in Wales. These inscriptions are epitaphs written in the Ogam script, where the characters are represented by strokes and notches incised along the edge of a stone. Ogam inscriptions are found all over Ireland, but are concentrated mainly in the southern counties, especially in Kerry in the south-west of that country. We find them also along the western seaboard of Britain, in south-west Scotland, the Isle of Man, in Wales (mostly

Wales' (AC fifth series, xii. 18-39), *Celtic Britain* (3rd ed. London, 1904), 247; J. B. Bury, *The Life of St. Patrick* (London, 1965), 288; Cecile O'Rahilly *Ireland and Wales* (London, 1924), 37-42, 59-65; T. F. O'Rahilly, *Early Irish History and Mythology* (Dublin, 1946), 421 ff.; F. Haverfield, *The Romanization of Roman Britain* 81; K. H. Jackson, LHEB 155-6; S. Pender in *Essays and Studies presented to Professor Tadhg Ua Donnchadha* (Cork, 1947), 209 ff.; M. Richards, *Journal of the Royal Society of Antiquaries of Ireland* xc. 133-62; Grace Simpson, *Britons and the Roman Army* 156-60; P. C. Bartrum, EWGT 4, 124; C. B. Crampton, AC cxvi. 57-70.

[124] C. 14.

[125] Irish pressure and harassing on the western seaboard explains the establishment of 'Saxon Shore' forts at Cardiff, Caernarfon, and (possibly) Holyhead, in the latter days of Roman occupation; cf. V. E. Nash-Williams, *The Roman Frontier in Wales* 94-99. Possibly related to this also is the general overhauling of the road-system apparent in the third century, first the main northern and southern coastal roads, and subsequently inland roads, especially those in the south-west, ib. 142. See also Wheeler, *Prehistoric and Roman Wales* 234, 'The Roman Amphitheatre at Caerleon, Monmouthshire' (*Archaeologia* lxxviii. 111-218), 'Segontium and the Roman Occupation of Wales' (*Cymmr.* xxxiii,1923); S. P. O'Riordain in *Proceedings of the Royal Irish Academy* li. 355ff; M. P. Charlesworth, *The Lost Province* 48; I. A. Richmond, PEW 169-71. But Grace Simpson (*Britons and the Roman Army* 178-9) states that "there is no evidence of Irish settlement in south-west Wales in A.D. 270. That oft-quoted date has no foundation, and the Irish settlements belong to the period after Rome's grip on the two regions (i.e. *Wales and the Pennines*) had loosened and been withdrawn." Cf. also Gildas, *De Excidio* cc. 19-23 (*Gildas* i. 45-55).

[126] See K. H. Jackson, LHEB 151-7; also his article, 'Notes on the Ogam Inscriptions of Southern Britain' in *The Early Cultures of North-Western Europe*, ed. C. Fox and B. Dickins (Cambridge, 1950), ch. 10.

in the south-west) and in Cornwall and Devon.[127] They date mostly from the fifth and sixth centuries. A significant feature of a large number (twenty-six) of the Ogam stones in Wales is that they are bilingual.[128] The Ogam is accompanied by a Latin inscription closely corresponding to it.[129] One such stone,[130] from Castell-dwyran, Carmarthenshire, commemorates Gwrthefyr. In Latin we have MEMORIA VOTEPORIGIS PROTICTORIS, and then in Ogam VOTECORIGAS in a Primitive Irish garb. It is reasonable to assume that this *Voteporigis* is the same as *Vortipor(i)*, one of the five British princes castigated so abusively in the *De Excidio Britanniae*.[131] He was fifth in descent from Eochaid mac Artchorp from the land of the Déisi in southern Ireland, who seems to have been brought to Dyfed in the late fourth century, probably to defend that area against raids by other Irishmen, and also possibly by Picts and Saxons. Another bilingual stone[132] found at Eglwys Gymyn in south-west Carmarthenshire contains the name *Cynin* (CUNIGNI), who was either a son or a grandson of Brychan Brycheiniog, upon whom tradition fathers so many ! [133] While these bilingual inscriptions may not offer us detailed and precise information, the fact of their existence in parts of Wales certainly suggests a state of bilingualism in these areas.[134] At the beginning of the fifth

[127] The Ogam inscription excavated at Silchester may be indicative of some Irish penetration into southern England. Cf. B. H. St. J. O'Neil, 'The Silchester Region in the Fifth and Sixth Centuries A.D.' (*Antiquity* xviii. 113-22). On their distribution in Britain cf. LHEB 153-4; and further E. MacWhite, ZCP xxviii. 294-308. On Irish influence in Cornwall, cf. Charles Thomas, 'Cornwall in the Dark Ages', *Proc. of West Cornwall Field Club* ii. 1957-8, 64-68.

[128] See V. E. Nash-Williams, ECMW 3. Nine are in Ogam only; of these four are in Pembrokeshire, two in Breconshire, and one each in Cardiganshire, Carmarthenshire and Glamorgan. Twelve of the twenty-six bilingual inscriptions are also in Pembrokeshire, five in Breconshire and four in Carmarthenshire, and one each in Cardiganshire and Glamorgan. In North Wales there are only three, two in Caernarvonshire (one at Treflys, Caerns. 106, possibly in Ogam only), and one in Denbighshire. All this serves to indicate the presence of the Irish, in the south-west especially, but also in Brecon and parts of the north. Cf. further Jackson, op. cit.

[129] Certain features of the Latin inscriptions in post-Roman Britain seem further to reflect the influence of Irish colonists, cf. LHEB 166-8.

[130] Dated *c.* 540-550 in ECMW 1; see also p. 107.

[131] *De Excidio* c. 31 (*Gildas* i. 72). Cf. also P. C. Bartrum, EWGT 10, 126.

[132] ECMW No. 142.

[133] Cf. VSBG 314-8; *Trans. Cymmr.* 1959, 78-83; EWGT 81-84.

[134] In some of these bilingual inscriptions we find Roman names, which we may regard as indicating that the Irish speakers had come under some degree of

century (and later), three languages must have been in use in Wales: Latin, the language of those in the service of the Empire, but in more general use in parts of the south-east (and possibly of the north-west also), British, in the main the language of the Ordovices, and also Irish which must already have been the speech of some areas.[135] All in all, at the end of the period of Roman occupation there was little to show for it in Wales, which, be it remembered, lay beyond both Chester and Caerlleon.

Such, then, was the position in the lowland and highland zones at the beginning of our period. Next we have to consider the events and changes which followed, and assess their significance, certainly a most hazardous undertaking, since so much of the history of those times is still a matter for speculation, as we have already noted. There has, however, been most fruitful investigation over the years, and here we may refer to scholarly works such as H. M. Chadwick, *The Origin of the English Nation* (Cambridge, 1907), Collingwood and Myers, *Roman Britain and the English Settlements* (2nd ed., Oxford, 1937), F. M. Stenton, *Anglo-Saxon England* (2nd ed., Oxford, 1947), D. Whitelock, *Anglo-Saxon England* (2nd ed., Oxford, 1947),[136]

Roman influence; cf. K. H. Jackson, LHEB 170. Also note the imperial title of *Protector* accorded *Voteporix* above, and cf. Jackson (*The Early Cultures of North-West Europe* 207): " on the one hand they clung to their Irish customs, on the other they were anxious to assimilate themselves to the admired culture in which they had come to live."

[135] Into south-west Scotland also Irish was to be introduced. Soon after the middle of the fifth century an Irish kingdom, Dálriada, was established in Argyll.

[136] Cf. also *The Beginnings of English Society* (Penguin Books, reprinted with revisions, 1965), and Professor Whitelock's inaugural lecture, *Changing Currents in Anglo-Saxon Studies* (Cambridge, 1958). Reference may be made to other works, such as M. D. Knowles (ed.), *The Heritage of Early Britain* (Bell, 1952); R. H. Hodgkin, *A History of the Anglo-Saxons* (3rd ed. Oxford, 1952); D. B. Harden (ed.), *Dark-Age Britain* (London, 1956); G. O. Sayles, *The Medieval Foundations of England* (reprinted London, 1958); P. Clemoes (ed.), *The Anglo-Saxons* (London, 1960); P. H. Blair, *An Introduction to Anglo-Saxon England* (reprinted Cambridge, 1960), *Roman Britain and Early England, 55 B.C.-A.D. 871* (Edinburgh, 1963); N. K. Chadwick, *Celtic Britain* (London, 1963). The archaeological evidence is presented by D. M. Wilson in *The Anglo-Saxons* (London, 1960); cf. also H. P. R. Finberg, *Lucerna: Studies of Some Problems in the Early History of England* (London, 1964); V. I. Evison, *The Fifth-Century Invasions South of the Thames* (London, 1965); J. Morris, *Britain and Rome: Essays presented to Eric Birley* ed. M. G. Jarrett and B. Dobson (Kendal, 1965), 145-85; D.T. Rice (ed.), *The Dark Ages*—ch. xii, C. Thomas—(London, 1965); D. P. Kirby, *The Making of Early England* (London, 1967); also Ordnance Survey, *Map of Britain in the Dark Ages* (2nd ed. 1966).

and *Studies in Early British History* (Cambridge, 1954), *Studies in the Early British Church* (Cambridge, 1958), *Celt and Saxon* (Cambridge, 1963), all three containing essays by various scholars and edited by Mrs. N. K. Chadwick. These works present a striking variety in basic outlook and conception as well as in method and treatment, but in all of them we find a scholarly analysis and discussion of the several problems, as well as a reasonably coherent presentation and exposition of at least some aspects of the history of these times. Full and accurate reconstruction is still not possible : we must be satisfied with trying to piece together the bits of reliable evidence that are recoverable.

It is well-known that this was the period of the Anglo-Saxon incursions and settlement. The severance of Britain from the Empire dates from *c.* 410 or *c.* 415,[137] and subsequent abortive attempts to reimpose imperial rule are of no lasting significance.[138] It would be wrong, however, to suppose that Roman order and civilization disappeared all at once. It probably survived till about the middle of the century, and Latin must have continued as an official language up till about that time.[139] Mrs. N. K. Chadwick in a comprehensive study[140] shows us that there is ample evidence of intellectual intercourse between Britain and Gaul in the fifth century.

Britain had sustained raids by barbarian enemies from the third century; from this period also there is evidence of the use by Rome of Germanic forces in this country[141]. But it was around the middle of the fifth century (indeed, possibly earlier) that Germanic peoples from the Continent, attracted by the country's wealth and resources, came not only to ravage but also to settle. This is roughly the time of the *Adventus Saxonum*.[142]

---

[137] Now apparently favoured; cf. H.M.Chadwick, SEBH 11 n.; I. A. Richmond, *Roman Britain* 185.

[138] Cf. RBES 290-301. Also S. C. Hawkes and G. C. Dunning, 'Soldiers and Settlers in Britain, Fourth to Fifth Century' (*Medieval Archaeology* v. 1-70).

[139] In the *Life* of St. Germanus of Auxerre Britain is a Roman province with an ordered ecclesiastical life. The saint is said to have visited Britain in the second quarter of the fifth century. Cf. further Hanson, SPOC 69-71.

[140] SEBH 189-253.

[141] Cf. L. Alcock, WHR iii. 230-1.

[142] Cf. J. N. L. Myres, 'The Adventus Saxonum' in *Aspects of Archaeology in Britain and Beyond* (1951), 221-41. Note also N. Tolstoy, *Trans. Cymmr.* (1964), 276-98; J.Morris, op. cit., pp. 150-70; R.P.C.Hanson, SPOC 13-20.

Gildas and Bede (as well as Nennius and the *Anglo-Saxon Chronicle*) tell us of the early settlements in the east.[143] We learn of Hengist and Horsa, who obtained lands in Kent from the British king Vortigérn,[144] apparently as *foederati*, employed in defence against Picts and Scots. However, there is archaeological evidence which suggests that there existed settlements in parts of the east from a much earlier time.[145] During the third quarter of the fifth century these Germanic invaders and colonizers must have made considerable progress, and this probably resulted in the destruction of the established pattern of life over much of the lowland zone.[146]

It was probably at some stage during this time that Ambrosius Aurelianus emerged. He is the leader (a *vir modestus*) mentioned in the *De Excidio*[147]: no doubt a man of good family, a romanized Briton who hailed from around Gloucester. Under his leadership the Britons may have succeeded in temporarily stemming the advance of the invaders around the years 470-480 A.D. Again in the *De Excidio* (as well as in other

[143] A Gaulish chronicle records that about this time (in the nineteenth year of Theodosius ll, i.e. 441-2), the provinces of Britain were reduced to subjection by the Saxons (*Brittanniae usque ad hoc tempus variis cladibus eventibusque latae in dicionem Saxonum rediguntur*). Ed. Th. Mommsen in the *Chronica Minora, Mon. Hist. Germ.*, vol. i, p. 617, under the name *Chronica Gallica* (Berlin, 1892, reprinted 1961). Cf. G. Ashe, *From Caesar to Arthur* (London, 1960), 131. But this was patently an exaggeration.

[144] There are, of course, very many complex problems connected with Vortigern, whose dealings with the Saxons take place in the south-east of England. But he also figures as a ruler in central Wales, married to a daughter of Maximus. He may have been the 'founder' of Powys, and the first post-Roman *gwledig*. We learn of his denunciation by St. Germanus, and of his encounter with the boy Ambrosius, who succeeds him as leader. The reader may be referred to discussions of various subjects connected with Vortigern by H. M. and N. K. Chadwick in SEBH 21-46, also 254-63. Further cf. A. W. Wade-Evans, 'Vortigern' (*Notes and Queries* 13 May, 1950, pp. 200-3); C. A. Ralegh Radford, 'Vortigern' (*Antiquity* xxxii. 19-24); N. K. Chadwick, '*Bretwalda . Gwledig . Vortigern*' (BBCS xix. 225-30); D. P. Kirby, 'Vortigern' (ib. xxiii. 37-59).

[145] Cf. Collingwood and Myres, RBES 386-7, and Map X*a*; R. R. Clarke, *East Anglia* (London, 1960), 129; Dauncey, *Antiquity* xvi. 51-63; Myres, *Council for British Archaeology* No. 11 (1961), 40; I. A. Richmond, *Roman Britain* 65; D. B. Harden (ed.), *Dark Age Britain. Studies presented to E. T. Leeds* (London, 1956), 3, 37; J. Morris, op. cit., pp. 149, 176-7.

[146] There is, of course, evidence that life here was already in an advanced stage of decline; cf. RBES 317-9.

[147] *De Excidio* c. 25 (*Gildas* i. 60). In Nennius (c. 48) he is *rex inter omnes reges* (var. *regiones Brittannicae gentis*). He may, perhaps, be equated with the Emrys Wledig of Welsh tradition, cf. R. Bromwich, TYP 345-6.

works) we have reference to a rather important battle fought early in the sixth century,[148] in which the Britons were victorious. This was the *obsessio Badonici montis*[149] 'the siege of Mount Baddon'. It is impossible to determine with certainty the site of this battle. The topic has been accorded much study and attention and need not be elaborated upon here. Suffice it to say that the most likely place appears to be Liddington, near the Wiltshire Badbury, and directly to the south of Swindon.[150] To this period probably belongs Arthur,[151] a *dux bellorum* who may well have been the hero of this battle, although there is no clear mention of him in the *De Excidio*. If the conclusions regarding the site of the battle are not hopelessly wide of the mark they enable us roughly to determine the extent of the progress made by the invaders by the beginning of the sixth century. It appears that the native Britons, who had been left to fend for themselves, still held the western and most of the northern parts of England. For the next forty or fifty years there seems to have been little fighting,[152] but about the middle of the sixth century the invaders resumed the offensive, and from then on till the end of the century they succeeded in gaining possession of the greater part of England.

As far back as the end of the fifth century and the beginning of the sixth we have evidence of Germanic settlements in the

---

[148] The *De Excidio* seems to date it *c.* 500-3, Bede *c.* 490-9, the *Annales Cambriae* 516. See RBES 480-1; also G. Ashe, *From Caesar to Arthur* (London, 1960), 295-8; N. Tolstoy, BBCS xix. 149-54.

[149] *De Excidio* c. 26 (*Gildas* i. 60). *Bellum badonis* in the *Annales Cambriae* (See *Cymmr.* ix. 154); *bellum in Monte Badonis* in Nennius (See BBCS xix. 118).

[150] Other places have, of course, been suggested. Kenneth Jackson in the *Journal of Celtic Studies* ii. 152-5 with some enthusiasm supports a location originally suggested by E. Guest, namely, Badbury Rings in Dorset, though he readily admits that this was not on the borders of the area occupied by the Saxons at this time. Arthur may have had his operational base at the Cadbury fortress in Somerset. Cf. also N. Tolstoy, BBCS xix. 143-9, where Bathampton Down overlooking Bath is suggested.

[151] Cf. K. H. Jackson, 'The Arthur of History', in R. S. Loomis (ed.), *Arthurian Literature in the Middle Ages* (Oxford, 1959).

[152] Cf. the *De Excidio* c. 26 (*Gildas* i. 62). There is also Procopius (*De Bello Gothico* iv. 19), from whom we learn of emigration to the Continent by the Anglo-Saxons, who apparently were unable at this time to push their settlements westwards. Further we may call in evidence the tradition of such a migration in the first half of the sixth century recorded by a ninth-century monk of Fulda. See ASE 7-8.

south also.[153]   In 477 Aelle had landed near Selsey, an event which marks the inception of the kingdom of Sussex. Later in 495 Cerdic, possibly half British by birth, and his son Cynric, landed on the shore of Southampton water.[154] Early in the second half of the sixth century, under Cerdic's successors, the West Saxons[155] renewed their expansion westwards. In c. 552 the Britons were defeated in the battle of Old Sarum in Salisbury. The most well-known of the West Saxon kings in the latter part of the sixth century was Ceawlin. He advanced towards the source of the Thames, in c. 577 the Britons were defeated in the battle of Dyrham near Bath, and it was not long before the West Saxons reached the shores of the Bristol Channel. When Ceawlin died (possibly around the year 600), Wessex consisted of a great part of southern England, and the territory of the Britons in the south-west was cut off from that of their kinsmen in the west and north.[156] Yet, as we shall see, this did not result in a complete severance of contact and communication between the two areas.

There is evidence of progress by the invaders in the north[157] also from the middle of the sixth century on. Archaeological investigation shows that they had settled in parts of central and east Yorkshire at least a hundred years before this time. It was here that the kingdom of Deira was formed. To the north there emerged the kingdom of Bernicia, which eventually consisted of all the country between the Tees and the Forth : according to Bede and the *Anglo-Saxon Chronicle* this kingdom was established by Ida (*c*. 547). From then on there must have been much fighting, fierce and prolonged, between the British

---

[153] Cf. RBES 393-5.
[154] Ib. 458, also 397-9.
[155] These probably came mainly from the upper Thames region, rather than from the south; cf. RBES 405. They could have advanced from the Wash along the ancient track known as Icknield Way, and also along the Thames from the river-mouth. Cf. H. R. Loyn, *Anglo-Saxon England and the Norman Conquest* (London, 1962), 31-33.
[156] See G. J. Copley, *The Conquest of Wessex in the Sixth Century* (London, 1954); J. N. L. Myres, 'Wansdyke and the Origin of Wessex' (*Essays in British History presented to Sir Keith Feiling*, ed. H. R.Trevor-Roper (London, 1964), 1-27); D. P. Kirby, 'Problems of Early West Saxon History' (*English Hist. Review* lxxx. 10-29).
[157] Cf. P. Hunter Blair, *The Origins of Northumbria* (Newcastle-upon-Tyne, 1948); also D. P. Kirby, *English Historical Review* lxxviii. 514 ff.

kingdoms of the north and the men of Deira and Bernicia, a
conflict referred to in the *Historia Brittonum* and echoed in the
poetry of Aneirin and Taliesin.[158] In 593 Ethelfrith came to the
throne in Bernicia, and Bede tells us that he conquered more territory from the Britons than any other English king.[159] According
to the *Historia Brittonum*[160] he was for the second twelve years
of his reign (605-616) king of Deira also. He had married the
daughter of the king of Deira, and thus united the two kingdoms,
which together consisted of a large area of country north of the
Humber, or Northumbria. In 603 he defeated Aedán son of
Gabrán, king of the Irish kingdom of Dálriada (Argyll) in
south-west Scotland. After some years, *c.* 616, he came into
conflict with the Britons of the west, the men of Powys in
particular, and defeated them in a battle at Chester,[161] in which
also (so Bede tells us) twelve hundred monks from the monastery
at Bangor Is-coed were slaughtered. After Ethelfrith's death in
617 Edwin came to the throne in Northumbria. He succeeded in
establishing his authority over all the English kingdoms except
Kent. He also enlarged the confines of his own kingdom.
It is likely that it was during his reign or immediately afterwards
that the south-east of Scotland was subjugated up to the Firth of
Forth. According to Nennius he subdued Elmet, a British
kingdom in south Yorkshire, and thus removed a barrier
between Deira and the Irish Sea. He seems also to have invaded
North Wales. But the struggle for supremacy in Britain was not
yet over. Edwin was confronted by new and dangerous enemies.
These were Cadwallon, an enterprising king of Gwynedd, and
Penda, the new king of Mercia. Under the latter in the second
quarter of the seventh century Mercia, in the heart of England,
emerged from obscurity and became for the first time a powerful
kingdom. An alliance was formed between Cadwallon and Penda,
and in 633 they defeated Edwin and killed him in a battle in
Hatfield Chase. For a little while Northumbria was at their
mercy, but in the following year Cadwallon was killed in battle,

[158] Cf. T. Parry, *A History of Welsh Literature*, trans. H. I. Bell (Oxford, 1962), 1-8.
[159] *Hist. Eccles.* i. c. 34.
[160] c. 63.
[161] See N. K. Chadwick, in *Celt and Saxon* (Cambridge, 1963), 167-85.

and with this defeat there vanished all hope of the Britons regaining dominion over the island of Britain. The Britons continued in league with Penda till he was in 655 defeated and killed in battle against Osuiu, king of Northumbria, who thus became overlord of most of England, and was recognised as supreme ruler by Britons, Picts and Scots, as well as Anglo-Saxons. For the Britons the unity of their land was thus finally and irretrievably destroyed, and the Britons of Wales were separated from their compatriots in the north.

Such then in outline appears to be the history of the lowland zone during these two centuries. By about the middle of the seventh century, only comparatively small areas of England remained unconquered. These lay in the north-west, the land to the west of the Pennines, Cumberland, Westmorland and north Lancashire,[162] in parts of the border country near Wales, and in the south-west. We are not concerned here with the details of the Anglo-Saxon conquest or colonization.[163] The large number of Celtic river-,[164] forest- and hill-names, as well as the names of Roman cities, which have survived among the English, strongly suggests that many people the invaders and settlers came into contact with were speakers of British,[165] who,

[162] These parts were soon subjugated by Northumbria. The only British kingdom that survived was Strathclyde in southern Scotland. Cf. LHEB 218-9.

[163] The late Rev. A. W. Wade-Evans denies that there ever was such a 'conquest'. He claims that historians (from Bede down) have gone astray in their interpretation of Gildas, and of the *De Excidio* as a sixth-century work. See his 'Prolegomena to a Study of Early Welsh History' in *The Historical Basis of Welsh Nationalism*, ed. D. M. Lloyd (Cardiff, 1950), 1-41; *The Emergence of England and Wales* (2nd ed. Cambridge, 1959). His researches into this dark period, researches extending over very many years, have done much to vindicate the importance and significance of the 'Celtic' element, although one must have reservations about at least some of his conclusions and theories.

[164] The evidence of river-names tallies with the sketch of the Anglo-Saxon conquest presented here. Extensive work has now been done in this field, and our knowledge has been greatly enriched as a result. In LHEB 220 in a map of England plotted with river-names of British origin it is shown that there is in general correlation between the changing degree of density of such names from east to west and the main stages in the conquest outlined above. The evidence of river-names is thus in harmony with the knowledge gained from other sources. See also Jackson, SEBH 221-9, 63-66

[165] See LHEB 241-9. For personal names and common names, see M. Förster, '*Keltisches Wortgut im Englischen*' in the *Festgabe für Felix Liebermann* (Halle, 1921). Cf. also E. Ekwall, '*Zu zwei keltischen Lehnwörtern im Altenglischen*' in *Englische Studien* liv, 1920; A. H. A. Hogg, 'The Survival of Romano-British Place-names in Southern Britain', in *Antiquity* xxxviii. 296-9.

however, must have readily abandoned it once they acquired the new speech. It is probable that the civilization they encountered here was in many areas as much Celtic as it was Roman by this time. Furthermore, very few would now be disposed to support the view that the native Britons, left to fend for themselves, were all annihilated or driven westwards. No doubt there was a movement of people away from the Anglo-Saxon advance, but there must have been at least some measure of intermingling and intermarriage,[166] except perhaps in parts of the east and south-east, in the areas first occupied. Although this part of Britain (i.e. England) may eventually have undergone a thorough transformation, it is difficult to believe that the new settlers destroyed everything they found here, and on arriving immediately initiated a completely new mode of living. But this is far too intricate and delicate a problem to be examined closely here. Archaeological and other problems relating to 'continuity' are still largely unsolved. It is clear that further critical investigation and sifting of evidence by archaeologists, geographers and others in fields such as settlement studies is required[167] before we can hope to study this question adequately, let alone resolve it.

Next, what of the highland area, in the north, west and south-west ? In these parts also we find change, but not a radical transformation. The changes we encounter here are such as result from assimilation and blending.

---

[166] Indeed the name Cerdic, the reputed father of the West Saxon dynasty, if it represents the Welsh *Ceredig*, may be taken as an indication of intermarriage. Cf. A. Anscombe, 'The Name of Cerdic' (*Cymmr*. xxix. 151-202); F. M. Stenton, ASE 25.

[167] Reference may be made to the following: 'The Character of the Conquest' in RBES 425-56; LHEB 229-41; R. Lennard, 'From Roman Britain to Anglo-Saxon England' (*Wirtschaft und Kultur*, Leipzig, 1938, pp. 34-73); E. T. Leeds, 'The Distribution of the Angles and Saxons Archaeologically Considered' (*Archaeologia* xci. 1-106); R. H. Hodgkin, *A History of the Anglo-Saxons* (3rd ed. Oxford, 1952), 161-78; J. N. L. Myres, 'The Survival of the Roman Villa into the Dark Ages' (*Archaeological News Letter*, Vol. vi, No. 2, 1955); Margaret Deanesly, 'Roman Traditionalist Influence among the Anglo-Saxons' (*English Hist. Review* lviii. 129-46); G. R. J. Jones, 'Settlement Patterns in Anglo-Saxon England' (*Antiquity* xxxv. 221-32); H. R. Loyn, *Anglo-Saxon England and the Norman Conquest* (London, 1962), 5-22; H. P. R. Finberg, *Lucerna : Studies of Some Problems in the Early History of England* (London, 1964), 1-20; L. Alcock, 'Roman Britons and Pagan Saxons: an Archaeological Appraisal' (WHR iii. 229-49). Cf. also *Angles and Britons: O'Donnell Lectures* (Cardiff, 1963).

Towards the end of the Roman period and later, when the vestiges of Roman life were being largely eradicated in the lowland zone, it seems to have acquired fresh vigour in these parts. This was in part the result of immigration from the more romanized lowland zone, caused by the Anglo-Saxon advance. The spread of the Christian faith must have been another factor[168]: many of the Latin words in the Brittonic languages relating to religion were probably borrowed during the fifth and sixth centuries.[169] In any event, there is abundant evidence of the influence of Latin culture in these parts. British leaders gave Latin names to their children, they set up memorial stones with inscriptions in Latin[170] and occasionally even claimed Roman titles. At times we find evidence of more intellectual involvement in Latin culture, as in the inscription commemorating Paulinus at Cynwyl Gaeo, Carmarthenshire, which contains two hexameter lines.[171] These people may well have regarded themselves as Roman citizens for quite a while, perhaps up till the middle of the sixth century,[172] and they must have continued to recognise Latin and to use it : the author of the *De Excidio* refers to it as *nostra lingua* 'our language'.[173]

For a long time, indeed up till the middle of the sixth century (and much later in some parts) the inhabitants of the highland zone probably did not directly feel the effect of the Anglo-Saxon advance. Although there seems to be evidence of a decline of material culture in western Britain from the fifth century,[174] these parts must have experienced about the same time some kind of revival, a Celtic revival.[175] It would be wrong, however, to suppose that the native Britons here were completely spared the agony of having to contend with intruders. In the north there were the Picts and the Scots (or Irish). In Wales, and also in Cornwall, we have Irish settlements.

---

[168] Roman culture was in part infused into these areas by direct contact with the Romano-Christian civilization of Gaul.
[169] Cf. LHEB 77; see also 116-21.
[170] Cf. ECMW 3-16.
[171] ECMW No. 139, dated *c.* 550.
[172] Cf. J. Loth, *Les Mots latins dans les langues britonniques* (Paris, 1892), 9.
[173] c. 23 (*Gildas* i. 54), but *Romana lingua* in c. 32 (ib. i. 72).
[174] Cf. L. Alcock, WHR iii. 244.
[175] Cf. Dillon and Chadwick, 'The Celtic Revival' in *The Celtic Realm* (London, 1967), 43-67.

There is plenty of evidence of the existence in the north and west during this period of a number of small kingdoms, no doubt formed in an endeavour to bring some sort of political order out of the chaos caused by the final collapse of Roman rule. These kingdoms were governed by rulers of courage and guile; they are the *tyranni* mentioned in the *De Excidio*. We learn of men such as Vortigern in Powys, Coroticus in Strathclyde, Maelgwn in Gwynedd, Voteporix in Dyfed, Constantine in Dumnonia, Mynyddog in the land between the Forth and Tyne, Urien in the north-west, with Carlisle as centre. They probably came from a class of wealthy native landowners, and their political traditions were in the main those of the tribe. Their emergence represents a resurgence of Celtic life in Britain, a manner of life by no means extinct which had, however, remained quiescent and largely dormant during the period of Roman rule.

Even now, we dare not claim that it is possible to present a complete picture of the political, social and economic scene during this period. Yet, our knowledge has been greatly improved, and as a general statement we can say that up till the beginning of the seventh century (and indeed later) there must have been a close link between Wales, especially North Wales, and the 'North', by which is meant parts of northern England and southern Scotland. The inhabitants of both these areas probably felt themselves as people of one land[176]; they were *Cymry* (<*Combrogi*), an appellation first used perhaps towards the end of the sixth century, when the progress of the Anglo-Saxons was threatening to divide their country in two.[177] The sense of kinship between North Wales kingdoms and the 'Men of the North' may well have persisted after the political link had been destroyed, as Mrs. Chadwick quite properly

---

[176] We learn of men like Kentigern and Taliesin who seem to belong to both areas; cf. Foster (PEW 228) : "at the end of the sixth century, a poet of the court of Powys could travel to a court on the edge of the Pennines and then on to Rheged." There is, of course, evidence of this connection from prehistoric times; cf. SCSW 70, SSSCL 50. We may also cite the Llanaelhaearn stone (Caerns. 87, fifth to early sixth century): ALIORTVS ELMETIACO, suggesting contact with Elmet in south Yorkshire; cf. Foster, op. cit. 217; also E. G. Bowen, *Llên Cymru* viii. 163-7.

[177] Cf. J. Rhys, *Celtic Britain* (3rd ed. London, 1904), 115-6; J. Rhys and D. Brynmor Jones, *The Welsh People* (London, 1900), 26; HW i. 164, 191-2.

suggests.[178] Wales, more especially South Wales, was also closely linked with south-west England, and there is evidence that here again contact was maintained even after the Anglo-Saxons had reached the Bristol Channel.[179]

Our knowledge of Wales during this period is derived in the main from the findings of the linguist, the archaeologist and the historical geographer. Very few records of events have been preserved. In the *Annales Cambriae* there is reference to pestilence in 547-550,[180] in which Maelgwyn Gwynedd perished, probably the yellow plague which started in Persia in 542 and then swept across Europe. In the *De Excidio*, where Maelgwn Gwynedd and Gwrthefyr (Voteporix) are mentioned by name, we learn of domestic struggles,[181] and in Taliesin's poem in praise of Cynan Garwyn of Powys (*c*. 580)[182] there is mention of fighting in different parts of Wales. Chieftains must have been in conflict with each other from time to time, but this part of the country can hardly have been as war-ridden over this period as were other areas to the east and north, especially during the sixth century, which is essentially the Age of the Saints.

Probably the most important event recorded of this period, as far as Wales is concerned, is that found in the *Historia Brittonum*, in that part of it which seems to derive ultimately from some northern British source of early date.[183] We are told that a chieftain named Cunedda, with his eight sons, came from the banks of the Firth of Forth to Wales.[184] He may have

---

[178] Cf. SEBC 78-79.

[179] One cannot determine how strong were the links at this time between the northern and southern areas of Wales. Cf. Fox (*The Personality of Britain* 73): "Throughout prehistoric times there were strong forces tending to make North and South Wales separate entities."

[180] Cf. further pp. 179, 209, 225 of this volume.

[181] cc. 21, 26, 32, 33 (*Gildas* i. 48, 62, 74, 76), not in every instance specifically in Wales, as we know it.

[182] I. Williams, *Canu Taliesin* (Caerdydd, 1960), 1; *The Poems of Taliesin*, ed. J. E. C. Williams (Dublin, 1968), 1.

[183] Cf. K. H. Jackson, 'On the Northern British Section in Nennius' in *Celt and Saxon* (Cambridge, 1963), 20-62.

[184] *Historia Brittonum* (c. 62): *centum quadraginta sex annis antequam Mailcun regnaret* 'one hundred and forty-six years before Maelgwn reigned.' c. 450 according to P. Hunter Blair, *The Origins of Northumbria* (Newcastle-upon-Tyne, 1948), 34-36; slightly before 400 according to A. H. A. Hogg, 'The Date of Cunedda' (*Antiquity* xxii. 201-5); c. 395 according to Collingwood, *Roman Britain* 289-90. See also H. M. Chadwick, *Early Scotland* (Cambridge, 1949), 147-9 (c. 460); R. Bromwich, SEBH 84; J. Morris, 'Dark Age Dates', in *Britain and Rome*, pp. 162-3; N. Tolstoy, *Trans. Cymmr.* (1964), 244 ff.

come (possibly by sea) because of persistent Pictish attacks, or the move may have been planned as part of a policy of settling war-lords and their followers at points of danger in border areas.[185] In many ways Cunedda is the most important figure in early Welsh tradition. From the cumulative evidence of the saints' genealogies, where many of the saints are placed in direct line of descent from him,[186] it seems reasonable to assume that he was a Christian, indeed a Christian who may have been instrumental in propagating the faith. Likewise he is the ancestor of several Welsh royal families. He must have been a romanized Briton : his immediate ancestors and some of his children had Roman names. He may well have been assigned the task of containing and repelling the Irish. At any rate, it is said that he drove them from British territories with great slaughter, and they never again returned to inhabit them. Further it is stated[187] that the territory of his sons extended from the Dee to the Teifi: they held very many districts (*plurimas regiones*) in the western area (*plaga*) of Britain. The names of his children occur as eponyms of later Welsh kingdoms and provinces in north and central Wales, such as Edeyrnion (Edern) and Ceredigion (Ceredig);[188] indeed Sir John Rhys has adduced evidence for supposing that the Ordovices, who seem to have inhabited those parts, collaborated with him.[189] There is, however, no reference to his sons in Anglesey, or on the opposite coast in Arfon, and it is quite possible that it was Cadwallon Lawhir, son of Einion Yrth, son of Cunedda and father of Maelgwyn Gwynedd, in conjunction with three sons of Gwron (another son of Cunedda), who finally overcame the Irish in these parts by defeating them in Cerrig y Gwyddyl in Anglesey early in the sixth century.[190]

[185] See RBES 289; M. P. Charlesworth, *The Lost Province* 27-39.
[186] Cf. for example, P. C. Bartrum, EWGT 54-67.
[187] In a note preserved in B.M. MS. Harleian 3859; see *Cymmr.* ix. 183.
[188] Cf. Bartrum, EWGT 13, 92.
[189] *Celtic Britain* (3rd ed. London, 1904), 302.
[190] In *Bonedd yr Arwyr* and a late triad it is stated that Cadwallon along with the three sons of Gwron ap Cunedda expelled the Irish from Anglesey, and completely defeated them in Llan y Gwyddyl in Caergybi (=Holyhead); see Bartrum, op. cit. 92, 93, R. Bromwich, TYP 256, also cxxxix-cxli, 296-7. An earlier triad mentions Cadwallon's war-band as fighting with Serygei the Irishman 'yg Kerric Gvydyl y Mon'; see TYP 167-9. Professor Bowen (SCSW 72) notes that dedications to descendants of Cunedda through Einion Yrth are concentrated in north-west Wales. He regards this as significant,

Less is known of the progress of the Britons to the south.[191]
It has been suggested that it was the Ordovices who engaged the
Irish here. They could have moved from present-day Radnor-
shire up the valley of the river Irfon and into the region of
Llandovery, Llandeilo and Llanelli, thus separating Dyfed
from the south-east.[192] The little kingdom of Brycheiniog
(Brecknock) was probably Irish, at least in part. We have
already referred to the evidence for the presence of the Irish in
Dyfed. The struggle for supremacy between Irish and Britons,
certainly one of the most important features of political life in
Wales in the sixth century, may well be echoed in the *Life of
St. David*, which relates how the chieftain Boia was defeated
by the saint.

Further investigation in the domain of toponomy, archaeology, historical geography etc., could well yield more precise
information. For the present we must allow that our evidence is
very meagre. Professor E. G. Bowen reminds us that "our
knowledge of the habitat and economy of the Welsh people in
the immediate post-Roman period is by no means as extensive as
that of immediate pre-Roman times."[193] The free tribesmen
were presumably still semi-nomadic, while non-free tribesmen
were settled close to the lord's *llys* in areas of good agricultural
land. It appears that most people lived on the lower fringes of
the hill-land, a feature of their material life which represents a

---

"as this is the area into which the original entry is presumed to have been
effected if the object was to deal with Irish settlers in these parts." It is also
worthy of note that the kingdoms said to have been founded by Cunedda's
sons are not in general in the extreme north-west, where there was the
greatest concentration of Irish settlements in this part of Wales.

[191] In c. 14 of the *Historia Brittonum* Cunedda and his sons are represented as
expelling the Irish from Dyfed, Gower and Cydweli: *Filii autem Liethan
obtinuerunt in regione Demetaram, et in aliis regionibus, id est Guir Cetgueli,
donec expulsi sunt a Cuneda et a filiis eius ab omnibus Britannicis regionibus.*
But there is no other evidence that Cunedda was connected with this part of
Wales.

[192] Cf. HW i. 121; *Hist. of Carmarthenshire* i. 122; also Bowen, BBCS viii.
383-5.

[193] SCSW 112. He rightly draws attention to the work of V. E. Nash-Williams
and H. N. Savory on the native settlements of this period. Cf. for example
BBCS xiii. 152-61, xiv. 69-75. See also L. Alcock, 'Wales in the Fifth to
Seventh Centuries A.D. : Archaeological Evidence' (PEW 177-211);
'Pottery and Settlement in Wales and the March, A.D. 400-700' (CE 281-302).
Notwithstanding the considerable advance made in archaeological studies
during the past twenty years, our picture is still tantalizingly blurred and
confused.

phase in the valley-ward movement of population.[194] There seems
to be evidence also of the re-occupation of earlier sites, both of the
Iron Age and of the Roman period.[195] Settlements such as those
in Dinas Emrys in Snowdonia and Dinas Powys in Glamorgan
were occupied,[196] and in some quarters we can detect signs of
prosperity, even of luxury, and of commercial contact with
Mediterranean lands, although money does not seem to have
been used. Furthermore, there may be some slight evidence for a
trend away from arable-farming and towards stock-raising during
this period.[197] The industries and crafts for which there is
evidence are such as would be supported in the main by a
farming economy : the services of the blacksmith and also of the
jeweller must have been in demand.[198] In the field of technology
and art there is increasing evidence of contact and intercourse
between the two sides of the Irish Sea.[199] Indeed, we are
probably justified in speaking of an Irish Sea culture province at
this time. Leslie Alcock[200] reminds us that "there need . . .
be no doubt that western Britain played its part, no less than
Ireland, in the Celtic metalwork of the two or three centuries
after 400 A.D."

As in Ireland, society within Wales at this time was probably
'tribal, rural, hierarchical and familiar'.[201] As in the highland
zone generally, there cannot have been any centralized power:[202]
the country must have consisted of a complex of petty kingdoms,
about which we have only very casual and superficial

---

[194] It is noteworthy, as Professor Bowen observed (SCSW 114, also 139), that
the sites of surviving Celtic churches are generally nearer the valley floors,
often probably in a position originally isolated. Cf. ib. 146-60.

[195] Cf. N. K. Chadwick, *Celtic Britain* (London, 1963), 91; also p. 162 for
further references.

[196] See H. N. Savory, AC cix. 13-77; L. Alcock, BBCS xvi. 242-50, xvii. 131-6,
Dinas Powys (Cardiff, 1963); Gardner and Savory, *Dinorben* (Cardiff, 1964).

[197] Cf. L. Alcock, PEW 191, 197.

[198] Cf. id. WHR ii. 1-7.

[199] Cf. id. PEW. 178-81, *Antiquity* xxxvi. 51-55; also G. R. J. Jones, WHR i.
111-32.

[200] *Celtic Studies in Wales* (Cardiff, 1963), 42.

[201] See D. A. Binchy, *Early Irish Society*, ed. M. Dillon (Dublin, 1954), p. 54.

[202] Cf. A. Cox, AC xciv. 40. A stone of the fifth-seventh century, now at
Penmachno, has VENEDOTIS CIVES which, according to Mr. G. R. J.
Jones (WHR iii. 32), "implies that an administrative entity corresponding
perhaps with the later Gwynedd (Venedotia) had already been constituted."
L. Alcock (PEW 193-4) suggests that the settlement at Dinas Powys probably
belonged to members of a princely dynasty of Morgannwg.

information. We are hardly justified in accepting the whole story of Cunedda and his sons as genuine history, but like all legends this 'origin' story also offers valuable clues. It certainly endorses the evidence which seems forthcoming from other sources that the British element in Wales (now affected by the impact of Latin culture) gradually succeeded in gaining the ascendancy over all the others, including the Irish, during these centuries. The language of the Irish, which must have been in use in certain parts, was receding by the end of the sixth century; eventually it disappeared completely, although there is no means of ascertaining when this happened.[203] The Celtic language which prevailed in Wales was that of the Britons.

And here we come to one of the most important aspects of the development of the Welsh people, and the emergence of Wales as a separate entity. We have seen that British was the native language of the Celts in Britain. At the beginning of our period both British and Latin (along with some Irish) must have been in use here, but both had been superseded over most of England by the end of it, that is, by the beginning of the seventh century. Latin survived only as the language of learning, culture and religion, while British was now confined to parts of the north-west, the west (including Wales, where its position had been strengthened), and the south-west. In the north-west it did

---

[203] It was, however, in use in the sixth century. Professor Jackson (LHEB 170-1) shows that there is in some sixth-century inscriptions evidence of the persistence of Irish in south-west Wales (and also in the Dumnonian peninsula). The Irish and their language were still present in north-west Wales in the sixth century, but here the evidence from the inscriptions is much slighter (ib. 172) : there are only three Ogams in this area.

Of the Ogam inscriptions in Wales only nine are without an accompanying 'Latin script' version. Of these, four are in Pembrokeshire, two in Breconshire, and one each in Cardiganshire, Carmarthenshire and Glamorgan (ECMW 3). Clearly the most intensively Irish areas were in Pembrokeshire and in parts of Breconshire. The vast majority of the inscriptions are bilingual. All these inscriptions can be dated within the fifth and sixth centuries, most of them before 550, see ECMW 6. Then, "by 600 the Ogam script had apparently ceased to be used as a monumental hand in Wales." (ib.). All this seems to be in accord with the view expressed above regarding the decline in the use of Irish.

As has been noted, the Irish element seems to have been strong in parts of Breconshire. That it could have penetrated thence to the south-east is suggested by the Irish form of the name *Illtud*, in contrast to *Elltud* of Llanelltud in Merionethshire, where the British element may have been dominant (possibly as a result of the Cunedda conquest). The Irish element could also have reached the south-east by sea. Cf. also Alcock, BBCS xviii. 221-7.

not survive for very long, although we do not know exactly when it became extinct.[204] In the west, more especially in Wales, it progressed and flourished. But during the two centuries of turmoil and upheaval its sound-system and structure had undergone drastic changes, and the language that emerged from the strains and stresses of those turbulent times and became the language of court, of law, of poetry, in the native British kingdoms, was markedly different from the old British of the Roman period : furthermore, it had assimilated hundreds of words borrowed from Latin. Such a change in itself constitutes evidence of social and political upheaval and consequent transformation. Details of the linguistic changes and a chronological history of them are presented in Kenneth Jackson's book, *Language and History in Early Britain*[205]. They need not be discussed here. Suffice it to say that from a highly inflected synthetic language, not unlike Latin in many respects, there evolved a medieval, or even a 'modern' language, shorn of its case terminations and with completely new features. This new speech was, of course, Welsh.

In the south-west of England the language that eventually emerged from the parent British was Cornish, which survived in Cornwall for over a thousand years. From an early period Britons from different parts emigrated to Armorica in north-west Gaul. They came from southern England, especially the Devon-Cornwall peninsula, and also, apparently, from other areas, including parts of South Wales and the Severn Sea. This emigration probably reached its peak in the second half of the sixth century.[206] The Britons who thus left for Armorica took their British dialect with them, and it is from their speech that the language we know as Breton developed.

---

[204] Cf. LHEB 219, where it is suggested that Cumbric might have survived in Strathclyde up till the eleventh century.

[205] See especially pp. 690-9: also his chapter 'The British Language during the Period of the English Settlements' in SEBH 61-82; and Ifor Williams, 'When did British become Welsh?' in the *Transactions of the Anglesey Hist. Soc. and Field Club* 1939, 27 ff.

For a general discussion of the Latin loanwords, see LHEB 76-80, 106-12.

[206] See J. Loth, *L'Émigration bretonne en Armorique du Vᵉ au VIIᵉ siècle de notre ère* (Paris, 1883); K. H. Jackson, LHEB 11-30; N. K. Chadwick, *The Colonization of Brittany from Celtic Britain* (The Sir John Rhys Memorial Lecture, British Museum, 1965). On the settlement of Britons in Galicia, Spain, cf. E. A. Thompson, CB 201-5.

As for Wales then, this was the time of great and profound
changes, which contributed to the growth and development of a
separate people and culture in this area of Britain. We have
already noted some of the dominant features: the impact of
Latin culture, the eventual dominance of the British element,
and the development of Welsh from the parent British language.
The one important movement which remains to be discussed
(in many ways the most abiding in its impact) was the conversion
of the people to the Christian Faith. To this we must now turn.

We know the names of very many saints or monks[207] (drawn
largely from the 'royal' families), who laboured in Wales during
these times, and who founded religious cells and settlements.
Little precise knowledge have we beyond the bare names, the
nuda - - - nomina as William of Malmesbury[208] says. Doble,
in reference to the Cornish saints,[209] is right in stating that "we
should be thankful that we have their names at all, for their
names are clues to what would otherwise have been entirely
forgotten."[210] From a much later period we have their *lives*.
These cannot be regarded as genuine biographies ; yet some of
the traditions which they incorporate may have some historical
basis, and they certainly deserve the kind of investigation and
analysis which we associate with scholars such as Canon Doble.

The earlier saints of the south-east, saints like Dyfrig
(Dubricius), Illtud and Cadog, may well have been operating
against a background of Christian culture, a culture inherited

---

[207] See N. K. Chadwick, ASECC 3-5; note especially J. Morris, 'The Dates
of the Celtic Saints' (JTS new series, xvii. 342-91).

[208] *Gesta Pontificum* (Rolls Series ed. Hamilton, 1870), 202.

[209] SC i. 109-10.

[210] We must rely largely on the evidence of archaeology (which consists
primarily of inscribed stones) and of dedications or hagiotoponymy.
However, it should be remembered that dedications serve mainly to
demonstrate the spread of the saint's cult or the power of his church;
cf. O. Chadwick, SEBH 175-88. In the case of the vast majority of churches,
our earliest evidence for dedications dates back no earlier than the eleventh
or twelfth century, and one need not assume that all churches must have been
associated with a saint from the beginning. Cf. further J. MacQueen,
St. Nynia (Edinburgh, 1961), 65-66; J. Morris, JTS new series, xvii, 354 n.
   The studies of ecclesiastical scholars such as A. W. Wade-Evans and
G. H. Doble, who have been primarily concerned with the *lives* of saints,
have yielded much useful and reliable evidence. For an understanding of the
cultural background we have the studies of Mrs. N. K. Chadwick, Mrs. R.
Bromwich, Miss K. Hughes and other scholars of what we may call the
'Cambridge' school.

from the Romano-British society. There is a tradition closely
linking Dyfrig and Illtud with St. Germanus. It is not possible
to determine how deep and wide had been the impression made
by Christianity in south-east Wales before the end of the Roman
period. It had probably made some sort of impact, as had Latin
culture generally in this extension of lowland Britain.[211] The
solution to this problem largely turns on the answer to the
question of the survival of Latin culture in these parts, a topic
far too intricate to be examined here.[212] We must also take
account of the possibility that the movement of people from the
north and east during this period might have been instrumental
in introducing Christianity into parts of Wales. Refugees may

[211] Roman traditions may have deeply affected life in Gwynedd also, but
further investigation is required before this can be firmly established.
Cf. E. G. Bowen, 'Archaeoleg a'n Llenyddiaeth Gynnar' (*Llên Cymru* viii.
150-67).

[212] On this intricate and controversial subject, see E. G. Bowen, SCSW 14-17,
SSSCL 61;   Aileen Fox, 'Early Christian Period' (pp. 106-7 in *A Hundred
Years of Welsh Archaeology*, Gloucester, Centenary Volume, 1846-1946).
    The evidence is, on the whole, inconclusive. The small early church at
Caerwent, where there was a Romano-British town, may be of Byzantine
origin. There is confirmation from other sources of contact between
Caerwent and the Byzantine world in the Dark Ages, which seems to point to
communication along the western sea-waters. Cf. further V. E. Nash-
Williams, *Archaeologia* lxxx, 235, BBCS xv. 165-6; L. Alcock, PEW 181-98;
G. C. Boon, BBCS xvii. 316-9, xix. 338-45, JRS lii. 196.
    We must also mention the villa situated at Llantwit Major. Here there
appears to have been some break in the continuity of life. In the fourth
century the main residential block seems to have been deserted, although the
labourers' quarters continued to be occupied. This seems to indicate
absenteeism on the part of the landlord, but with the estate continuing to
exist as an economic unit. Later, probably in the fifth century, a number of
bodies were buried there. Cf. AC xciii. 255-6; cii. 89-163; BBCS xiii.
163-6; LRB 93-94; *Athenaeum* Oct. 20th, 1888; *Cardiff Naturalists. Soc.
Trans.* xx. 50 ff. Another villa, at Ely near Cardiff, did not continue beyond
325 A.D., see M. P. Charlesworth, *The Lost Province* 21. R. E. M. Wheeler
seems to favour the view that the fortification of this villa is connected with
the inroads of the Irish; and he tentatively suggests that the destruction of
the villa at Llantwit is also connected with them; see JRS xi. 67-85. Yet
another villa, nearer Caerwent, seems to have lasted at least until c. 364-378;
see Wheeler, *Antiquaries Journal* iii. 374. More recently new sites have been
discovered on the coast and in valleys north-west and west of Barry, and in at
least three of these there is evidence of fourth-century occupation; H.
Thomas BBCS xvii. 293-6; cf. JRS xlix. 102, Fig. 35.
    There is much to be said for the view that in the south-east Romano-
British Christianity (which could at least in part be a survival from Roman
times) might have been reinforced and revitalized by a more monastic
movement (possibly with 'Macsen Wledig' traditions), which could reach
these parts by way of the old Roman roads, such as the road leading from
Maridunum up the Tywi valley and into the vale of Usk, past the Brecon
Gaer and down to Abergavenny and Monmouth.

well have come from places like Silchester and Cirencester, where there were Christian communities,[213] but one cannot assume without firm evidence that missionary activity was a feature of such movements. In any event, we have to consider what vitality was left in the Christianity of Britain at the end of the Roman era, one of those fundamental questions that confront the student of this period.

It has already been observed that some kind of episcopal system must have been established in Britain during the period of Roman occupation. A closely knit and ordered civil administration readily lent itself to such a system, which reflected the system of Roman civil government. But where such a civil organisation was lacking this form of ecclesiastical government and administration was far less suited and appears to have been less in evidence. One ought not to be surprised to find that eremitism seems to have flourished in the less populous parts of Gaul.[214] We have, of course, evidence of the monastic movement in Gaul during the fourth and fifth centuries, a movement austere, passionate, democratic, which we associate more especially with Martin, that somewhat unconventional bishop of Tours and evangelizer of rural Gaul (c. 315-397).[215]

According to P. A. Wilson, 'Romano-British and Welsh Christianity : Continuity or Discontinuity' (WHR iii. 5-21, 103-20), the thesis "that Christianity in the south-east is in direct line of descent from Roman Britain while in the south-west and north-west it is a later importation from western Gaul" is "inherently improbable" (p. 8). The author relies mainly on the surviving literary evidence, and concludes that it "points unmistakably in the direction of 'continuity'" (p. 10). Again, "The case presented argues decidedly in favour of 'continuity' between the church in Roman Britain and the church in sub-Roman Wales." (p. 117). W. H. Davies (CB 131-50) subscribes to a largely similar thesis.

Finally, we must take account of the evidence there is for the survival (if not revival) of paganism towards the end of the Roman period. Some time after 364 A.D. a pagan temple to Nodens (evidently a Celtic deity, at least in part) was erected at Lydney, on the north side of the Severn estuary. This may reflect Irish influence, but its true significance still remains to be determined. Cf. H. Williams, CEB 38; M. J. Wheeler, *Report of the Excavation of . . . Lydney Park, Gloucestershire* (Oxford, 1932); T. G. E. Powell, *The Celts* (London, 1958), 130; I. A. Richmond, *Roman Britain* (London, 1963), 110-13; L. Alcock, PEW 178-81; R. G. Collingwood and R. P. Wright, *The Roman Inscriptions of Britain* (Oxford, 1965), p. 100, No. 306; R.P.C. Hanson, SPOC 168-9.

213 Cf. G. C. Boon, *Roman Silchester* 119-31.
214 Cf. ASECC 46.
215 His biographer was Sulpicius Severus, who was also his disciple; cf. p. 9, n. 45.   The *Life* of St. Martin is translated in F. R. Hoare, *The Western Fathers* (London, 1954). Cf. also N. K. Chadwick, PLECG 89-121.

The monastic movement derived ultimately from the east, from Egypt and Syria, and it was interpreted to the west by the famous eastern monk and writer Cassian,[216] who established monastic communities in the vicinity of Marseilles. A contemporary of his, Honoratus,[217] founded a monastic settlement on one of the islands of Lerins,[218] off the coast of the French Riviera. To the communities and schools of Marseilles and Lerins,[219] founded in the early fifth century, many holy men (including, possibly, Patrick, Illtud, Paul Aurelian and Samson) seem to have gathered. The progress of monasticism at this time was, no doubt, due to the frustration and despair experienced in the wake of the barbarian incursions and the collapse of Roman order. In Gaul it was firmly established by the middle of the fifth century, and its influence was already pervading the secular church there. In Britain there is as yet no sure evidence [220] that such a movement was making an impact. But Magnus Maximus (*d.* 388) who, according to Sulpicius Severus,[221] became a close friend of Martin, must have come under the influence of his dynamic, militant monasticism, and this influence no doubt reached Wales through Maximus's widow Helena, and her sons Constantine and Peblig. Victricius of Rouen, a disciple of Martin, had visited Britain about 396. Ninian and Patrick, both Romano-Britons who advanced the frontiers of Christendom in Scotland[222] and Ireland respectively, were probably influenced

---

[216] See O. Chadwick, *John Cassian* (Cambridge, 1950, 2nd ed. 1968). Cf. also N. K. Chadwick, op. cit. 212-39.

[217] His biographer was his disciple, St. Hilary of Arles.

[218] A. Cooper-Marsdin, *History of the Islands of the Lérins* (Cambridge, 1913). Cf. N. K. Chadwick, 'Foundations of Western Monasticism. The Monastery of Lerins' in PLECG 142-69.

[219] These appear to have been affected by semi-Pelagianism, which we may regard as indicative of intellectual vitality and alertness. Cf. N. K. Chadwick, PLECG 170-211.

[220] Three of the Britons at the Council of Rimini in 359 had no private means (Sulpicius Severus, *Chronica* ii. c. 41). It is, however, extremely doubtful if we should take this as indicating that they had been affected by the monastic ideal. (But cf. N. K. Chadwick, PLECG 107; R. P. C. Hanson, SPOC 33-34). Indeed it could be argued that for another century there is evidence in Britain of a church of learned and prosperous bishops; cf. P. Grosjean, AP lxxv. 173; R. P. C. Hanson, SPOC 35. Yet there may be evidence of a monastery at Glastonbury in the fifth century; cf. Hanson, ib. 153-4, also Thomas, CB 96.

[221] *Dialogues* ii. 6, Monceaux, Watt.

[222] On Ninian and the introduction of Christianity into Scotland early in the fifth century, cf. W. D. Simpson, *St. Ninian and the Origins of the Christian*

by the monastic movement in Gaul. This movement must also have affected Germanus of Auxerre, who came to Britain in 429. Everything points to an intimate connection with the Continent, a connection later impaired but not broken by the Anglo-Saxon incursions. Here we may mention that there are certain small scraps of information which may be called in evidence, such as the reference to Riocatus (possibly a grandson of Vortigern[223]), a bishop and monk who seems to be bringing home to Britain books from southern Gaul.[224]

We shall later briefly examine the evidence which can be adduced to show that during our period (and especially in the sixth century) Christianity entered Wales mainly from the west, and directly from the Continent. In Wales, where there were few, if any, urban nuclei, the forms and organisation which the new faith assumed were in the main those of the monastic establishment. Indeed this was a feature of the Celtic church generally, especially in the sixth century. Doble reminds us that "the most characteristic feature about the Celtic church was its preference for the monastic and eremitic life," and further that "the history of the Celtic Church is largely a history of monks and monasteries."[225] The monastic institutions founded during the fifth and sixth centuries, beacons of peace and truth amid the dark and treacherous turmoils of those times, must have proved

Church in Scotland (Edinburgh, 1940); W. Levison, 'An Eighth-Century Poem on St. Ninian' (Antiquity xiv. 280-91); N. K. Chadwick, Trans. of the Dumfriesshire and Galloway Natural History and Antiquarian Society, third series, xxvii. 9-53; P. A. Wilson, ib. xli. 156-85; C. Ralegh Radford and G. Donaldson, Whithorn and Kirkmadrine: Official Guide (Edinburgh, 1953); E. A. Thompson, 'The Origin of Christianity in Scotland' (Scottish Hist. Review xxxvii. 17-22; P. Grosjean, 'Les Pictes apostats dans l'épitre de S. Patrice' (AB lxxvi. 354-78); J. MacQueen, St. Nynia (Edinburgh, 1961); J. Bulloch, The Life of the Celtic Church (Edinburgh, 1963), 34-61; K. Hughes, The Church in Early Irish Society (London, 1966), 26-29; A. C. Thomas, CB 93-121.

223 Possibly to be identified with Riagath, son of Pascent, son of Vortigern, as listed in a ninth-century genealogy; see Bartrum, EWGT 8 (Briacat), 46.

224 So Sidonius Apollinaris, Epistolae—Mon. Germ. Hist. viii. 157. English translation in O. M. Dalton, Letters of Sidonius (Oxford, 1915), ii. 188 ff. This may have happened c. 475 (cf. P. A. Wilson, WHR iii. 115-6). He is said to have visited Faustus (a close friend of Sidonius) and to be taking back one of his books. We cannot be quite sure where he was going, whether to Britain or to Brittany : what we are told is that it was to Britons (Britannis tuis). He is styled bishop and monk (antistes ac monachus). Cf. also G. Ashe, From Caesar to Arthur (London, 1960), 120-2.

225 SC. iv. 154.

more convenient centres than the diocesan *curia* for the kind of society which obtained here.[226] Organised on a semi-tribal basis, they must have been important and influential establishments in their areas.[227] Mrs. Chadwick observes that the "most outstanding feature of this Celtic Church was the widespread extent and power of the monastic foundations. By the sixth century these had come to give it an individual character and local tradition to which it clung passionately in the face of attempts from Rome and Canterbury to bring it into full conformity with continental usages."[228]

We have, of course, no details of the establishing of such centres apart from what is told us in the later *lives*, which at times undoubtedly echo historical events and situations from the sixth century and earlier, when local chieftains must often have striven to resist the progress of the saints. From many sources we are reminded of the serious problems and difficulties that beset these early missionaries. Patrick's letter to Coroticus (a Christian

---

[226] It must be realised that monasticism does not imply a rigid, uniform system. There was considerable variety in the customs and methods adopted, and the form the organisation took largely reflected the views and character of the founder. It would also be wrong to draw too rigid a distinction between monks and bishops. On the Continent we have a fusion of clerical and monastic life, a fusion exemplified in the life and work of men such as Martin of Tours. Cf. K. Hughes, *The Church in Early Irish Society* (London, 1966), 55-56, 70-71, 82-83.

One must refer to the evidence of a few inscriptions of the fifth or early sixth century, which appear to reflect an episcopal organisation. Two contain the title *sacerdos* ? 'bishop' : one from Llantrisant, Anglesey (later 6th century A.D. ECMW 63); the other from Bodafon, Caernarvonshire ('5th-early 6th century A.D.' ib. 86). Another two have *presbyter* 'priest', both at Aberdaron, Caernarvonshire ('5th-early 6th century' ib. 84). Cf. further Wheeler, *Roman Archaeology in Wales : A Tribute to V. E. Nash-Williams* (1957).

Note also the *De Excidio* c. 65 (*Gildas* ii. 156) : *malitiae episcoporum vel ceterorum sacerdotum aut clericorum in nostro quoque ordine*, also cc. 66, 67, 69 (*Gildas* i. 156, 168, 174); and see O. Chadwick, 'Gildas and the Monastic Order' (JTS v (1945). 78-80); I. Ll. Foster, PEW 214-6. There is also the *Life of St. Samson*, an early witness, which offers some evidence: we are told, for instance, that Samson obtained the *bishop*'s sanction before he went to Ireland (c. 37).

[227] We have the larger establishments such as those at Llanilltud Fawr, Nantcarfan, Penmon, St. David's, Llandeilo Fawr, etc., which were missionary centres, as well as the numerous hermitages of individuals or small groups of saints, 'seeking the desert', who set up their cells in more desolate and secluded spots, on hill-tops, promontories or islands. The larger establishments appear to have been situated closer to inhabited settlements. Cf. further Bowen, SSSCL 191-225.

[228] ASECC 70. Cf. also CEB 306-403; HW i. 143-61, 202-19; CCL 57-61.

ruler) provides direct evidence of a saint's troubles. In the *Lives* of the Saints, notably the *Life of St. Samson*, we learn of popular beliefs, ideas, customs, usages, etc., which impeded the progress of the new faith.[229] Then there are the references to the five *tyranni* in the *De Excidio*. The standards and interests of the lay rulers, living as they were in an environment of relentless cruelty and oppression, could hardly remain unaffected by the progress of the saints. The latter's activities could well damage their political power and authority. One is not surprised to find that most of the references to Arthur in the *vitae* of Cadog, Carannog, Padarn, Illtud and Gildas (Caradog of Llancarfan) are not very respectful.[230] Maelgwn Gwynedd was in frequent conflict with the saints, as may be gathered from the *vitae* of Cadog, Padarn and Cybi.[231] Yet we learn from the *De Excidio*[232] that he was a Christian, at least nominally. So were other rulers of the period.[233] Cynan, son of Brochfael Ysgithrog, who was ruler in Powys in the latter part of the sixth century, had a brother Tysilio, who was a saint. However, in Taliesin's poem to Cynan (*c.* 580)[234] no Christian influence can be detected.

But from what sources and along what routes came this new power, which was thus to disturb and ultimately to control the interests and outlook of the secular leaders also ? Thanks to the conflict and turmoil already described, the routes leading to Wales from the east must have been hazardous for much of the time. As archaeologists and historical geographers have shown, there was a major reorientation of life, both cultural and commercial, in the fifth century. Whereas under Roman rule life had been directed mainly towards the south-east, the western parts of Britain now looked mostly towards the west and south. Extensive use was probably made of the western sea-routes, which meant that there could be direct contact between Wales

---

[229] Cf. F. Jones, *The Holy Wells of Wales* (Cardiff, 1954), 21-23, 39-41.
[230] See G. Ashe, *From Caesar to Arthur* (London, 1960), 178-80; also A. W. Wade-Evans, *Welsh Christian Origins* (The Alden Press, Oxford, 1934), 107-10.
[231] See R. Bromwich, TYP 437-41.
[232] cc. 33-35 (*Gildas* i. 76-83).
[233] Cf. ib. cc. 27, 33, 67, 76.
[234] See I. Williams, *Canu Taliesin* (Caerdydd, 1960), 1, *The Poems of Taliesin*, ed. J. E. C. Williams (Dublin, 1968), 1; I. Ll. Foster, PEW 229-30. Cf. also VSBG 114.

and the Continent. Indeed, the monastic movement could come direct from Gaul, or northern Spain, or even from the Eastern Mediterranean. There was also intensive traffic between Wales[235] and Ireland. And finally, there must have been direct contact between South Wales and Cornwall, and also Brittany. Within the zone constituted by these areas the early saints could travel with comparative ease and safety, and there is reason to believe that they were great travellers.[236]

[235] More especially the south-western and north-western parts. The findings of archaeologists, both prehistoric and early historic, serve to remind us of connections with Ireland. Reference has already been made to the Ogam stones and the Irish settlements. The Irish element is represented in the *Life of St. David*. There is also the evidence of British Latin loanwords in Irish, which points to contact with Ireland in the fifth and sixth centuries; cf. LHEB 122-48. But relatively few settlements have been left by Irish *peregrini* in Wales. As one would expect, dedications to Irish saints (except those to St. Brigid) are found mostly in the south-west and north-west; cf. SCSW 96-99. That there was a close relationship between some Welsh and Irish establishments, especially in the sixth century, cannot be denied, although there is little evidence of it in the activities of the saints studied in this volume. There is, of course, evidence of close contact and association between Welsh and Irish at later periods; cf. for example SEBC 124-8.

There appears to have been direct contact between Ireland and the Continent also; cf. Bowen, SSSCL 51-52, and especially 112-46. We have the reference in a Leyden manuscript of the twelfth century to the flight of the learned men of Gaul to Ireland at this time, a flight caused by the devastation of the Huns, Vandals, Goths and Alani, and which proved beneficial to the cause of learning in Ireland. Cf. N. K. Chadwick, SEBH 237-8; also P. Grosjean, *Celtica* iii. 85, *Fritz Saxl 1890-1948: a Volume of Memorial Essays from his Friends in England* (ed. D. J. Gordon, London, 1957), 72; P. A. Wilson, WHR iii. 111. It is very doubtful whether this notice can be regarded as contemporary; but it is not on that account devoid of value.

The progress of Christianity in Ireland is not discussed here, as it has been my intention to concentrate on what little we can learn about the evidence for the saints in Wales. The missionary activity of the Irish church, notably the work of Columba (521-597), the founder of Iona, and that of later monks of Iona, is not to be disregarded, although one should pause before pronouncing upon its effect on Wales as such. Cf. A. O. and M. O. Anderson *Adomnan's Life of Columba* (London, 1961); J. A. Duke, *The Columban Church* (Edinburgh, 1932, reprinted 1957); D. A. Bullough, 'Columba, Adomnan and the Achievement of Iona' (SHR xliii. 112-30, xliv. 17-33); J. Bulloch, *The Life of the Celtic Church* (Edinburgh, 1963), 50-61; M. O. Anderson, 'Columba and other Irish Saints in Scotland' (*Hist. Studies* v. 26-36).

[236] See E. S. Duckett, *The Wandering Saints* (London, 1959), for an account of the Celtic pilgrim saints in the British Isles and on the Continent. There can be little doubt that the Celtic saint was often attracted by the 'facilities' offered by a deserted place. His movement in part represented a withdrawal from society. A new land frequently offered better opportunities and greater freedom, which may help to explain the journeyings which some of the early saints appear to have made from one land to another, for example from Wales to Brittany. Also cf. Bowen, SSSCL 70-72.

The late Dr. V. E. Nash-Williams in his monumental work, *The Early Christian Monuments of Wales*, shows that the Christian monuments of the fifth and sixth centuries, bearing inscriptions in Latin or Ogam, or both[237], are concentrated mainly along the coast. They are found more especially in the west, in the north-west and south-west, in Anglesey, Caernarvonshire, Merionethshire, and in Pembrokeshire and Carmarthenshire.[238] Without going into details, we can say that such a distribution certainly points to a movement reaching Wales by way of the western seas. The significance of the Ogam inscriptions has already been discussed. The Latin inscriptions exhibit features akin to those of the Early Christian inscriptions of the western Roman Empire, notably those of the Lyon-Vienne region of Gaul,[239] and they may justifiably be taken as evidence of a movement (possibly involving at least some Christian refugees) into Wales and the neighbouring Celtic regions by sea from these parts.[240] These monuments (both Latin and Ogam) are also concentrated in the Brecon

---

[237] According to the table in ECMW 3, out of a total of 139 inscriptions, 104 are in Latin only, 26 have Latin and Ogam, and 9 Ogam only. For an analysis of the formulae used, cf. J. D. Bu'lock, 'Early Christian Memorial Formulae' (AC cv. 133-41).

[238] See ECMW 2, also the map facing p. 10. They are distributed as follows : Anglesey 11, Caernarvonshire 18, Merionethshire 11, Denbighshire 3, Flintshire 1, Montgomeryshire 1, Radnorshire —, Cardiganshire 9, Pembrokeshire 36, Carmarthenshire 22, Breconshire 17, Glamorgan 9, Monmouthshire —, Herefordshire 1. It will be noticed that in the more romanized parts in the south-east, notably in Monmouthshire, these monuments are hard to come by.

See also R. A. S. Macalister, *Corpus Inscriptionum Insularum Celticarum* (1945 and 1949), Nos. 318-520, 968-1068; C. A. R. Radford and I. Williams, AMCA xciv-xcv, civ-cxvii; K. H. Jackson, LHEB 149-93.

A considerable number are found in Cornwall, whence they spread into Devon and Somerset; and some belong to the Isle of Man and to the old British kingdom of southern Scotland.

In all they total over 150. For references to more recent finds, cf. CB 143.

[239] Cf. Nash-Williams, AC xciii. 34, xciv. 2; Ralegh Radford, AMCA xciv, cvi; Jackson, LHEB 163-4; Bowen, SSSCL 52-53.

[240] Cf. ECMW 4. There is also the evidence of Mediterranean pottery discovered in Cornwall, Wales, Scotland and Ireland. Cf. Radford, *Dark Age Britain* 59-70; Thomas, *Mediaeval Archaeology* (1959) iii. 89-111, also *Cornish Arch.* (1967) vi. 35-46; Alcock, *Celtic Studies in Wales* (Cardiff, 1963), 40. This evidence of contact with the Mediterranean is certainly of importance and significance in an investigation of the sources of those missionary activities which affected the Celtic lands in this period.

area,[241] a circumstance which seems to indicate a movement inland along some of the Roman valley routes.[242] It has been shown that the early monks must have made use of the old Roman road-systems in South Wales, as the field of their missionary activity expanded.[243] Then from South Wales the movement

[241] This area in turn seems to have been a centre of missionary activity. Cf. Doble (SC ii. 31-32-33): "Now we know that from Brecknock went forth numerous missionaries who evangelized Hereford to the east and Glamorgan, Carmarthen and Pembroke to the south and west . . . Thus it looks as if S. Decuman belonged to a group of Brecon saints who founded monasteries in south-west Wales, from which missions to Somerset and Cornwall were sent out . . . he may have been associated with the great saints of Cardigan and Pembroke, Carantoc, Petroc and Brioc, who did such an important work in Somerset, Cornwall and Brittany."

Note also Professor Bowen (SCSW 26-27), who draws attention to the distribution of dedications to the saintly sons and daughters of Brychan, concentrated around Brycheiniog, but with extensions in different directions: "We have, thus, every reason to associate the establishment of these and other churches dedicated to the children of Brychan with an early re-diffusion of Celtic Christianity from Brycheiniog in the fifth and sixth centuries." (ib.)

[242] Cf. A. Fox, AC xciv. 40; *A Hundred Years of Welsh Archaeology* (Gloucester, Centenary Volume 1846-1946), 109. Also L. Alcock (PEW 206) : "On the whole, the relationship of Roman roads and stones is probably to be thought of not as a causal one, but as a coincidence imposed by the constraints of a mountainous terrain."

[243] See for example Bowen, SCSW 22-25. Professor Bowen draws attention to the location and distribution of dedications to members of the family of Macsen Wledig, which are found in areas roughly corresponding to those of the Gallo-Roman memorials (see p. 21, n. 116). Both are concentrated in the south-west and north-west, but with evidence of an extension eastwards. We find evidence of the Macsen Wledig cult in Monmouthshire and western Herefordshire, areas which are completely bare of early Christian inscribed stones. Conversely the latter are found in Breconshire, where there is little evidence of the Macsen cult.

Likewise the Ogam stones concentrated mainly in the south-west show an extension eastwards. And the location of a certain type of memorial stone (with a simple cross and the Christian monograms IHS and XPS) along with the distribution of 'Dewi' churches suggests a cultural contact between St. David's peninsula and western Herefordshire; cf. SCSW 61.

Without going into details, we can say that the collective evidence of the Macsen Wledig dedications, the early Christian inscribed stones, and the Ogam stones, indicates an extension or movement well eastwards from the western areas of Wales. It could only have reached these areas by sea, and from the sea use was apparently made of the ancient routeways inland, which led to the network of Roman roads.

But in the north there is also evidence of movement from south to north on either side of the mountain mass. The cult of Beuno, however, who has more dedications than any other saint of North Wales, seems to have moved from Powys into north-west Wales; cf. SCSW 81, 86.

See the map showing the network of Roman roads in I. D. Margary, *Roman Roads in Britain* (London, 1957) ii. 48.

was diffused further[244] throughout western Britain (and Ireland), to south-west England, more especially Cornwall, and also to Brittany.[245]

In a survey of this kind one should not get entangled in problems relating to individual saints, their work and their travels, or in questions of doctrine, discipline, order and organisation. Here I propose merely to refer to certain of the more important aspects of the lives and labours of the saints discussed by Doble in his 'Welsh Saints' series. These are Dyfrig (Dubricius), Illtud, Paulinus, Teilo and Oudoceus (Euddogwy). He has, of course, dealt with other Welsh saints, such as Meugan, Cybi, Carannog, Cadog, Briog, Dochau, Pedrog, Padarn, and Tysilio; but these figure in his 'Cornish Saints' series,[246] and are, therefore, not included in this collection.

With the probable exception of Oudoceus, whose identity and period are as problematical as ever,[247] these saints were among the foremost religious leaders in areas of South Wales during this formative period. We find dedications to some of these early saints from South Wales also in south-west England

---

[244] Here we may, perhaps, be permitted to mention as evidence (however late, and therefore suspect) a letter from the chapter of St. David's addressed to Pope Honorius II (between the years 1124-1130), and preserved in the *De Invectionibus* of Giraldus Cambrensis; cf. C. Brooke, SEBC 207-8, also 233. See J. Conway Davies, *Episcopal Acts and Cognate Documents relating to Welsh Dioceses, 1066-1272* (Historical Society of the Church in Wales, 1946-8) i. 250: "Also it is true that by that church several archbishops and bishops ordained to the office of preaching the Catholic faith were sent to the island of Ireland and also to many nations of other lands, . . . Among those, St. Samson, . . . fleeing from the imminent danger of the plague, crossed over to the monastery of Dol, of the people of Brittany, with the honour of the pallium."

[245] On the progress of Christianity in Brittany, cf. R. Largillière, *Les Saints et l'organisation chrétienne primitive dans l'Armorique bretonne* (Rennes, 1925); also N. K. Chadwick, *The Colonization of Brittany from Celtic Britain*, 279-80, and Bowen, SSSCL 160-90.

[246] Meugan SC ii. 34-44; Cybi iii. 105-32; Carannog iv. 31-52; Cadog iv. 55-66; Briog iv. 67-104; *Docco* iv. 105-9; Pedrog 132-66 (also AB lxxiv. 188); *Saint Sulian and Saint Tyssilio* ('Cornish Saints' series, No. 37, 1936); *Saint Patern* (ib. No. 43, 1940).

[247] The *Book of Llandaff* places him third in the succession of bishops there (after Dubricius and Teilo). As E. D. Jones (NLWJ iv. 135) reminds us, his *Life* is not found in the B.M. MS. Cotton Vespasian A xiv, and its compilation may well be part of the project of composing the *Book of Llandoff*. Saints Dubricius, Teilo and Oudoceus, along with Peter, are co-titulars of the cathedral. Cf. P. C. Bartrum, 'The Chronology of the Early Kingdom of Glywysing' (*Trans. Cymmr.* 1948, 279-93); J.W. James,'The *Book of Llan Dâv* and Bishop Oudoceus' (JHSCW v. 23-37).

and in Brittany. This does not, of course, necessarily mean that
the saints themselves all travelled to these parts or that they
settled in them. What it does demonstrate is the direction in
which their cultus spread, whether this happened during their
lifetime or later. And all this serves to remind us once more of
the close links between South Wales, south-west England and
Brittany : as has already been suggested, for quite a while these
areas must have constituted a cultural zone within which there
was considerable coming and going.[248] It is especially noteworthy that *many* of the Welsh saints of this period have churches
dedicated to them in Cornwall (and also, but to a lesser degree,
in Devon and Somerset), and in Brittany.[249] Time and again
does Doble remind us of this. We may, for example, refer to his
conclusions regarding St. Mawgan : "The result, then of our
researches would seem to lead us to the conclusion that Maugan
or Malgand was an abbot, probably an abbot-bishop, of an
important monastery in Demetia, the modern Pembrokeshire,
and that he shared with S. Brioc and S. Cadoc and other saints of
South Wales in the great movement of monastic expansion and
missionary enterprise which began in the sixth century and
covered Wales, Cornwall and Brittany with churches and

---

[248] Cf. Doble SC i. 31, 36, 110, ii. 25, 30, 34, 92, iii. 57, 63, 103, 126, 139,
iv. 1, 31, 63-64, 65, 100, 130, 132; D. Attwater, *The Penguin Dictionary of
Saints* (1925), 227 (Malo), 281 (Petroc). Cf. also J. Marx, *Nouvelles
recherches sur la littérature arthurienne* (Paris, 1965), 77 ff.; Bowen, SSSCL
108-111.
  There is possible evidence also of a political connection between Armorica
(Brittany) and south-west England at this time, i.e. in the first part of the
sixth century; cf. R. Bromwich, SEBH 122-3.

[249] In the case of Cybi and others such as Iestin, Custennin Gorneu and Cyngar,
who are of the same family, there seems to be evidence of movement in the
opposite direction,—saints from Cornwall labouring in Wales (and possibly
for a while in Ireland also): see SC iii. 105-32. But our knowledge of these
saints is too inadequate to justify firm judgments; cf. Doble. op. cit. 112.
There is evidence also of *peregrini* moving from Brittany to Wales, led by
St. Cadfan; but this should not be urged too forcibly; cf. SCSW 91-96,
SSSCL 189-90.
  It is reasonable to suppose that some of the Britons who emigrated to
Armorica, more especially those who went in the sixth century, had already
been converted to the Christian faith. This possibility should certanly be
borne in mind when examining the spread and diffusion of the saints' cults.
Mansuetus (*episcopus Britannorum*), one of the nine bishops present at an
informal council held at Tours in 461, could be from Brittany; cf. H.
Williams, CEB 282; also P. A. Wilson, WHR iii. 118-9; R. P. C. Hanson,
SPOC 21, 65-66. Faustus also may have hailed from Brittany, cf.
pp. 3, 45, n. 224.

monasteries".[250]   In his study of St. Carantoc he shows how parishes in the Newquay district of Cornwall are called after monks from Cardiganshire and Pembrokeshire, "who settled here and afterwards founded a fresh settlement in the north-west of Brittany".[251] Finally, we may quote from his study of St. Cadoc : "South Wales during this period (i.e., *the fifth and sixth centuries*) was covered with flourishing monasteries, founded in many cases by members of the princely houses of Brycheiniog, Ceredigion, and Dyfed who had become monks. A great expansion of monasteries followed, and monasteries were founded all over the north in Somerset, in Devon and Cornwall, and in Brittany".[252]

Two of the saints discussed by Doble in this series belong to south-east Wales. Dyfrig, or Dubricius, is associated especially with the west and south of Herefordshire, with centres at Hentland and Moccas. He lived c. 475. About the same time, or a little later (c.475-c.525) lived Illtud. There is an early reference (in the *Life of St. Samson*) to his wide learning, and the persistent traditions regarding a monastic school at Llantwit Major (or less probably, at some other place) can hardly be discounted. Both Dyfrig and Illtud, along with Cadog (and possibly *Doccus*[253]) belong to the earlier generation of saints. It would be too hazardous to try and determine with certainty the source and origin of their movement. They appear to have laboured mainly in that part of Wales where there might be survivals (or at least reminiscences) of earlier Romano-British Christianity, which could have been kindled anew and set ablaze by the fire of a more 'evangelizing' movement from the west. They would thus have belonged, at least in part, to that earlier tradition in which Patrick and others from the late Roman period, such as

---

[250] SC ii. 43-44.   Cf. also Bowen, SSSCL 93-99.
[251] ib. iv. 50.
[252] ib. iv. 63. It is worthy of note that many Welsh saints with dedications in Cornwall and Brittany have left little trace of their cults in Wales. Cf. Doble (SC iv. 64) : "Ordinarily, the founders of Welsh and Irish monasteries did not leave those countries, and Welsh saints who founded monasteries and parishes in Brittany, like S. Samson, S. Paul Aurelian, S. Malo and S. Brioc, usually have little or no cult in the country of their origin".   See further Bowen, 'The *Peregrini*', SCSW 87-103.
[253] Located in Cornwall, Somerset and Glamorgan, and apparently a little earlier than the others. But the traditions regarding him are faint and scanty, cf. Doble, SC iv. 105-9; J. Morris, JTS new series, xvii. 372-8.

Pelagius, had been nurtured. In any event, the zone of their cult seems to extend from the south-east along the Somerset-Devon coast into Mid-Cornwall, and thence to Brittany.[254]

Paulinus, or Peulin, may be the same as Paul Aurelian,[255] one of the founders of the Faith in Brittany. He is mentioned as a teacher of David and Teilo, and is possibly earlier by a generation than both. There are good reasons for supposing that he hailed from east Carmarthenshire.

To the same region belongs Teilo, a saint widely venerated in South Wales and in Brittany. He lived in the sixth century and was probably a contemporary of David.[256] Both belong essentially to the south-west, to the part where there could hardly have been many early Christian survivals, and where Irish rather than Roman culture had been predominant. Along with Padarn[257] (who may, however, have been a little earlier and more in contact with Roman culture), they must have been prominent in a movement which had, apparently, emanated from the west, a movement more ascetic and less intellectual in character than earlier movements. The progress of their mission was most marked in the parts least affected by Roman culture.[258] Teilo founded Llandeilo Fawr in Carmarthenshire, and it was probably from this centre that his cult was diffused to other areas. It was at a later stage that his name became linked with Llandaff where he was claimed as the second of its bishops.[259]

These saints, of course, represent only a small proportion of those missionaries who laboured in various parts of Wales (both north[260] and south) during this period. The initial task of

254 SCSW 103.
255 But cf. SC i. 36.
256 Cf. D. S. Evans, 'An Approach to the Historical Dewi—Some Comments' (*The Friends of St. David's Cathedral, 1963 Report*, 7-13).
257 But the origins of Padarn may lie in south-east Wales. Cf. SCSW 55; also Doble, *Saint Patern* ('Cornish Saints' series, No. 43, 1940).
258 A movement to be distinguished from that with which the saints of the south-east, Dubricius, Cadog and Illtud, were associated; cf. SCSW 33-48, especially pp. 44-45. The area in which Dewi and Teilo (and Padarn) worked was then, as now, culturally distinct from the south-east.
259 But cf. C. A. Edwards, 'St. Teilo at Llandaff' (JHSCW v. 38-44).
260 For the saints of the north and their movements see Bowen, 'The Saints of Gwynedd' (*Trans. Caerns. Hist. Soc.* ix. 1-15), 'The Northern Cults' (SCSW 66-86). Cf. also C. N. Johns, ''The Celtic Monasteries of North Wales' (*Trans. Caerns. Hist. Soc.* xxi (1960), 14-43). Here I have limited myself to two areas, the south-east and the south-west, to which the saints discussed in this volume primarily belong.

formal conversion may well have been completed by the end of the sixth century.[261] A great deal from this period still remains obscure, although we are able gradually to unearth some of the evidence which has lain hidden for so long as a result of ignorance, prejudice and the lapse of time. Through the haze of the centuries a picture is gradually emerging of a new people, appearing from the ruins of Romano-British order and civilization. We can with confidence regard as historical personages the names and characters produced by the researches of scholars, saints such as Dyfrig, Illtud, Cadog, Samson, Gildas, Paul Aurelian, Padarn, David, Teilo, Deiniol, Beuno, Kentigern, Cadfan, Seiriol, Cybi, chieftains such as Vortigern, Cunedda, Ambrosius, Arthur, Gwrthefyr, Maelgwn Gwynedd, Cynan Garwyn, bards such as Talhaearn, Aneirin, Taliesin, Bluchbard, Cian. These men belonged to widely different spheres, and the nature of their work varied greatly, but they all contributed positively and creatively to the growth and development of a new people. The Welsh people born of this period in a part of the highland zone which the Anglo-Saxons never conquered, represent a blending and fusion of both old and new. Here we have a new political set-up, a new cultural awakening, a new language, and, what is more important, a new Faith. The Welsh language and the Christian faith, together the two basic elements in the birth of a new people, have survived to our own day as the essential ingredients of Welshness. Such is the continuity over thirteen centuries within which all changes, movements and impulses have to date been contained and assimilated. Professor E. G. Bowen inclines to the view that"there is continuity of settlement on the site of existing churches from the days of the saints themselves".[262] This continuity so persistently evidenced on all sides and in all spheres, physical and cultural, material and spiritual, explains, indeed constitutes that bewildering phenomenon which the scholar with his limitations can only describe as the History of Wales.

[261] Cf. C. A. Ralegh Radford (AC cxi. 4) : "The conversion of the British Celts was not only begun, but, in my view, completed, before the establishment of the Rule of St. Benedict and before the time of Pope Gregory the Great (590-603)".

[262] SCSW 141.

SAINT DUBRICIUS[1]

THE earliest mention we have of Dubricius is in the *Vita Samsonis*, written by a monk of the monastery of Dol in Brittany, probably at the beginning of the seventh century.[2] It is, of course, entirely free from the tendentious corruptions introduced into the story five centuries later in the interests of the see of Llandaff.

In c. 13 of this *Life* the *papa* Dubricius[3] comes to Eltut's monastery (*domus*) on a Sunday and ordains Samson deacon, two other brethren being ordained presbyters at the same time. During the customary prostration, and again when the bishop lays his hand upon Samson, a dove descends upon the latter, but is seen only by the bishop, the *magister* (Eltut) and the deacon who had chanted the gospel and was holding the chalice. We observe that Dubricius is introduced into the story without any explanation as to who he was and where he came from.

In c. 15 "the same bishop" ordains Samson presbyter. The miracle of the dove, we are told, was repeated, but is only briefly referred to.

Soon after (cc. 20 and 21) Samson leaves the monastery and goes to "a certain island lately founded by a certain holy presbyter called Piro". In c. 33 we are told that Bishop Dubricius, who was accustomed to spend the greater part of Lent in this island, receives Samson kindly on his return thither from his home at the beginning of Lent, together with his father and uncle. Dubricius is said to be dwelling in the island "in his own house" (*quippe in sua domo commanebat*). Not long afterwards the holy *papa* Dubricius sends for a deacon, who had accompanied Samson on his journey, and listens with interest

---

[1] *Published in 1943, Billing and Sons Ltd., Printers, Guildford and Esher, in the 'Welsh Saints' series, No. 2, with a foreword by the Lord Bishop of Hereford.]

[2] Duine thought "between the years 610 and 615." In any case it cannot be later than the middle of the ninth century, and is clearly much older. *See also p. 8.]

[3] *Dubricio papa* in four MSS., *Dubritio* or *Dubricio episcopo* in four.

to the story of what had happened. He decides to make Samson cellarer (*pistor*). This arouses the jealousy of a brother who had formerly held this office, and he accuses Samson of wasting the honey stored in the monastery. Dubricius visits the cellar, but first sends a boy to warn Samson of his intention to do so. Samson makes the sign of the cross over the jars, and the bishop, on his arrival, finds them quite full. Moved with admiration, he destines Samson for further promotion. Not long after Piro dies. Dubricius calls the brethren together after matins, and at his suggestion Samson is unanimously chosen abbot in Piro's place.

Not long after Samson's return from a visit to Ireland a synod is held (c. 42) in a place of which the name is not mentioned. The elders (*majores*) send for Samson and receive him on his arrival as "an angel of God". He "is appointed, against his will, abbot of the monastery, which, they say, had been built by S. German". The writer adds that the brethren had come together for the purpose of holding a consecration of bishops in this monastery, which they were accustomed to do on the feast of S. Peter's Chair.[4] This festival was approaching, and several bishops were expected to take part in the service. On their arrival two candidates are decided on. It was, however, the custom (*antiquitus traditum*) to consecrate not less than three bishops at the same time. In a dream Dubricius is informed by an angel, "as he himself used afterwards to relate", that Samson was to be the third. He immediately has "all the best counsellors of the congregation" awakened, and tells them of the vision. Samson is unanimously elected, and consecrated next day. The service is again attended by miraculous manifestations, one being visible to all and the other only to *papa* Dubricius and two distinguished monks.

The author of the *Vita Samsonis* introduces Dubricius again in Book ii, which is a homily read at Dol on the saint's festival. He tells a long story about Samson, after his consecration, making a journey to visit *papa* Dubricius, who was ill, in a place the name of which is not given. (It is not clear why he did not insert this episode, where we should naturally have expected to find it, in Book i. It is certainly very unsuitable in

---

[4] *beati Petri apostoli cathedrae* [22 February].

its present position.) Dubricius asks Samson to take charge of a
certain young man, to whom he was much attached, a deacon
named Morinus. Samson takes the boy, makes the sign of the
cross on his forehead and kisses him, but not without some
misgivings, of which he gives a hint by remarking to Dubricius
that the net in the parable (Matt. xiii. 47, 48) gathered bad fish
as well as good. Dubricius is pained, but conceals his annoyance
by silence. Samson perceives it, however, and to please the
papa entrusts to Morinus the care of his episcopal chrism.
Some time after, while Samson and the deacon were praying
together in church, the former perceived a devil in the form of a
little black boy on Morinus's shoulder, whispering into his ear.
The deacon is taken ill, and confesses to Samson that he has
been from childhood in intimate association with an evil spirit.
He dies, and Samson orders his body to be taken out of the
monastery, nor is anything more said about Dubricius.

The author of the *Vita Samsonis* tells us that he had visited
Wales, and that he "had been in Eltut's magnificent monastery"
(c. 7) and also in the island of Piro (c. 20). Most of the stories he
relates about Samson in Wales have to do with these two places.
We are not, indeed, explicitly told where the monastery of which
Samson was made abbot after his return from Ireland and in
which he was consecrated bishop was, but it seems to be
Llanilltud (Llantwit), as it is stated to have been built by
S. German, and Eltut is said (c. 7) to have been a disciple of,
and ordained priest by, S. German. Nothing is said about
Eltut in the story of Samson's consecration, and it has been
inferred from this that he was already dead, or had (according
to the tradition recorded in the *Vita Iltuti*) gone to Brittany.

To sum up, the *Vita Samsonis* shows us that Dubricius was a
greatly revered character at Llantwit Major and Caldy Island[5] in
the seventh century. He is seven times called *papa* and four times
sanctus papa or *Sanctus Dubricius papa*. In confirmation of the
story of his frequent residence in the monastery on the island of
Piro "in his own house", in which he acts with authority, sole
and supreme, it is noteworthy that "an early inscribed stone, in

---

[5] M. Fawtier (*La Vie de S. Samson*, Paris, 1912, pp. 31-43) has challenged the
identification of the *Insula Pironis* with Ynys Bŷr (Caldy Island), but no other
site has yet been suggested.

Ogam and Latin, has been discovered on Caldy Island. The now imperfect Ogam inscription reads, MAGL DUBR, which seems to mean 'the tonsured servant of Dubricius'."[6] We observe, too, that the last of the nine charters prefixed to the *Vita Dubricii* in the *Liber Landavensis* purports to be a grant of land at *Penn Alun* (now Penally), near Tenby, immediately opposite Caldy Island, 'to God and Archbishop Dubricius'.

Dubricius is not mentioned in the *Vita Pauli Aureliani*, and our next source of information about him is in the *Liber Landavensis*, compiled five hundred years after the *Vita Samsonis*.

The object of the author of this famous book[7] is to prove the antiquity and grandeur of the see of Llandaff, and in particular to claim for the *parochia* (diocese) *Landaviae* all the property which was believed to have belonged to two of the most famous saints of South Wales, Dubricius and Teilo. Much of this was now included in the dioceses of Hereford and St. David's, and to recover it the energetic Bishop Urban struggled indefatigably throughout his episcopate.

Dubricius was undoubtedly one of the earliest of the Welsh saints.[8] The oldest part of the original manuscript[9] of the *Liber*

---

6 LBS ii. 370, and Professor Macalister in AC (1938), 281-2. *The reading of the Ogam inscription in R. A. S. Macalister, *Corpus Inscriptionum Insularum Celticarum* (Dublin, 1945), i. 405, is MAGL[I]DUBAR[. . .]QI. In ECMW 180 the reading is MAGL[IA(?)] DUBR[ACUNAS(?) MAQI]INB. This inscription cannot serve as evidence of Dubricius's association with Caldy. Cf. E. D. Jones, NLWJ iv. 130, n. 1.]

7 As the *Vita Sancti Teliavi* in Vesp. A.xiv., which is identical (except for certain omissions) with that in the *Liber Landavensis*, is there stated to have been written by a brother of Bishop Urban (*a Magistro Galfrido* [*i. Stephano* has been interlineated above] *fratre Urbani Landavensis ecclesiae episcopi dictata*), it has been inferred that he was the author of the *Book of Llandaff*. It is possible, however, that the latter is not Geoffrey, but a clerk of Llandaff who revised his work (cf. pp.164-6).

8 *There has been no lack of speculation as to his dates. One of the most recent attempts is that of N.Tolstoy; cf. *Trans. Cymmr.* (1964), 303: "David and Dubricius were contemporaries and associated with each other, and it is, therefore, probable again that the real date of Dubricius's death is 532." The Rev. A. W. Wade-Evans (ib. p. 129) gives 556 as the year of the saint's death (cf. also *Anglo-Welsh Review* x. 1960), while R. W. D. Fenn in *Province* xi. 65 mentions a date not later than 540 or 541.]

9 This manuscript is written in several different hands. The earliest begins on col. 77, p. 68 of the printed edition published by J. Gwenogvryn Evans in 1893 (all references made will be to that edition). *Cf. further E. D. Jones, NLWJ iv. 123-57; and see p. 12 n. 70 for references to more recent discussions of this book.]

Landavensis consequently begins with an attempt to reconcile
the Welsh traditions about this saint with what the writer knew
of early British ecclesiastical history from other sources, in order
to make a convincing argument in favour of his case.   This
section is headed *De primo statu Landavensis ecclesiae, et Vita
archiepiscopi DUBRICII.*

In the *De primo statu Landavensis ecclesiae* the writer
describes the beginnings of Christianity in Britain, borrowing the
names of Lucius, king of the Britons, and of Pope Eleutherius,
and the date 156, from Bede's *Ecclesiastical History* (Lib. i, c. 4).
He adds the statement that the letter sent to Eleutherius by
Lucius was carried by two messengers called *Eluanus* and
Meduuinus,[10] whom the Pope baptized and ordained.   He then
refers to the mission of SS. Germanus and Lupus to Britain and
ascribes to them the division of the country into dioceses.
The blessed Dubricius, *summus doctor*, is appointed by them
archbishop over the whole of "Southern Britain", having been
elected by the king and the whole *parochia*, and they fix his
episcopal see at the *podum* (monastery) of *Lanntam*, founded in
honour of S. Peter the apostle, with the consent of King *Mouricus*.
The extent of the diocese is defined so as to include the territories
which Urban claimed,[11] and the property and rights of the
parochia Landaviae, and its *refugium* or sanctuary, are enumerated.
The procession of the clergy bearing crosses and relics and the
king carrying the gospel-book on his back around the limits
of the sanctuary is described.   Dubricius then sent some of his
disciples to take charge of churches which had been given him
and for others he founded churches.   He consecrated bishops
for the dioceses of "Southern Britain", among others Daniel to be
bishop of the city of Bangor.   Some he made abbots, Ildut
being appointed abbot of Lannildut, and on others he conferred
the presbyterate and the minor orders.   This section ends with

[10] It has been suggested that the writer got this name from *Llanfedwy*, near
Rudry, in the extreme east of Glamorgan.   There is a chapel of *Saint-
Elouan* in Brittany (see Loth, *Les Noms des saints bretons*, 37 and 131). A *S.
Elwin* is honoured in West Cornwall, and *S. Ailwini, Conf.*, appears in the
kalendar in Vesp. A. xiv on 20 November.

[11] The statement that the diocese contained 500 *tribus* is interesting.   Wrmonoc
(*Vita Pauli*, c. 19) tells us that King Philibert, in founding the diocese of
Léon, gave S. Paul 100 *tribus*.   Perhaps, however, he really means 'five
cantrevs.'

the statement that "the *locus* of Mochros on the bank of the Wye, which in the former time the blessed man Dubricius had first inhabited, was given by King Mouric to the church of Llandaff and its pastors for ever, and it was decreed that the former *locus* should always be in subjection to the latter."

It seems impossible that the author can have had any kind of authority for his statements about Dubricius in the *De primo statu Landavensis ecclesiae*, and they must be regarded as almost entirely drawn from his imagination.[12] In what follows, however, he does give us the traditions about the saint which he found existing in Wales in the twelfth century, and contents himself with adding a few phrases here and there. Llandaff is not mentioned in the *Life of S. Dubricius* (except in the appendix describing the translation of the saint's body thither), which is written entirely from the point of view of *Mochros*.

The *Life* is preceded by nine charters granting land, mostly in Herefordshire, to "Dubricius, archbishop of the see of Llandaff". It will be convenient to deal with them after examining the *Life of S. Dubricius* which follows them.

The cartularies of monasteries (and the *Liber Landavensis* is meant to be a cartulary) usually contain a *Life* of the founder or of the saint honoured there. The body of S. Dubricius had recently been brought to Llandaff, and lessons containing the story of his life were required for his festival, which was now observed there each year on November 14. The *Life of S. Dubricius* is material for such lessons. The writer, however, had not the leisure to work it up into homiletic form, as has been done for S. Teilo.

The *Life* is very different from what the *De primo statu* would lead us to expect. It consists of local Herefordshire legends, which the author of the *Book of Llandaff* may have found in an older *Life* used in a church dedicated to S. Dubricius, perhaps *Mochros*, and which he has supplemented by borrowing from the *Vita Samsonis* and by adding an appendix.

---

[12] The author has read Nennius, since he refers to Brutus as "the first inhabitant of the region". He has also read the *Annales Cambriae*, from which he borrows the date of Dubricius's death, in spite of its being inconsistent with his own words in the *De primo statu*, and perhaps the name of St. Deiniol. There may possibly, however, have been in fact a connection between Dubricius and Deiniol (cf. note 72).

The *Life* begins abruptly with the story of *Pepiau,* king of *Ercych,* on his return from a military expedition, discovering his daughter *Ebrdil* to be pregnant. He sentences her, first, to be drowned in the Wye, and then, as the current continually brings her back to the bank, to be burnt. She is found next day alive, holding at her breast her child, which had been born on a stone that still stands on the site in remembrance of the miracle. The place is called *Matle,* because the blessed man was born there. The mother and child are taken to the king, and the touch of the babe's hands cures the latter of an infirmity from which he had long suffered, which required the constant ministrations of two attendants to wipe the drivel from his face, and in consequence of which he had been nicknamed in Welsh *Clavorauc* (*Latine Spumosus*). The king conceives a special affection for the child and makes him heir of the place where he was born. The derivation of the name *Matle* is again given, more explicitly— the writer states that *Mat* means 'good' in Welsh and *le* means 'place'. With *Matle,* the king grants to the child the whole 'island' which is called, after his mother *Inis Ebrdil,* and is also known as *Mais Mail Lochou* [this name is not explained]. The boy grows and is sent to school. After he has become a man, his fame for wisdom and for knowledge of the old law and of the new law (i.e. the Old and New Testaments) spreads so widely that students from all over Britain, not only boys, but wise men and teachers, flock together to learn from him. A list of his disciples is given: *In primis sanctus Teiliaus. Samson discipulus suus. Vbeluius. Merchguinus. Elguoredus. Gunuinus. Congual. Arthbodu. Congur. Arguistil. Iunabui. Conbran. Guoruan. Elheharn. Iudnou. Guordocui. Guernabui. Louan. Aidan. Cinuarch.* Besides these, he had under his care a thousand clerks, for a space of seven years, at the monastery of Hentland (*in podo Hennlann super ripam Gui*), training them in the knowledge of letters and of wisdom, divine and human, and showing in himself a pattern of religious life and perfect charity. He then [removed from Hentland (no reason being given for his doing so) and] spent another space [of time—the number of the years is not mentioned] in the place of his birth—that is, in *Inis Ebrdil,* choosing a spot (*locum*) in a corner of that island, on the river Wye, convenient because of its being well wooded and abounding in fish. Here he remained, with his innumerable disciples, for many years, continuing his teaching (*regendo studium*). He called the place *Mochros*. The writer carefully explains the etymology of the name, which he says is derived from the Welsh *moch* = 'pigs' and *ros* = 'place', and relates a topographic legend to say why it bore this name. An angel, he says, had appeared to Dubricius in a dream one night and instructed him to build a settlement and a church in the name of the Holy Trinity (*funda et conde in nomine Sanctae Trinitatis habitaculum simul et oraculum*) at the place he had already marked out for this purpose, the exact spot to be indicated by his finding there a white sow with young. Immediately on awaking, the saint with his disciples obediently went round the place (or "site of the monastery"—*locum*), and, as the angel had promised, a white sow with her pigs started up from her lair. On that spot he built the settlement and church, and there for many years he lived as a monk (*regulariter vixit*), preaching and teaching the clergy and people, and through his teaching, which shone throughout Britain "like a candle upon a stand" (Matt. v. 15), the whole British nation preserved the true Faith without any stain of false doctrine.

After a few commonplaces of panegyric, the author inserts into his narrative the story of the jealous ex-cellarer and the honey-jars, borrowed from cc. 33-36 of the *Vita Samsonis*, but retold in his own words and considerably elaborated and added to. He does not, however, mention the island of Piro as the scene of the incident, but says it happened in the *locus* and *domus beati Ilduti*. He also recapitulates the stories in the *Vita Samsonis*, cc. 13 and 15. The insertion has been most clumsily made in the middle of a sentence describing the miraculous cures wrought by Dubricius.[13]

The writer then returns to the *Life* he is copying, and proceeds to give the promised instance of Dubricius's miracles. A certain ruler of royal blood (*potens vir regali prosapia procreatus*), named *Guidgentiuai*, came to him and, kneeling, asked him to

---

[13] The original *Life* must have run: *et ut quiddam de multis enarrem, confugientibus populis ex solito*. The long passage *vir beatae memoriae . . . remunerando* (BLD 81, 82) has been inserted between *enarrem* and *confugientibus*.

deliver his daughter *Arganhell*, who was possessed by a devil and
had to be tied up to prevent her throwing herself into fire or
water.   Dubricius prostrated himself, and prayed to God, by
the intercession of the blessed Peter, the prince of the Apostles,
and of all the Saints, to succour the afflicted girl, who straightway recovered her former health and passed the rest of her life in
(the consecrated state of) virginity under the holy man's
protection[14] as an anchorite or nun.

The *Life* proper concludes with the story of how the saint
retired to Bardsey Island and died there :

> The blessed man, seeing that his life (*or* vital powers) sufficed not
> for himself and for the people too, oppressed by certain infirmaties[15]
> and by old age, resigned the laborious task of the episcopal office,
> and (resuming) the eremitical life, in company with several holy
> men and with his disciples, who lived by the labour of their hands,
> he dwelt alone for many years in the island of Enli and gloriously
> finished his life there.   It has been for ages a proverbial saying
> among the Welsh that this island is 'the Rome of Britain', on
> account of its distance—it is situated in the extremity of the
> kingdom—and of the danger of the sea-voyage, and also because
> of the sanctity and charm of the place: sanctity, for twenty
> thousand bodies of saints, as well confessors as martyrs, lie buried
> there: and charm, since it is surrounded by the sea, with a lofty
> promontory on the eastern side and a level and fertile plain,
> where there is a fountain of sweet water, on the western.   It is
> entirely free from serpents and frogs, and no brother has ever died
> there leaving one older than himself to survive him.[16]

The writer adds, in a passage which from its broken and
ungrammatical construction seems to be corrupt, that the
natives of the island venerated Dubricius with a special cult,
invoking him, among the other saints of the island, as an
intercessor with God and the defender of the whole *patria*.
He complains of the scantiness of information about the saint,
due either to the records having been burnt during hostile raids
or removed when the monks on the island had been forced by

---

[14] *sub refugio sancti viri.*   Possibly there may be a reference to the saint's
refugium or sanctuary.
[15] Cf. *Vita Samsonis*, Lib. ii. c. 7: *Dubricium . . . qui quadam aegritudine corporis
vexabatur.*
[16] The description of *Enli* is word for word the same as in the *Life* of St. Elgar
the hermit on pages 1 and 2 of the *Book of Llan Dâv.*

these raids to desert it, but claims that this *Life* is based *monumentis seniorum et antiquissimis scriptis litterarum*.

The translation of the saint's body by Bishop Urban to Llandaff took place in 1120 (the body was removed from *Enli* on Friday, May 7, and received, with a procession, at Llandaff on Sunday, May 23), and is described in a passage of considerable length and great detail, in striking contrast to the exiguous and vague *Life* to which it serves as an appendix, and the writer ends by saying that it was on this occasion that the insignificance of the older minster of Llandaff was recognized and the construction of a larger one in honour of Peter the apostle and the holy confessors Dubricius, Teilo and Oudoceus undertaken. The author prefixes to the story a statement, which he had taken from the *Annales Cambriae*,[17] that Dubricius died on November 14, 612. It did not occur to him that he had previously told us that the saint was a contemporary of S. German of Auxerre, which would make him nearly two hundred years old in 612.

The *Life of Dubricius* used by the compiler of the *Liber Landavensis* is not really a biography at all. It is a collection of traditions and local legends, made centuries after the time of the saint. It is silent about many of the things we most want to know. It does not tell us who was the saint's teacher or where he was educated. It does not mention his being consecrated bishop, and not a word is said about his exercising any episcopal functions until he resigns them. Till then he is represented only as a master. This is puzzling, since in the *Vita Samsonis* he appears as a bishop, not a teacher, while Iltut is the *magister*. There is no reason, however, to doubt that Dubricius really was connected with the places with which the traditions recorded in the *Vita Dubricii* associate him.

The opening section of the *Life of Dubricius* is a legend about *Matle*, intended to explain the connection between Dubricius and an older saint venerated in the neighbourhood—*Ebrdil*. The author tells us that close to *Matle*, perhaps surrounding it,

---

[17] 612. *Conthigerni obitus, et Dibric episcopi*. The writer may also have borrowed the name of "Daniel, bishop of Bangor", from the *Annales Cambriae*—584. *Depositio Danielis Bancorum*.

was some church land called *Inis Ebrdil*. This must have included the *Lann Ebrdil* mentioned in a charter on page 192 of the *Book of Llan Dâv* as being close to *Mochros* (it comes between *Mochros* and *Bolgros*). The *Insula Ebrdil* appears in another charter (on p. 76). North-east of Usk, in Llan Denny, was another *Lann Emrdil* or *Efrdil* "*in Brehes*" (*Book of Llan Dâv*, p. 159—the form *Llann Eurdyl* has been added in the margin of the manuscript). There was also a *Finnaun Efrdil* on the Monnow (in Llangynvil, near Welsh Newton) referred to in a charter on page 173 and in another on page 264 of the *Book of Llan Dâv*. The charter on page 78 which gives the boundaries of Llandeilo Fawr mentions a stream called *Euyrdil*, and it is significant that this charter is one of those prefixed to the *Life of S. Dubricius*, and that the connection between Llandeilo Fawr and Dubricius is insisted on both there (p. 77) and elsewhere in the book (p. 133). It is possible that a saint of very early date (perhaps really a male saint), whose career had been entirely forgotten, has come to be regarded as Dubricius's mother, and an unedifying story linking the two has been invented or adapted, as seems to have happened in the case of S. David and S. Nonna.[18]

Pepiau or *Peipiau* appears (in the form *Peibio*) as a legendary king in Welsh folklore.[19] Rhigyfarch tells us that S. David "cured Peibio,[20] the blind king of Erging, by restoring light to his eyes". The writer may have learned his nickname *Clavorauc* from the charter he gives on page 163, but the extraordinary story[21] he tells to explain it shows his imperfect knowledge of Welsh, since the word really means 'leprous', though the Welsh word for 'drivel' (*glafoer*) is not unlike it. It is, of course, quite possible that a Welsh king may have been a leper, and have been known, after his death, as 'Peipiau the Leprous', so that King *Peipiau Clavorauc* may be an historical character, though the story about him and *Ebrdil* is not historical.

---

[18] The authors of *Lives of the British Saints* reject the story.
[19] In the story of *Culhwch and Olwen* in the *Mabinogion* two kings called *Nynnyaw* and *Peibyaw* are changed into horned oxen on account of their sins. There is a parish of Garth *Beibio* in Montgomeryshire, and an Ynys *Beibio* near Holyhead; LBS ii. 363.
[20] *Pepiau, but more correctly *Proprius*; see J. W. James, *Rhigyfarch's Life of St. David* (Cardiff, 1967), 8, 33-34.]
[21] Originally, no doubt, intended as a joke.

The statement about Dubricius's school at *Hennlann* is no doubt a genuine tradition. Several of the most famous Celtic saints, like Iltut in Wales and Maudez and Budoc in Brittany, are described as *magistri* in a monastic school, to which thronged great numbers of pupils, eager for learning and thirsting for perfection. *Hen-lan*—'The Old Lan'—is a common name in Wales and Cornwall.[22] In Celtic times the sites of monasteries, schools and churches seem to have been not infrequently abandoned, and new sites sought, for reasons which were afterwards forgotten. Another *Hennlann*, called *Hennlann Titiuc*, is twice mentioned in the *Book of Llan Dâv* (pp. 183 and 231). The *Hennlann* of the *Vita Dubricii* is called *Hennlann Dibric* in the list of churches headed *De Terra Ercycg* on page 275, and is (with one exception—Llanwarne) the only place called after our saint in the book. It is now Hentland,[23] four miles west-north-west of Ross. Hentland is near the ancient Roman city of Ariconium, from which the little Celtic kingdom of *Ercic* or *Erging*, now the hundred of Archenfield, seems to have got its name. The site of Ariconium is in the parish of Weston Penyard, two miles east-south-east of Ross. It may well be that Hentland was found to be too close to the Saxon border for safety, and a more remote site was chosen.

The list of the disciples of Dubricius, which is introduced in a very abrupt manner must be an insertion of the author of the *Liber Landavensis*, and cannot have been found by him in the original *Life*. Every one of the names is found in some other part of the book (in several cases two or more being grouped in the same order in which they stand in the list of disciples), and it seems impossible to avoid the conclusion that he took the names he found in the charters and other ancient material he had collected for his book and used them, when he came to write the *Vita Dubricii*, to make a list of the disciples of his hero,

---

[22] There is a parish of Helland near Bodmin, and a Helland in Mabe (*Hellan* 1321), where the foundations of an ancient church have been discovered. A *Hen lann* (its site is unknown) is mentioned in one of the marginal entries in the *Book of St. Chad* (see BLD xlvii).

[23] Sir Allen Mawer, the secretary of the English Place-name Society, tells me "there is no doubt about the identification of Hentland. The early forms are *Hentlan* 1291 Tax Eccl., *Hantlan* 1316 Feudal Aids, *Henthlan* 1331 Reg. Bps. of Hereford."

such as he had met with in other *Lives* of saints.[24]   He had an
additional reason for compiling this list. We have seen that in
the *De primo statu* Dubricius is asserted to have had churches
given him which he assigned to his disciples, and to have
founded others which he dealt with in the same way—a very
unlikely story, but one which enabled him to claim a large
number of churches, many of which must have been founded
independently and at different periods, for the block of territory
which the diocese of Llandaff claimed as the inheritance of
Dubricius. He now names these disciples.

As one of the objects of the *Liber Landavensis* was to assert
the rights of Llandaff over all the Dubrician churches, many of
which now belonged to the diocese of Hereford, so another,
equally dear to the heart of the writer, was to claim for Llandaff
all the churches once belonging to the monastery of Teilo, many
of which had passed into the hands of the bishop of St. David's.
He is therefore careful to give Teilo the first place among the
disciples of Dubricius: *In primis sanctus Teiliaus*. In the *Vita
Sancti Teiliavi* he tells us that "we read" of Teilo's instruction
as a child by S. Dubricius, the archbishop, before becoming a
pupil of Paulinus, and he repeats the statement a few lines
farther on, showing that he felt it specially needed calling
attention to. In the charter, *De Penn Alun*, prefixed to the *Life of
Dubricius, Lann maur* (i.e., Llandeilo Fawr in Carmarthenshire) is
described as the place "where Teilo, the pupil and disciple of
S. Dubricius, lived".[25] The fact that in Erging a church of
Dubricius and one of Teilo were found side by side in the same
churchyard—*Hennlann Dibric et Lann Teliau in uno cimiterio*[26]—
may have suggested the idea of a connection between the two
saints to our writer, but it is possible that there really were
genuine traditions about such a connection at Hentland and at
Llandeilo Fawr.

The author of the *Book of Llandaff* was perfectly aware that
Samson was a disciple of Iltut, and had never been at Hentland,
but he considered, we must suppose, that his having been

---

[24] E.g. in the *Vita Pauli Aureliani* and the *Vita Iltuti*.
[25] BLD 77; cf. p. 133.
[26] Ib., p. 275. In the next line Llanwarne is called *Lann Guern Teliau ha
Dibric*.

ordained by Dubricius justified his being described as one of his disciples. In the *Vita S. Teiliavi* (BLD 109) he again claims Samson and Teilo as both disciples of Dubricius.

Ubelvivus appears in the list of the bishops of Llandaff (pp. 303 and 311) as the successor of S. Oudoceus, and is the bishop to whom the charters on pp. 160-2 are granted. He is a witness to four of the charters prefixed to the *Vita Dubricii*—viz., those granting *Lann Custenhinn Garthbenni, Tir Conloc, Porth Tulon* and *Penn Alun* (pp. 72, 76, 77).

The next three in the list of disciples—*Merchguinus, Elguoredus* and *Gunuinus*—appear together, and in the same order, in the *Life of S. Oudoceus* (pp. 131, 132), as being, with the abbots of Llanilltud, Nantcarfan and Llandochau, the electors when Oudoceus was chosen to succeed Teilo.

Merchguinus is the second of the "clerks of Dubricius" who are witnesses in the charter granting *Porth Tulon* to Dubricius (p. 76), *Ubelvivus* being the first. The king who granted the land bore the same name.

Elguoret is the second of the witnesses (*Arguistil* being the first) to the charters granting *Lann Garth* and *Lann Teliau Porth Halauc* to S. Teilo (pp. 121, 122), and seems to be the *Elguaret* who was a clerical witness to the charter granting *Lann Coit* to Bishop *Arguistlus* (p. 166). M. Loth has pointed out[27] that there is a village called *Saint-Eloret* in the parish of Goudelin, east of Guingamp in Brittany.

Gunuinus is described as *magister* in the *Life of S. Oudoceus* (p. 131). He appears to be the same as the *Gunnbiu* who is found on the next page in that *Life* and the *Gunbiu magister* who witnesses the charter granting *Cilciuhinn, Lann Gemei* (? in Gower) and *Lan Teliau Talypont* in Glamorgan to S. Oudoceus (p. 140). A *lector* named *Gunviu* witnesses two charters to Bishop *Berthguin*, the fourteenth bishop of Llandaff (pp. 182, 189), in each case preceding *Confur*.

Congual may be the *Cingual*[28] whose monastery in Gower, called *Lann Cingualan* on pp. 90 and 144 of the BLD was violated by King *Grifud* (ib., p. 239; his *ager* is mentioned in

[27] *Les Noms des saints bretons*, p. 37. He observes that "*El-guoret* pour *El-woret* donne régulièrement *Eloret*."
[28] *Lann Conuur* on p. 144 of the BLD is spelt *Lann Cynuur* on p. 145.

the same charter). A layman called *Congual* signs a charter granting land to Dubricius on p. 76, and a clerk of that name is described as *equonimus* on p. 218, and signs a charter on p. 235. There is a *Saint-Gonval*[29] in Penvenan, near Tréguier in Brittany, and a *Saint-Conval* in Hanvec, north of Châteaulin.[30] S. Conval is honoured in the diocese of Aberdeen on September 28, and is patron of Eastwood[31] and Inchinnan in Renfrewshire, of Cumnock and Ochiltree in Ayrshire, and of Kirkconnel and Kirkpatrick Fleming in Dumfriesshire (a *S. Congal* is patron of Durris in Kincardineshire and Holywood in Dumfriesshire). There is a Breton tenth-century *Vita Cunvali*.[32]

A *Lann Arthbodu* (also called *Cella Arthvodu*) in Gower is mentioned in the *Book of Llan Dâv* among the property recovered by Bishop Oudoceus (p. 144).

Lann Conuur, also called *Cella Conguri*, follows *Lann Arthbodu* on p. 144 (there is a *Lann Cynuur* on pp. 145 and 239).

Arguystil appears in the list of the bishops of Llandaff, where he occupies the ninth place, and a charter, by which King *Idon* grants *Lann Coit* (presumably Llangoed to Brecon[33]), *presenti Arguistlo pontifici*, is found later in the *Book of Llan Dâv* (pp. 166, 167). He is the first clerical witness after Dubricius in the charters granting *Lann Custenhinn* (p. 72), *Lann Iunabui* (p. 73), *Cum Barruc* (p. 74), *Tir Conloc* (p. 76), and *Penn Alun* (p. 77). In the charter of *Lann Cerniu* the first clerical witness is *Elgistil*, followed by *Iunabui* and *Cenguarui*, as *Arguistil* is followed by *Iunabui* and *Cinguarui* in that of *Lann Iunabui*, which looks as if *Elgistil* and *Arguistil* were the same person, but *Elgistil* is distinguished from *Arguystil* in the list of the bishops of Llandaff, where he occupies the sixth place. Four other *Arguistil*s (the name means 'pledge') appear in the *Book of Llan Dâv* (pp. 225, 246, 276). A saint of this name is the eponym of

[29] The story of *Le baptême de minuit* in Anatole Le Braz, *Légende de la mort*, ii. c. 84, pp. 68f., is about this chapel.

[30] Soc. Arch. du Finistère, 1904, p. 39.

[31] Festival on May 17.

[32] Published by M. André Oheix (Paris, Champion, 1911), cf. Duine, *Mémento*, Nos. 61 and 160, and *Saints de Domnonée*, p. 14. There is a *Tregonwell* in the parishes of Crantock and Manaccan in Cornwall.

[33] Near *Llandeilo* Graban.

Sant-Allouestre (1280, *Argoestle*), near St.-Jean-Brévelay, north of Vannes in Brittany.[34]

Iunabui signs the charter granting *Lann Cerniu* to Dubricius (BLD 73) and those of *Lann Iunabui* (Llandinabo), where he is called *presbiter*, *Cum Barruc* and *Penn Alun* (pp. 73, 74, 77). He must be the *Iunapius* who signs the charters of *Lann Custenhinn* and *Tir Conloc*. In the former he is also called *Iunapeius* and is described as the cousin of King *Peipiau*,[35] the charter grants the land to him as well as to Dubricius. He is the "Bishop Iunapeius" to whom the charters of *Lann Loudeu* and *Lann Budgualan* (pp. 163, 164) are granted, but in the list of the bishops of Llandaff his name has been spelt *Lunapeyus* (p. 311). In the *Vita S. Teliavi Iunapeius* is one of the former disciples of Dubricius who join Teilo after the latter's return from Brittany.

Conbran signs charters granted to Dubricius on p. 77 (preceding *Guoruan*), to Teilo on p. 122, and to Oudoceus on pp. 140, 146, 148, 149, 154 and 156. A *Conuran* is a clerical witness on pp. 72 and 76 (in each case preceding *Goruan*) and 167. A *Cinbran* appears on pp. 157 and 276, and a *Cunbran* on p. 150.

Guoruan seems to be the *Goruannus* who appears in the list of the bishops of Llandaff as tenth bishop (following *Arguystil*) and who is clearly the *Guruannus episcopus* who punished *Teudur*, king of *Brecheniauc*, for the murder of King *Elgistil*, and received from him the grant of *Lann Mihacghgel Trefceriau*, near Llan-gors (BLD 167). The name of *Goruan* follows that of *Conuran* in the charter of *Lann Custenhinn* (ib., p. 72). *Guoren* is a clerical witness to a charter on p. 75, and *Guoruan* follows *Conbran* in the charter of *Penn Alun* (p. 77). One of the three hermits of *Merthir Clitauc* was called *Guruan* (p. 195).

Elheharn must be the *Elharnn* who signs the *Lann Iunabui* charter (p. 73), and perhaps is the *Elheiarun* who signs that of *Cum Barruc*. As *Elhearn* he signs immediately after "Archbishop Dubricius" in the charter of *Cil Hal* (BLD 75), and after *Guoruan* (whom he follows in the list of the disciples of

---

34 The name appears in Cornwall at *Lanalwstel* (1250) and at *Tremaruustel* in Kea.

35 The words *consobrino suo* have been taken to mean that *Iunapeius* was the cousin of Dubricius.

Dubricius) in that of *Penn Alun*,[36] and he is the last clerical witness in the second *Cum Barruc* charter (p. 163). He signs the charter of *Lann Loudeu* as "*Helhearn,*abbot of *Lannguorboe*", and that of *Lann Cinmarch* as "*Elhearn*, abbot of *Lann Guruoe*" (? Garway, or perhaps, St. Devereux on the river Worm). The pedigree of a saint, *Elhaiarn*, is given in *Bonedd y Saint* (No. 35 in E) : he is described as "of Cegidfa in Powys", and as being a son of *Keruael*,[37] son of *Kyndrwyn* of *Lystin Wynnan* in Caer Einion. *Aelhaearn o Gegidfa ym Mhowys* has been added, on November 2, to the kalendar in Vesp. A. xiv. A saint of this name is eponym of Llan-aelhaearn in Caernarvonshire and of Capel Aelhaearn in Gwyddelwern (Merioneth), and of Parc-Saint-Elouarn in the parish of Plogonnec near Quimper in Brittany (it is significant that this parish contains a very important chapel of Saint-Théliau).

Iudnou signs before *Elharnn* in the charter of *Lann Iunabui* (p. 73) and after *Elhearn* in that of *Penn Alun* (p. 77). As "*Iudnou*, abbot of *Bolcros*" (Belley-moor in Madley), he signs the charter of *Lann Loudeu* before *Helhearn*. A layman of this name signs several charters.

Guordocui signs (after *Elhearn* and *Iudner*) the *Cil Hal* charter (p. 75) and (after *Iudnou*) that of *Penn Alun* (omitted in Vesp. A. xiv). He signs (after *Iudon*) the *Lann Garth* charter (p. 122). He seems to be the "*Guordoce*, abbot of *Lann Deui* (Much Dewchurch)", who signs the *Lann Loudeu* charter (p. 164) and that of *Lann Cinmarch* (as *Gurdocoe*).

Guernabui signs the charters of *Cil Hal* and *Penn Alun* after *Guordocui*. In that of *Lann Budgualan* (p. 164) he signs as *princeps Garthbenni, et alumnus eius Gurguare.*[38] Presumably he is the *Guernapui Guritpenni* of the *Lann Cinmarch* charter (p. 166). A *Guenopoui* signs after *Aidan* in the *Mafurn* charter (p. 163).

Louan appears to be the *Iouann* who signs the *Lann Custenhinn*, *Tir Conloc* and *Penn Alun* charters.[39] *Aidan* is the

---

[36] P. 77. His name and the two following names are omitted in Vesp. A. xiv.; see BLD 359.

[37] *Hygaruael* in two manuscripts, *Hyrgaruael* in one, *Eharnuael* in one, recte *Caranuael*. See Wade-Evans, AC 1931, p. 166. *Now see VSBG 322, no. 36, and Bartrum, EWGT 60, no. 36.]

[38] In the preceding charter *Gurguare* is the *alumnus* of *Guenuor*, *abbas Lanngarthbenni*.

[39] We have already had an example of how *L* and *I* have been confused.

"Bishop *Aidan*"of the *Mafurn* charter (p. 162), and is fifth in the list of the bishops of Llandaff, but otherwise is not mentioned.

Cinuarch is the patron of the "Church of *Cynmarch*, the disciple of S. Dubricius", near Chepstow, which was granted to Bishop *Comeregius* by King *Athruis* (BLD 165). The king went in procession round the land, sprinkling the boundaries "with dust from the sepulchre of *S. Cinuarch*, the disciple of S. Dubricius".

It is to be noted that "*S. Tisoi*[40], *alumnus* of S. Dubricius", whose *podum* (Llansoy in Monmouthshire) was granted to Bishop *Berthguin* (BLD 187), does not appear in this list of Dubricius's disciples.

We are next told that Dubricius, after leaving *Hennlann*, spent a further period of time in *Inis Ebrdil*. This must be a wide district containing *Matle*, for it is described as *in natiuitatis suae solio*, while we have been already told that *Matle* owed its name of 'the good place' to the fact that "the blessed man was born there". *Inis Ebrdil* was also called *Mais Mail Lochou*, which appears to be the *Campus Malochu*[41] mentioned in the charter on p. 165 as including *Lann Guoruoe* (see p. 72 of this work). Madley[42] is near Moccas, which is undoubtedly the *Mochros*

---

[40] One of the disciples of S. Paul of Léon was called *Toseocus* (Wrmonoc, *Vita Pauli*, c. ll.). *Soy* might be from an older *Se-oc*.

[41] The name seems to survive in that of *Mawfield* Farm in the parish of Allensmore, the church of which is about three and a half miles south-east of Madley Church. For the prefix *Mais*(='plain') cf. *maes Hewed* in *Annales Cambriae* (Rolls Series, p. 21)—i.e., 'the plain of Hyfaidd', the district around New Radnor. It is to be observed that Arclestone, now Arkstone Court, close to Allensmore, belonged to the bishops of Llandaff all through the Middle Ages, the sole remnant of all the Dubricius lands in Herefordshire claimed by the *Liber Landavensis*.

[42] Sir Allen Mawer tells me that "the early forms for Madley are *Medelagie* in Domesday (1085), *Madele* in Heref. Cath. Ch. (1200), and *Maddeleye* (ib., 1221). There is also a form *Maudel* in the Calendar of Charter Rolls (1280), which suggests that there may be something in the form beginning with *Magd-* and raises slight doubts in one's mind as to whether the identification of Madley and *Matle* is correct." It has been suggested that Madley= 'Mada's Meadow'. Possibly this part of Herefordshire was saxonised when the *Lib. Land.* was written and its author took an Anglo-Saxon name for a Welsh one. In any case, his explanation of *Mat-le* is very far-fetched. There is a place called *Childerstone*, on church land quite near Madley (a little to the west), to which he seems to refer and which is certainly English.

of the *Life of S. Dubricius*.[43]   Apparently the church of *Matle* was originally dedicated to S. Dubricius, since in the story of the two men of *Lannerch Glas* (BLD 194) we are told that one of them suggests to the other that they should go "to Matle, to the church of S. Dubricius, and there swear upon his altar to live henceforth in brotherly peace".   The author of the *Life* knew the neighbourhood of *Matle* very well indeed.   He gives us no less than four place-names, with explanations of the meaning of the names in Welsh in three cases, and stories accounting for their bearing those names.   He knows, too, the tradition about the stone which marked the site of the saint's birth, though he does not tell us what it was called.   He carefully describes Dubricius's monastery at *Mochros* and its exact position on the Wye.

It seems possible, from the statement in the *De primo statu* that King *Mouric* "decreed that the former *locus* [Mochros] should always be in subjection to the latter [Llandaff]", that the monastery at *Mochros* was still in existence, in a very attenuated form, when the *Liber Landavensis* was written.[44]   In any case, it is indisputable that it was still regarded as having been the centre of Dubricius's activities.   The *Vita* gives a topographic legend about it to account for its name.[45]   The finding of a sow with young on the site of a famous monastery is a favourite theme in Celtic *Lives* of Saints.   It appears in c. 15 of Wrmonoc's *Vita Pauli Aureliani*, written in 884, and in the much later *Lives* of S. Cadog and S. Brynach in Vesp. A. xiv., and in that of S. Kentigern.   The direction given by the angel to found a *habitaculum* "*in nomine sanctae Trinitatis*" looks like an interpolation made by the author of the *Liber Landavensis*.   Wrmonoc twice describes the foundation of a monastery by S. Paul of Léon as consisting of the building of *habitacula et parvum oratorium*.   Our author repeats the words *oraculum simul et habitaculum*

[43] Sir Allen Mawer says: "early forms *Mocres* 1242 Fees, *Mocros* 1291 Ch., *Mockers* 1291 Tax Eccl. confirm it.   The DB form *Moches* is unfortunately clearly defective."

[44] In the charter on p. 192 *Mochros*, followed by *Lann Ebrdil*, comes in a long list of churches in this part of Herefordshire, ending with *Lann Garan* (cf. pp 84 and 87 of this work), given to Bishop *Berthguin* after they had been desolated by a Saxon invasion.

[45] Mr. Wade-Evans points out that *Mochros* really means, not 'swine place', but 'swine moor' or 'swine peninsula'.

without the addition *in nomine sanctae Trinitatis* a few lines
farther on. The statement that a church was dedicated in the
name of the Holy Trinity is characteristic of the work of Norman
hagiographers.[46] Our author tells us (p. 161) that Bishop
Vueluiu "founded a church" at *Bolgros* "in honour of the
Holy Trinity and of S. Peter and of SS. Dubricius and Teliavus",
and on the next page tells us that the same bishop "founded a
locus (at *Lann Guorboe*) in honour of the Holy Trinity". Similar
statements are found in the *Vita Iltuti*[47] and the *Vita Cungari*.
The use of *oraculum* to mean a church is interesting and
unusual[48]; our author employs it again in the *Vita Oudocei*
(pp. 138 and 142), and in the *Life of S. Clitauc* (p. 194).[49]

The story selected by the writer of the original *Life of
Dubricius* to illustrate his thaumaturgic powers, immediately
before which, as we have seen, our author has very awkwardly
interpolated the section about Dubricius's relations with
S. Samson, is again based on Herefordshire legends. The name
of the demoniac girl, *Arganhell*, which seems to be a diminutive
of *arian* 'silver', is found as a place-name in two charters—
those of *Cil Hal* (BLD 75) and of *Lann Tipallai* (p. 173). In the
former "the boundary is from the great swamp to Arganhell",
while "the boundary of Lanntipallai" begins from *Licat Arganhell*
('the spring of Arganhell'). Mr. J. G. Evans identifies *Cil Hal*
with Pencoyd in Herefordshire (other scholars question this)[50]

---

[46] S. Benedict of Aniane dedicated (*c.* 800 A.D.) the church of Aniane in the
name of the Trinity, "anticipating", says Mr. E. Bishop (*Liturgica Historica*,
1918, p. 212), "a devotion which spread in the later middle ages, but was
alien to the mind and feeling of those earlier times".

[47] C.7. *Construens - - - illico habitaculum, presule Dubricio designante cimiterii
modum, et in medio, in honore summae et individuae Trinitatis, oratorii
fundamentum.* Cf. c. 16, *dilectio Sanctae Trinitatis erat ejus dulcedo*, and c. 18,
in sanctae et individuae Trinitatis honore servire. Cf. p. 84 note, 71, of this
work.

[48] Du Cange gives *aedes sacra in qua oratur* as one meaning of *oraculum*,with a
vague reference to the *Acta Sanctorum.* Cf. I Kings viii. 6.

[49] Wrmonoc gives us two interesting names for specially holy places in the
Celtic monastery on the Ile de Batz: *Locum quem usque hodie proprio nomine
Secretum appellant* (*Vita Pauli*, c. 17), and *in loco cui modo Signaculum*
[*Aroedma* has been interlined above] *nomen est* (ib. c. 23).

[50] A marginal note to the *Cil Hal* charter, written in the hand called D by
Mr. Evans, says that the *palus magna* and *Arganhell* are "In Goweer"
(Gower),but the king who grants the charter is *Erb, rex Guenti et Ercic*, and
Pepiau is one of the witnesses, which seems to prove that this is a baseless
guess.

and *Lann Tipallai* with 'The Parsonage Farm' in St. Maughan's (in Monmouthshire, but adjoining Herefordshire). It is to be observed that St. Maughan's is the *Lann Bocha* granted to "Saint Peter and Archbishop Dubricius" by *Britcon* and *Iliuc* (BLD 74) in the charter which precedes that of *Cil Hal* (which in turn is followed by one dealing with the Golden Valley in Herefordshire), and that *Lann Tipallai* follows *Lann Mocha* in the charter on pp. 171f.

The name of *Arganhell*'s father, *Guidgentiuai*, occurs again later in the *Liber Landavensis*. On p. 151 we read that "Bishop Oudoceus received Villa Greguri [Gabalfa, near Llandaff] from Guedguen, son of Brochmail", the only witnesses being *Rex solus* [*et*] *Guidgen cum suis*. On p. 159 *Brochmail filius Guidgentiuai* grants *villam Meneich* (in the title of the charter *Lann Menechi*) to Oudoceus. There is obviously some confusion here, but *Guidgen* and *Guidgentiuai* must be the same person (it has been suggested that *Tiuai* is an epithet attached to the real name). In c. 68 of the *Vita Cadoci* (which contains much material also utilized by the author of the *Liber Landavensis*, as we shall see) *Jacob*, abbot of the *cathedra* of S. Cadog, gives a horse to King *Mouric*, who bestows it on *Guodgen*, son of *Brocmail*. Among the witnesses are *Guedgen*, son of *Brocmail*. Nothing more is said about him. It is clear that *Guidgen* was a once-famous character, whose name was long preserved in Welsh tradition, though all knowledge of what he did had been forgotten in the twelfth century.

The vivid description of *Enli*[51] seems to be due to a personal visit to the island. The few traditions about it which our author here relates are of great interest, and it is a pity that so little should have come down to us of a place which seems to have fascinated the primitive saints of Wales. He himself complains that the desolation resulting from constant invasions had destroyed all records of its past history. One of the *Enli* legends which had survived and which he has preserved for us is

---

[51] Repeated in the *Vita Elgari* contained in the *Lib. Land.*, the handwriting of which is later than that of the *Vita Dubricii*. Elgar is there represented as seeing visions of "Dubricius, archbishop of Southern Britain, Daniel, bishop of the church of Bangor, S. Patern, and many others whose bodies are buried in the island."

identical with that which Wrdisten tells us was related in his
time (the second half of the ninth century) by aged monks of
Landévennec, in Brittany, about their own abbey.[52]

We have seen, in studying the *Vita Dubricii*, that there is a
close connection between its statements and those found in
other parts of the *Liber Landavensis*. It will be useful now to see
what further light (in addition to passages already quoted) the
charters[53] it contains may throw on the Welsh traditions about
the saint existing in the twelfth century.

The first four charters in the book, together with the sixth
and seventh, purport to be grants of land made to "Archbishop
Dubricius" by King *Peipiau* and his family. We learn some
details about him, such as the names of his father, of his father-
in-law, and of his sons (pp. 73 and 163), which are not mentioned
in the *Vita*, and we observe that in no charter is Dubricius said
to be his grandson, or in any way related to him.

The first deals with an estate (*mainaur*) at what is now
Welsh Bicknor.[54] It is constantly mentioned in the *Liber
Landavensis*[55] and was evidently a place of special importance.
It bore the name of *Custenhin* or Constantine, and the charter
mentions "King Constantine's *jaculum*" (apparently a ferry
across the Wye[56]). The writer adds that Constantine was
Peipiau's father-in-law.[57] There are some other interesting

---

[52] "In the first monastery no one could die . . . the monks compelled
Winwaloe to pull down the abbey and rebuild it towards the east, by the
shore . . . . Shortly afterwards the oldest monk died and others followed,
but still in order of age, ... And this was long the rule in the monastery
and has only recently been changed." *Vita Winwaloei*, Lib. ii., c. 26
(Doble, *S. Winwaloe*, p. 21, 2nd ed; * or SC ii 74-75.])

[53] They are called 'charters' here for convenience, but of course they are
really only summaries of the contents of charters or of entries on the margins
of gospel-books like the *Book of St. Chad*. It will be observed that none of
the Dubrician charters deal with Hentland, Madley or Mochros.

[54] It is called *ecclesia Sancti Custenin de Biconovria* in a St.-Florent charter of
1144 (*Bibl. de l'Ecole des Chartes*, 1879, p. 182).

[55] In the charters of *Lann Loudeu* and *Lann Budgualan* its *abbas* or *princeps* has in
each case an *alumnus* (BLD 164): King *Clotri* is punished for having broken
an oath made on the gospels and relics on its altar (pp. 176-8). In its
cemetery was a chapel called *Lann i Doudec Sent*, which suggests a
connection with S. Paulinus and Llan-gors (p. 276).

[56] Baxter and Johnson, *Mediaeval Latin Word-List* (Oxford, 1934).

[57] It will be observed that the second charter is that of *Lann Cerniu*, which on
p. 192 is called *Cenubia Cornubium* and is stated to be *super ripam Dour*.

details in this document. The king holds the *grafium*[58] (i.e. the real charter granting the land) on the hand of S. Dubricius, "that it might be a house of prayer and penitence . . . and an episcopal *locus.*" The words *domus penitentiae* remind one of the very common[59] Breton *pénity*, meaning a chapel founded by some famous Celtic saint (the last syllable is the Breton *ty* 'house'). The expression *episcopalis locus* might possibly be a latinization of the Welsh *escop-ty* ('bishop-house') which appears in the Laws of Howel the Good as meaning, apparently, an episcopal monastery with special privileges.[60] The charter concludes by stating that Dubricius "left there his three disciples and consecrated that church."[61] Unfortunately the six clerical witnesses are all found in the list of the saint's disciples in the *Vita*, so that the exact meaning of the statement is not clear. The land is stated to be granted by the king to "Dubricius and to Iunapeius his cousin" (apparently the king's cousin),[62] but *Iunapeius* comes fifth in the list of clerical witnesses. It would seem that the grant was really made to *Iunapeius*, and that "to Dubricius" only means that the estate was part of the Dubrician territory. The second lay witness is *Custenhin*. Presumably he is the eponym of the *lan*, and is called a witness in the same way as in the *Book of St. Chad* God and Teilo are called as witnesses to gifts to the monastery of Teilo. On the

---

Now it is remarkable that a *Kustennyn Gorneu* appears in *Bonedd y Saint* as an ancestor of S. Cybi [*see EWGT 58], and that *Llangystennin* in Caernarvonshire is close to *Llangernyw* in Denbighshire. The problem of disentangling the confusions between the various Constantines is a very formidable one. (It seems possible that *Cerniu* might be derived from the name of the Cornovii who inhabited the Welsh border in Roman times, and that the name may have been carried to Cornwall, where a good number of saints honoured in Archenfield are eponyms of parishes in the east of the county. The *Lib. Land.* mentions a Teilo church called *Tref i Cerniu* in Pembrokeshire). The author of the *Annales Cambriae* inserts the entry *Conversio Constantini ad Dominum* under 589.

[58] The word *graphium* is found in the *Vita Carantoci* in Vesp. A. xiv., and in Asser's *Life of Alfred*, also in the *Rule of S. Benedict.*

[59] See Largillière, *Pénity*, Quimper, 1927. He deals with twenty famous Penities.

[60] Wade-Evans, *Life of St. David* (London, 1923), 89, 94-95.

[61] One may compare this statement with the frequent entries *Hergualdus episcopus consecravit . . . et ordinavit . . . in presbiterum* which appear on p. 275f. of the BLD.

[62] *Consobrino suo* has been taken to mean that he was Dubricius's cousin, but, as *socri sui* immediately before means *Peipiau*'s father-in-law, the *suo* after *consobrino* may well refer to *Peipiau* too.

other hand Mr. Wade-Evans considers that in reality "King Constantine was the original donor or founder of Lann Cus-tenhin", which was consequently called after him, just as King *Erb*, another supposed great-grandfather of Dubricius, is the founder of *Cil Hal* and signs its charter (BLD 75) as first lay witness, followed by *Peipiau*.[63] "This proves," he says, that these two charters, "even when stripped of their Landavian accretions, are not true copies of originals, but composite productions, wherein the benefactors and ministers of the two monasteries are respectively brought together."[64]

The third charter is granted by King *Peipiau* to S. Dubricius and to his successors in the see of Llandaff, and conveys to him the *podum Junabui*, called in the title *Lann Iunabui*. Here again the grant cannot really have been made to Dubricius in person. Unless this is understood, it would be very disconcerting to find that a monastery called after *Iunapeius* is given to his master, and that *Iunabui presbiter* is among the clerical witnesses. It will be observed that this charter contradicts the statement (which we have already seen to be very improbable) in the *De primo statu* that Dubricius gave churches to his disciples. The word *podum* or *podium*, used as identical with *lann*, is a favourite term with the author of the *Liber Landavensis*, who uses it again and again, but seems to be otherwise unknown in this sense, though Du Cange gives *domus rustica* as one of its meanings.

The fourth charter deals with *Cum Barruc*, in the Dore valley, where also was *Tir Conloc*, the subject of the seventh. The fifth grants "to Saint Peter the apostle and Archbishop Dubricius of the archmonastery of Llandaff, and all his success-ors", *Lann Bocha* (now St. Maughan's in Monmouthshire). The eighth is the grant to Archbishop Dubricius of *Porth Tulon*

---

[63] This charter has much perplexed those who have tried to get accurate historical and genealogical information from these documents. Cf. LBS ii. 364, 365, 370.

[64] Unpublished notes kindly lent to me. There is a *Strickstenning* (so spelt *c.* 1650) in the parish of Much Birch near Hentland (see Bannister, *Place-names of Herefordshire*, p. 179). The name is very like the Cornish place-name *Triggstenton* (found in the parishes of Tywardreath and St. Endellion), which, C. G. Henderson thought, may contain the name *Constantine* or *Constenton*.

in "the region of *Guhir*" (Gower).[65]   It tells us that the place owed its name to a virgin called *Dulon* whom her father *Guorduc* "immolated" to Dubricius, who consecrated her as a nun. The name appears again on p. 90 of the BLD in the bull of Calixtus II as *Lann Teiliau Portulon*. The last of the supposed Dubrician charters is that of *Penn Alun*. Its significance will be understood when the connection of Dubricius with Caldy Island, already dealt with, is remembered, for the island, though possessing a Benedictine priory and several chapels, has for many centuries been within the parish of Penally. "Caldey Island," says Lewis's *Topographical Dictionary of Wales*, "is within the limits of this parish for all ecclesiastical purposes." Penally was the birthplace of S. Teilo, and the charter also tells us that Llandeilo Fawr, "where Teiliaus the *alumnus* and disciple of Dubricius lived," was granted to Dubricius at the same time, together with the "territory of the Church of the *Aquilenses*"— i.e. Llanddowror. No doubt there was in the twelfth century a tradition, perhaps based on fact, connecting Dubricius with these Teilo churches. The author of the *Liber Landavensis* has inserted (pp. 127-9) a long story, clearly based on Carmarthen-shire legends and not invented by himself, about the seven *Dybrguyr* or Watermen, who were disciples of S. Teilo at Llandeilo Fawr and "afterwards spent a long time in the company of S. Dubricius". In the *Vita S. Oudocei* he refers again to *Pennalun et Lannteiliau Maur et Landyfuyrguyr, quae prius fuerant archiepiscopi Dubricii* (p. 133).

A particularly interesting statement is found in the charter on pp. 225-6, headed *De Merthir Iun et Aaron*, in which *Gulfert*, *Hegoi*, *Arguistil*, the sons of *Beli*, and their household, grant to Bishop *Nud* "all the territory of the holy martyrs Julius and Aaron [at Caerlleon], which had formerly belonged to Saint Dubricius in the former time."[66] If this could be accepted as

---

[65] An Oudoceus charter on p. 144 mentions the *Ager sancti Dubricii in patria Guhyr*. A *S. Tula* appears in a group of Celtic saints (including *Canidir*, *Siloc* and *Triohoc*) in a litany in the British Museum (MS Galba A. xiv.).

[66] The exact meaning of the phrase so often recurring in the *Liber Landavensis*— *quod prius fuerat Sancti Dubricii in priore tempore*—is not clear. It may simply mean 'at an early period', or it may refer to the desolation of the Dubrician churches in Herefordshire described on p. 192, or the author may have had in his mind some other notion with regard to the original jurisdiction exercised by Dubricius to which we have lost the clue.

true, it would connect Dubricius with the British Church in the days of the Roman Empire.

The charter on p. 167 mentions an oath taken by two kings of *Brecheniauc per sancta sanctorum* "on the altar of S. Dubricius", but we are not told where it was.

The twelfth century saw a renaissance of literary activity in Wales, as in other parts of Europe. Not long after the *Liber Landavensis* had been compiled at the place from which it gets its name, a monk of Brecon priory began a Welsh legendary, which has come down to us in the British Museum manuscript Vesp. A. xiv. It was in this century, too, that Geoffrey of Monmouth's famous *History of the Kings of Britain* appeared. The important place held by Dubricius in Welsh tradition is shown by the way all these writers introduce him into their narratives.

The author of the *Vita Iltuti* in Vesp. A. xiv says (c. 7) that, after his conversion, "Aeltutus went to Dubricius, bishop of Llandaff, who enjoined upon him penance for his past sins and gave him the tonsure". Iltut then built a monastery, "Bishop Dubricius planning the cemetery".

The author of the *Vita Gundlei* in the same collection says (c. 10) that "when the most holy Gynlyu began to be sick and the end of his life approached, he sent for his son Cadoc and for Dubricius, bishop of Llandaff. And they came to the sick person and gave him penance, exhorting and comforting him with salutary doctrine. After which the bishop gave him absolution and the apostolical benediction."

In the *Vita Sancti David* by Rhigyfarch we read (c. 50) that after messengers had been sent three times to S. David to invite him to attend the synod of Brefi, and he had refused each time to come, out of humility, "at last the most holy men and the most faithful brethren, Daniel and Dubricius, are sent", and David finally consents.

In Geoffrey of Monmouth we have the fully developed legend of S. Dubricius. He is appointed archbishop of Caerlleon by Aurelius Ambrosius (Lib. viii., c. 12). In Lib. ix, c. 1, "Dubricius, archbishop of the City of Legions", crowns the youthful Arthur.   In c. 4 he addresses Arthur's soldiers in a loud voice from the top of a hill, in a speech which Geoffrey gives in full.   In cc. 12 and 13 Dubricius, described as "Primate of Britain and Legate of the Apostolic See, of so meritorious a piety that he could make whole by his prayers any that lay oppressed of any malady", places the crown on the king's head at Caerlleon at the feast of Whitsuntide and celebrates the religious services in the churches of the martyr Julius and of the blessed Aaron [it seems possible that Geoffrey may have got the idea of this story from the charter in the *Liber Landavensis* already referred to (BLD 225)].   In c. 15 he resigns the archi-episcopal see, "piously longing after the life of a hermit" (this detail, too, might be borrowed from the *Liber Landavensis*) "and David, the king's uncle, was consecrated in his place".

All these fancies were, very soon after their appearance, inserted into the Llandaff *Vita* by Benedict of Gloucester, whose new *Life of Dubricius* is found (together with an abbreviated version of the original) in Vesp. A. xiv. Benedict's *Life* is summarized by John of Tynemouth in *Nova Legenda Angliae*.

The evidence from topography and from references to the saint in liturgical documents will be found to confirm the impression derived from the study of the very incomplete and unsatisfactory efforts of medieval hagiographers.

The Reformation destroyed nearly all the liturgical books of Wales.   If it had not been for this we should no doubt have found much more about Dubricius in the service-books of Llandaff, where there was a chapel of the saint in the cathedral, which possessed his relics.[67]   The diocese of Hereford obtained most of the country which had been the principal scene of his activities.   An examination of the missals and breviaries of the Use of Hereford shows that the cult of S. Dubricius survived in

---

[67] John ap Iefan, treasurer of Llandaff, in his will (dated November 1, 1541) directed that he should be buried in this chapel, which seems to be the present Mathew chapel.   The cathedral possessed until 1558 "S. Dubrice hedde of silver & an arme of the seyd Seynte of silver" (LBS ii. 380).

this diocese into the Middle Ages. His name appears in a few, but not all of the kalendars they contain, while no other local Celtic saint finds a place there.[68] Two of the entries are of very great interest.

The kalendar of the twelfth-century Hereford noted breviary belonging to the chapter library of Hereford has the words *Dubricii episcopi et confessoris*, with *S. deuerecke* added in a later hand, on November 14. The importance of this entry is obvious—the addition of the vernacular form of the saint's name proves that the place in Herefordshire called *St. Devereux* are undoubtedly dedicated to Dubricius (which hitherto has been only an assumption).

The kalendar of the Hereford (manuscript) missal in the library of University College, Oxford, has on March 11 the following entry (addition): *Dedicatio ecclesiae albae in honore Sancti Dubricii, principale*. This is the dedication festival of *Whitchurch*, on the Wye, near Monmouth. The same missal has *Sancti Dubricii episcopi et confessoris, principale* on November 14 (on December 15 *Festivitas Sci dubricii, principale festum* was written by mistake, but afterwards scored through and partly erased).

In the small fifteenth-century Hereford breviary belonging to the chapter library of Worcester, a late hand has added Dubricius on November 14. Mr. Dewick's MS. of the Hereford missal has *Dubricius* as a red-letter day on the same date. The other kalendars which have come down to us omit him, neither is his name in the litany. No proper collect, antiphons or lessons for his feast are found in any breviary.

When we come to tabulate the churches dedicated to S. Dubricius and the places called after him, we are not surprised to find that, like the places mentioned in his *Life*, they are mostly grouped together in the west and south of Herefordshire.

The churches of two Herefordshire parishes in the deanery of Archenfield are given in Ecton's *Thesaurus* (1742) as dedicated to *S. Dubritius*—viz., those of Whitchurch (p. 214) and Hentland

[68] See *The Hereford Breviary* (Henry Bradshaw Society), Vol. III, pp. xxxi, 255, 261, 262.

(pp. 215, 221). Ballingham is also dedicated to him.[69] He is the eponym of St. Devereux, a parish in Archenfield near Kilpeck, called *S. Dubritii* in the *Valor Beneficiorum Ecclesiasticorum in Anglia* (ed. 1680, p. 128). In the parish of Woolhope was formerly a chapel of St. Devereux, called *capella S. Dubritii* in the *Valor*,[70] showing that the territory of the saint formerly included both banks of the Wye. Possibly two of the at present unidentified Dubrician churches in the *Liber Landavensis* might be placed here. It is very significant that until recently the parish of Lugwardine near Hereford, north of the Wye, in the deanery of Weston, possessed five chapels in Archenfield, one of them at a distance of no less than twelve miles.[71] All of them are mentioned in the *Liber Landavensis*. Two of them (Hentland and Ballingham) are dedicated to S. Dubricius, one (Llangarran) to S. Deinst (i.e., apparently, to S. Deiniol[72]), one (Little Dewchurch) to S. David, and one (St. Weonard's— *St. Waynard* in Ecton) to the *Sant Guainerth*[73] of the *Liber Landavensis* (pp. 275, 277). Preb. Seaton (*History of Archenfield*, p. 69)

---

[69] *Herefordshire*, by G. W. and J. H. Wade, p. 92; LBS ii. 380. *Also Bowen, SCSW 36-39.]

[70] *Hopewolnith cum cap S. Dubritii et Brokehampton annex.* On April 18, 1514, Bishop Mayew granted an indulgence for the support of the chapel (*sacellum*) of the Trinity at *Hope Wolwith* (Woolhope), commonly called Saint Dubricius, *a Domino Dubricio per angelicam visionem miraculose infra parochiam de Hope Wolwith, ubi Deus, per eiusdem famuli sui Dubricii merita, plura miracula operare dignatus est, constructum*: also for devout visits there (*Registrum Ricardi Mayew*, p. 285). This is of great interest as proving the survival of the popular cult of S. Dubricius in Herefordshire.

[71] In 1330 Bishop Thomas de Charlton provided that the revenues of Lugwardine, which, with its dependent chapelries, had recently been given to the Dean and Chapter by Johanna de Bohun, Lady of Kilpeck, should, after due provision for the maintenance of a vicar of Lugwardine be used for the salaries of a number of vicars choral in the cathedral, so as to ensure that the daily office of the B.V.M. in the Lady Chapel should be sung with due solemnity. The bishop's ordinance speaks of the *ecclesiam parochialem de Lugwardyn . . . cum suis capellis de Langaran, Sancti Waynardi, et Henthlan*, A TEMPORE CUJUS PRINCIPII MEMORIA HOMINIS NON EXISTIT *eidem annexis et dependentibus ab eadem* (Register of Bishop Charlton, printed by the Cantilupe Society, pp. vii and 35; cf. also Bishop Orleton's Register, p. 386, note, and Bishop Trillek's Register, p. 116).

[72] S. Deiniol is associated with S. Dubricius, as we have seen, in the *Vita S. David* and in the *De primo statu*. There was a chapel of S. Deiniol at Penally, with a holy well. The church of *Lanndiniul* is mentioned on pp. 171-2 of the *Liber Landavensis* (*Lann Dineul* on p. 32) and has been identified with Llanddinol (Llanddeiniol), the Welsh name of Itton in Monmouthshire.

[73] The same saint is eponym of Llanwenarth, two miles west-north-west of Abergavenny (*Llanwaynard*, 1402)

adds Bolstone. These medieval ecclesiastical arrangements are of great antiquity, often going back (in France as in England) to Celtic times, and the subjection of a group of churches of S. Dubricius and other Celtic saints to what has been for ages an unimportant country parish may prove a valuable clue to the early history of this part of Herefordshire.[74] Moccas[75] is now dedicated to S. Michael and Madley to the Nativity of the B.V. Mary.[76]

Dubricius is stated in Lewis's *Topographical Dictionary of Wales* to be the patron of Gwenddwr, south of Builth, in Breconshire.[77]

There is a "holy well, called Ffynnon Ddyfrig, at Garn Llwyd, opposite Llanfeithin, about a mile from Llancarfan"[78] in Glamorgan.

---

[74] An interesting parallel is provided by Sellack—the *Lann Suluc* of the *Liber Landavensis*, evidently one of the most important monasteries in Archenfield. In Ecton we find that in 1742 it possessed three chapels—King's Chapel (on the opposite side of the Wye), Pencoyd and Marstow. The *Liber Landavensis* tells us that "in the time of King Edward Bishop Herwald consecrated Lann Tiuoi [=Foy] and ordained in it Joseph son of Brein as priest *sub titulo Lann Suluc*" (p. 275-6), so that Foy, too, must have belonged to Sellack before it was given to Gloucester abbey. The *Liber Landavensis* mentions the consecration of a presbyter at *Lann Marthin* (Marstow) immediately after recording a similar event at *Lann Suluc*, though they are a considerable distance from each other. In 1742 Ecton states (p. 211, note 1) that "Moreton Magna, *Selleck* and *Lugwardine* are in the Bishop's immediate jurisdiction and are exempt from all Archidiaconal Visitation." He refers to Willis's *Survey*, p. 837. It is worth noting that the abbey of Gloucester received in 1356 an annual pension of 20s. from *Baysham* (i.e., Sellack). Thirteen other parishes paid similar pensions, including *Mockes* (3s.) and *Maddeleye* (2s.). The abbey also possessed a priory at Kilpeck, several parish churches in the diocese, and tithes in other parishes. Here, as in the diocese of Llandaff, Gloucester seems to have inherited much ancient Celtic monastic property.

[75] The authors of LBS say (ii. 380) that "when the church of Moccas was undergoing restoration, at some depth was found a stone rudely carved with interlaced work", and that there is a holy well at Blakemere close by. Rev. A. Payne, late rector of Moccas, tells me that the well is not called after the saint, and has no building over it. It is in a field on the left side of "Holy Well Lane", which leads from Blakemere to Preston-on-Wye.

[76] Can this dedication have been suggested by the legend of the birth of S. Dubricius? S. Mary has displaced ancient Celtic saints at Kenderchurch, Kentchurch and Foy.

[77] Mr. Wade-Evans gives the reason for believing this statement to be true in his *Parochiale Wallicanum*, p. 21, note 4.

[78] LBS ii. 380. The 'Pwll Dyfrig', on the banks of the Gwaun, near Fishguard, referred to on this same page of LBS, is a mistake due to Fenton, who in turn derived it from Owen, as Mr. Wade-Evans has explained in AC 1919, pp. 105-6. The place is really called *Pwll Dyrys*—i.e. 'the tangled hollow'.

The parish church of Porlock in Somerset is called *ecclesia S. Dubricii* in the foundation deed of the Harington chantry in 1476 and in wills of 1533 and 1536.

To sum up : it is clear that Dubricius was one of the chief figures in the creation of Christian Wales. Owing to the fact that no *Life* of him was written till many centuries after his death, we really know very little about him. He was not the founder of the see of Llandaff, but he certainly is the first bishop recorded as exercising episcopal jurisdiction in the district which afterwards became the see of Llandaff. The fact that his first foundation was near Ariconium (from which the Celtic kingdom of Erging seems to have got its name[79]) suggests that Ariconium may have been the source of the Welsh Christian movement of the fifth and sixth centuries,[80] and the legends of the Children of Brychan (Brecon being so close to Archenfield) seem to contain a dim reminiscence of this. Dubricius bore a Celtic,[81] not a Roman, name, and was therefore of native British extraction. He lived in a monastery in a country district, not in a city. On the other hand, the nearness of the Roman city of Ariconium to Archenfield and the fact that Dubricius was at any rate in the twelfth century believed to have possessed land at Caerlleon remind us that Welsh Christianity came originally from Romano-British sources. The dedication of Porlock church to Dubricius seems to indicate that he (or monks from one of his houses) played a part in the great missionary expansion which, starting from South Wales, covered the coast of Somerset with churches and monasteries.

---

[79] As the Welsh kingdom of Gwent was called after the Roman city of Venta Silurum.

[80] *Cf. R. W. D. Fenn, 'St Dyfrig and Christianity in South East Wales' (*Province* xi. 22-25, 60-67.)]

[81] The name *Dyfrig* is derived from *dwfr* 'water' (this may have suggested the story about *Ebrdil*). *Dubric* was an ordinary Welsh name and is found as that of a clerical witness in three charters in the *Liber Landavensis* (pp. 209, 210, 211).

NOTE ON THE HISTORY OF MOCCAS

An interesting glimpse into the history of Moccas between the time of S. Dubricius and the Norman Conquest is afforded by three successive charters in the *Book of Llandaff* (pp. 163-6).

In the first *Gurcant*, son of *Cinuin*, king of *Ercicg*, grants the *podum* (=monastery) of *Lann Loudeu* (Llan Loudy) to Bishop *Iunapeius* (who has given his name to Llandinabo). After the bishop's name in the list of witnesses come those of six abbots of neighbouring monasteries, the first being *Comereg* of *Mochros*. In the next chapter the same king, "sitting on the sepulchre of his father, and for his soul", grants *Lann Budgualan* (Ballingham) to Bishop *Iunapeius*, and again, the first witness is *Comereg, abbas Mochros*. In the third *Athruis*, king of Gwent, grants seven churches to Bishop *Comeregius*. The abbot of *Mochros* is now bishop. In the procession round the land "Bishop Comeregius, with his clergy, was present, and the king carried the gospel-book on his back". In the list of the bishops of Llandaff in the *Liber Landavensis*, *Comeregius* is placed eighth, but *Cymelliauch*, the twenty-third bishop, is the "Cameleauc, bishop in Archenfield", who, as we learn from the *Anglo-Saxon Chronicle*, was captured by the Danes in 915; so that *Comereg*, after he became bishop, probably continued to reside in Herefordshire. In any case the charters referred to show that *Mochros* long remained an important centre of church life.

Later on, the *Book of Llandaff* has a story of how, after an invasion of Herefordshire by the Saxons, in which great destruction was wrought and the whole country depopulated, King *Iudhail* reconquered it and handed over to Bishop *Berthguin* a large number of churches in this neighbourhood, including *Mochros*.

SAINT ILTUT[1]

UNTIL the Norman Conquest we have practically no sources of information about the Welsh saints except what may be found in the writings of Breton hagiographers.

The earliest document which tells us anything about S. Iltut is the *Vita Samsonis*, written at Dol, perhaps about the year 610.[2] We are introduced to him in c. 7, in which the youth Samson is taken by his parents "to the school of an illustrious master of the Britons, named *Eltut*.[3] Now Eltut was a disciple of Saint German and in his youth had been ordained presbyter by S. German." In describing Eltut the writer dwells on two things about him which are regarded as his chief titles to fame—his erudition and his wisdom, the latter being shown especially in his power of prophecy, of which he proceeds to give us an example :—

> Now this Eltut was the most learned of all the Britons[4] in the knowledge of Scripture, both the Old Testament and the New Testament, and in every branch of philosophy—poetry and rhetoric, grammar and arithmetic; and he was most sagacious[5] and gifted with the power of foretelling future events. I have been in his magnificent monastery, and if I were once to begin to relate all his marvellous works I should be led too far away from my subject. But one thing we will record, in order to confirm what has just been said, which was related to us by catholic brethren

---

[1] *Published in 1944, University of Wales Press Board, Cardiff.]

[2] See Duine, *Mémento des sources hagiographiques de l'hist. de Bret.* (Rennes, 1918), No. 2, and *Origines bretonnes* (Paris, 1914), pp. 25f. *See also p. 8 n. 37.]

[3] In the list of chapters at the beginning of the *Vita* the name is spelt *Eltudus*.

[4] The phrase recalls the statement of Gildas (*De Excidio* c. 36) that *Maglocunus* (Maelgwn, king of Gwynedd) "had had for his instructor the most eloquent master of almost all Britain." It has been suggested that Gildas means Iltut. But one would expect in that case some tradition to this effect to have survived in Wales. We have a list of Iltut's disciples in two hagiographical documents, as we shall see, and Maelgwn's name is not among them. *But see P. Grosjean, *Fritz Saxl. 1890-1948: A Volume of Memorial Essays from his Friends in England*, ed. D. J. Gordon (London, 1957), 71, 75-76.]

[5] The exact meaning of *Genereque* MAGICUS *sagacissimus* is not clear. Seven MSS. read MAGNIFICUS.

who were in that place.[c. 8.]   For when he was fallen sick and
was about to die, he sent for two other abbots to come and visit
him, of whom one was called Isanus and the other Atoclius.
And when he saw them, he saluted each in his accustomed way,
and said to them: 'I rejoice, dearest brethren, that you have come,
because the time is at hand that I should depart and fall asleep in
Christ, and you shall[6] duly honour me [at my obsequies].   But
be of good cheer, for your own departure shall in each case quickly
follow mine, though not with equal happiness for you both.
I indeed shall be received tonight by the hands of angels, about
midnight, in the presence of you all, and my brother Isanus shall
see my soul carried away under the appearance of an eagle having
two golden wings, and he shall also see, under the appearance of
another eagle, but flying heavily with a pair of leaden wings, the
soul of that other brother [Atoclius].   And after forty days brother
Isanus shall himself also happily come to Christ, as he saw me
come in the vision I have described.   But thou, brother Atoclius,
hast greatly loved the things of the world, and so, though thou shalt
appear in the likeness of a pure and winged creature,[7] thy wings
shall not have the pureness of gold.   Thou art, indeed, pure[8] and
hast preserved thine innocence from thy youth until this day, but
thou art heavy in thy wings through the leaden weight of avarice.
May God Almighty deign to pluck those wings from thee.'

He continued speaking after this fashion throughout that day and
the night following.   At about midnight, as he had said, after
bidding farewell to the brethren, he departed happily from the
flesh, amid the chant of hymns and the customary rights, and the
blessed Isanus saw his soul in a vision, exactly as he had said, and
he likewise saw the soul of the other brother, as the old man had
foretold, and with difficulty was it, through his efforts, redeemed,
by the prayers of saints and many masses sung, but finally Isanus
saw it purified and absolved from the worst of its offences. He told
all these things (which he alone saw) to the brethren, and they all
marvelled and held him in great honour, and he himself came
happily to Christ on the day predicted, according as the old man
had promised.

---

6 The MS. in the Bibl. de l'Arsenal in Paris reads *prebebitis*.
7 The *similitudo* of the *animal pennatum* seems to be based on the *similitudo
quattuor animalium . . . pennas habebant* of Ezek. i. 5-8. The *plumbeum pondus*
may possibly be a dim reminiscence of Zech. v. 7-9.
8 There is a most unfortunate confusion in this passage, caused by the use of
mundus in its two different meanings of 'world' and 'pure' in two successive
sentences.   The second *mundus* must mean 'pure' not 'the world' (as Canon
Taylor has translated it in *The Life of S. Samson of Dol*), since there is clearly a
comparison between the pure winged creature, which yet has leaden wings
that weigh it down, and the soul of Atoclius, who has preserved his *antiqua
sanctitas* but is yet *gravidus . . . propter plumbeum avaritiae pondus*.

After this digression, the writer returns to the story of Samson being brought to the school at Llantwit. He is presented to Saint Eltut by his mother, "together with the gifts which it was customary to offer on such an occasion". Eltut kisses the boy and foretells his future greatness in glowing language, but cuts his prophecy short and refuses to say more when pressed to do so by Samson's parents.

In c. 10 he restrains the youthful Samson's wish to engage in prolonged fasts. The next chapter describes how Eltut and Samson discuss together a difficult theological problem, without success—till finally the answer is revealed to Samson in prayer and he tells the master.[9]   C. 12 contains the episode of the brother bitten by a snake : after an altercation between Samson and Eltut, the latter gives him leave to visit the patient and he heals him. The master now decides that Samson shall be made deacon. He is present at his ordination by the *papa* Dubricius, and sees the miracle of the dove hovering over Samson and settling on his shoulder when the bishop lays his hand upon him, the only other person privileged to do so being the deacon who had chanted the Gospel and the Prayer and administered the chalice. We are next told (c. 14) that Eltut had two nephews in the monastery, one of whom was a presbyter, who were jealous of his affection for S. Samson—especially the presbyter, who feared that it might lead to his being "deprived of his hereditary right in the monastery".[10]   They determined to poison him. The story contains an interesting and detailed reference to a monastic custom in use at Llantwit of periodically giving a beverage of crushed herbs to the monks for purposes of health. The chief offender is punished by God for his attempted crime, and the abbot and brethren ask Samson to obtain pardon

---

[9]   For the *spirituales theoriae* of c. 11 see an article by the late Dom Gougaud in *Rev. d'asc. et de mystique*, October, 1922.

[10]   The idea of the post of superior of a newly founded religious house, still in its first fervour, being regarded as hereditary, might surprise us, but it must be remembered that we are dealing with a Celtic monastery. An interesting example of the extent to which in Wales, at a much later period, spiritual rule might be regarded as a family right is afforded by an entry in the *Annals of Tewkesbury Abbey* in the year 1230, referring to this very church (*Llandirwit*), which states that there had been "disputes between Peter, abbot of Tewkesbury, and certain persons who wished that a brother of William, lately parson there, and his kin should succeed him by hereditary right, *as is the custom among the Welsh*."

for him. An account of the ordination of Samson as a presbyter, by God's will and the master's request, is inserted (c. 15) in the middle of the story. The miracle of the dove, again witnessed by the master and the deacon, was renewed.

Samson now wished to lead a more retired and ascetic life, and thought of leaving the crowded and tumultuous monastery[11] and of visiting the *insula* of a certain distinguished man and holy presbyter, named Piro, and sojourning with him, but feared lest the old man, his teacher, might be grieved at the idea. But a messenger from the Lord appeared to Saint Eltut in a dream and instructed him to enquire of Samson what his wishes were and to assist him in carrying them out, for God was with him and was guiding him in all things. On awaking, Eltut did as he had been commanded, and bade farewell to Samson, saying, "None in our generation shall be greater than thee." Then, smiting upon his breast in grief, he gave orders that he should be conducted to Piro's island.

Nothing more is said of Eltut in the *Vita Samsonis*. He is not mentioned in the chapters[12] describing Samson's appointment as abbot "in the monastery which, it is said, had been founded by S. Germanus" (presumably Llantwit), and his consecration there as bishop, though Dubricius takes an active part in the election and "the best advisers of the Congregation" and "the Council" of the monastery are consulted.

We need not doubt that the anonymous author of the *Vita Samsonis* is speaking the truth when he asserts that he had visited the monastery of Eltut and received a good deal of information from the monks there. The portrait he gives us of its founder as a famous *magister* has led to his being introduced in the same capacity into the *Lives* of S. Magloire, S. Lunaire, and S. Paul Aurelian, and into the Breton *Life* of S. Gildas (the latter being the work of a monk named Vitalis, who had read and rewritten the *Vita Pauli*), and is imitated (together with the story in c. 12) by Wrdisten in his *Vita Winwaloei*. The author of the *Vita Brioci*, who makes Iltut, in company with Brioc and Patrick, a disciple of S. Germanus of Paris, may have

---

[11] *Grave valde apud se reputans illud monasterium quippe quod jam tumultuosum ac expandiosum per patriam erat.*
[12] Cc. 42-44.

had in mind the statement in the *Vita Samsonis* that Iltut was "a disciple of S. Germanus" [of Auxerre]. But the story of the death of Eltut in c. 8, which is one of the most interesting features of the whole book, is much more original and convincing than any of the other stories about the saint. It bears every mark of antiquity and may be a genuine glimpse into the Age of the Saints in Wales. We seem to see the figure of a real saint and prophet, and to feel the veneration inspired by his personal holiness in the monastery he had founded, and remembered long after his death. It is a full and well-told narrative, not a scrap of vague tradition elaborated by the hagiographer with imaginary incidents and invented speeches, such as we find in most other *Lives* of Celtic saints, and the details in it ring true. It shows us the eponym of *Lann Isan* in Pembrokeshire[13] as a contemporary of Iltut, who is here represented as possessing jurisdiction over a group of monasteries in South Wales. The story presents two problems, which must be briefly referred to here, though we shall have to deal with them again later. First, does it form part, as M. Fawtier thinks,[14] of an ancient *Life* of S. Iltut ? The writer says that it was "told him by catholic brethren who were in that place", which seems to indicate that it was *not* taken from a written *Life*. On the other hand, it is rather a long story to be handed down by tradition alone. Secondly, it appears to show beyond dispute that the tradition of Llantwit in the seventh century was that Iltut died there. Why then does not the writer make clear *when* he died ? The author of the second *Life* of S. Samson, a clerk of Dol who rewrote the first *Life* in better order and better style some time during the first half of the ninth century,[15] has attempted to remedy this and other deficiencies, and has rearranged the story of *Isanus* and *Atoclius*, together with other digressions and insertions of his predecessor (such as the story of Dubricius and the deacon Morinus), in what seemed to

---

[13] Also spelt *Lanyssan* and *Lann Issan*. It is mentioned on pp. 56, 62, 124, 255 and 287 of the 1893 edition of the *Book of Llan Dâv*. It is now St. Ishmael's. *Lan Ismael* is one of the more important of the "Seven bishop-houses of Dyfed" in the Laws of Howel the Good. Llanishen in Glamorgan is *Lann Nissien* on pp. 241, 242 of the BLD, *Lanyssan* on p. 321. An *Atoc* appears as a witness in the BLD (p. 150); cf. Loth, *La Vie la plus ancienne de St. Samson* (Paris, 1914), p. 17, note 4.

[14] *La Vie de saint Samson* (Paris, 1912). 39.

[15] Duine, *Mémento*, No. 2, p. 32.

him a more logical order. The description of the death of Iltut
is now a story told to Samson after he had left Wales by a monk of
Llantwit who meets him at Golant in Cornwall after the miracle
of the dropping well.[16] Unfortunately we have no reason to
believe that the later writer had any evidence for this new setting
of the story. Nor, if true, would it explain why Iltut is omitted
in the narratives of Samson's appointment as abbot, consecration
as bishop, and farewell to Wales. It does, however, show that
there was no tradition at Dol in the ninth century that Iltut
died there, as stated in the twelfth century *Vita Iltuti*.

About two hundred and fifty years after the composition of
the first *Vita Samsonis*, in the year 884, another Breton writer, a
native of Léon, called Wrmonoc, who had been a monk at Landévennec under the celebrated abbot Wrdisten, wrote a *Life* of
the founder of St.-Pol-de-Léon. The first book of his *Vita
Pauli Aureliani*[17] deals with his hero's life in Wales and with a
visit to Cornwall on his way from Wales to Brittany. In it the
writer shows a knowledge of two sets of Glamorgan traditions.
He has heard of a once-famous character called Paul of Penychen,
who is introduced several times into the *Vita Cadoci* (written
about two hundred years later). He has also heard of, and
perhaps read, a *Life* of Iltut. He seems, too, to have some
knowledge of a now-lost *Life* of Iltut's disciple Paulinus, a saint
honoured in Carmarthenshire, from which he borrows the stories
he gives in c. 7 of his work. The founder of St. -Pol-de-Léon
was known both as *Paul* and *Paulinus*,[18] so Wrmonoc decided to

---

[16] *Cum enim de hoc miraculo inter se congratularentur, unus affuit ex discipulis
Heltuti, qui et ipse simul cum Sansone in illo monasterio edoctus fuerat. Quem
sanctus Sanson interrogavit, dicens: 'Vivit adhuc magister meus? omnem rem,
quaeso, replica mihi per ordinem. At ille respondens dixit: 'Cum aegrotaret
magister tuus Heltutus . . . duos abbates ad visitandum se invitavit'.*
The story is retold, mainly in the same words as in the first *Life*, but partly
paraphrased, with some details altered. He remedies the failure of the earlier
writer to mention Atoclius's death by stating that it took place fifteen days
after that of Heltut. Samson is made to express his sorrow at the news of
the death of his old master in a suitable speech (edition by Dom Plaine,
Paris, 1887, p. 36).

[17] I have paraphrased this *Vita* in *S. Paul of Léon* ('Cornish Saints' series,
No. 46). *SC i. 11-28.]

[18] See *S. Paul of Léon*, pp. 26, 27. *SC i. 32-33.]

identify his hero with the Glamorgan Paul as well as with the Carmarthenshire Paulinus. He first says that he came "from a province called in the language of the Britons *Penn Ohen*"—he attempts to explain the name. But the stories related about Paul of Penychen did not suit his narrative at all, so he abandoned them in favour of the history of the saint of Carmarthenshire, whose "family . . . lived in the region which in their language is called *Brehant Dincat*" [i.e. Llandingad at Llandovery]. "Saint Paul, while still of tender years, asked his father to send him to the school of a certain master, who was *a burning and a shining light*".[19] It will be well to summarize the next few chapters in order that the reader may be able to compare them with the corresponding chapters in the *Vita Iltuti*.

C.2. *How he was trained in sacred studies at Iltut's School.*

There was a certain island called Pyrus within the borders of the *patria* of the Demetae, in which lived a certain Iltutus,[20] a man of noble birth and great learning, walking in the narrow way which leads to life. He had many disciples, who flocked to him from every side, and his fame was spread throughout every place in the island of Britain, which was illuminated by his doctrine. Paul was handed over by his parents to the school of this master.

C. 3. *Of his fellow-disciples, and of the miracle wrought by them with the knowledge of their master (conscio magistro).*

Iltut had many young men distinguished for piety and learning among his disciples, but four of them far outshone the others, and by the command of the master were placed in a position of authority (*magisterium*) over them. These were Saint Paul, Saint Dewi (*Devius*) who was called *Aquaticus*; also Samson, the holy bishop whose deeds are recorded in his *Life*; and lastly Saint Gildas. All these four joined with their master in a notable miracle. The place which they call the Monastery of Iltut was of very limited area and hemmed in by the sea. The four disciples asked their master

[19] John v. 35.
[20] Wrmonoc invariably spells the name *Iltut*.

to pray to the Lord that He might cause the sea to retire, and so enlarge his domain. Iltut agrees, and goes apart to pray by himself, asking them to do the same [Wrmonoc records the lengthy prayer he made on this occasion]. Then, accompanied by his disciples, he went down to the shore at low tide, when the sea used to withdraw to the distance of a mile or more, and traced, with the point of his staff, a furrow, beyond which he forbade the water to pass, and it has never since that time transgressed his command. Iltut gave thanks to God, with his disciples— to whom he attributed the merit of the miracle, which they as steadfastly ascribed to him. The land which was thus reclaimed from the sea is exceedingly fertile, and never ceases, to this day, to yield abundant crops for the monastery of the aforesaid master.

C.4. *How he drove back the birds to the sheepfold as if they were sheep.*

Not long afterwards the aforesaid spiritual father commanded the same four disciples to take turns in watching the ripening crops in this piece of ground throughout the day, to prevent it being injured by the seagulls. When Paul's turn came, he did not pay sufficient attention to his task and the birds swallowed all the grain. He was so frightened by the consequences of his negligence that he was afraid to show himself at the monastery, and spent a whole day and night in prayer. Next day he arose early and summoned his fellow-disciples, and they drove the birds before them, as if they were a flock of sheep, into a barn, which was soon filled with their clamour. The master heard of what had happened, and he and the other monks prostrated themselves before Paul and glorified God for what He had wrought through His youthful servant, and with the disciples sang a song, as with one voice.

C. 5. *Of the familiar conversation which followed between him and the master.*

When the song is finished, Paul raises his master and his fellow-disciples from their prostrate position. He ascribes the miracle to their merits and not to his own. He also asks the master to allow the birds to return to the sea unharmed. Iltut replies in a long discourse exhorting Paul not to hide his talent in the earth. He permits the birds to depart, and offers to make over the whole monastery to Paul. The latter modestly refuses the offer in a highly rhetorical and carefully prepared speech. The disciples listen with admiration to this conversation. The birds are then released and fly back to the sea.

Wrmonoc goes on to tell us (in chapters 6 and 7) how, not long after this miracle, Paul resolved to live as a hermit in the wilderness, and, with Iltut's permission and approval, left the monastery and sought the seclusion of a certain desert place which adjoined his father's possessions [Llanddeusant]. Nothing more is said of Iltut.

The author of the *Vita Pauli* is a shameless plagiarist. Throughout his work he has his master Wrdisten's *Vita Winwaloei* before him and embroiders his narrative continually with phrases and sentences copied from it. But the narrative itself is based (so far as Book I is concerned) on a set of Welsh and Cornish traditions. Where did he find them? The author of the *Vita Samsonis*, as we have seen, states that he has visited Llantwit and learned what he relates about Eltut from conversations with the brethren there. Wrmonoc has *not* been in Wales. He twice mentions *transmarini* and quotes their gossip as proof of the existence of an avenue of stones (in Scilly or Mount's Bay) called *Semita Pauli*. He quotes (in c. 7) hearsay evidence for the existence of a monastery in Wales, founded by Paul and called after his two brothers (Llanddeusant in Carmarthenshire)— *quod nunc . . . multis decoratum aedificiis* DICUNT. It is evidently from similar sources that he learnt about Mark's burial at *Caer Bannhed* (? Castle Dore) and about the inscribed stone at Castle Dore which bears his other name *Quonomorius*. These considerations are a necessary preliminary to the discussion of an exceedingly difficult problem which must now be faced. Its solution would throw a flood of light on the subject.

If the reader will compare the above extracts with the analysis of chapters 11, 13, and 14 of the *Vita Iltuti* which will be given on pp. 109 and 110, he will see that these chapters and cc. 3 to 7 of the *Vita Pauli* must have a common source. In both versions Iltut is a famous *magister*, the list of disciples is the same (except that Wrmonoc has *Paul* while the *Vita Iltuti* has *Paulinus*), both versions have the miracle of the sea retiring and that of the birds driven into the barn—the latter immediately following the former in each case. The only serious difference is that in the *Vita Pauli* the miracle of the birds is ascribed to Paul, while in the *Vita Iltuti* it is ascribed to Samson. In the story of the birds there is, as we shall see, some verbal agreement between the two documents.[21]

A very simple explanation of this remarkable similarity would be to suggest that the author of the *Vita Iltuti* has copied Wrmonoc. But this seems untenable. There is no evidence that the *Vita Pauli Aureliani* was known in Wales at all during the Middle Ages. If the author of the *Vita Iltuti* had seen it and copied it, he would not have stated that one of Iltut's disciples was *Paulinus* (which is almost certainly the original tradition) and he would have shown some acquaintance with other parts of the *Vita Pauli*. He has two references to *Letavia*, but only knows Dol—he would have mentioned Léon if he had read Wrmonoc. It is much more likely that both writers are copying from a now-lost Welsh source. M. Fawtier, as we have seen, believes in the existence of a primitive *Life* of Eltut. He thinks[22] that it was older than the *Vita Samsonis*, and that it contained, in addition to the 'core' of stories common to Wrmonoc and the *Vita Iltuti*, a statement that Eltut was a disciple of Germanus and the story of Eltut's death, both of which are found in the *Vita Samsonis* but omitted in the two later *Lives*. But there are considerable difficulties in the way of accepting M. Fawtier's view. The differences between the picture of Eltut in the *Vita Samsonis* and that in the 'core' we are dealing with are very serious indeed. They have, as a matter of fact, only two common features—the description of Iltut as a *magister* and the statement that Samson was one of his disciples. It is inconceivable that the author of the *Vita Samsonis* should have omitted, for example, the story of the birds, if he had

---

[21] This story is also found in the *Vita Sansonis* contained in the *Liber Landavensis*.

[22] Op. cit., pp. 38-40.

read it in a Llantwit *Life* of Iltut, especially as in the version in the *Vita Iltuti* and in that given by the *Liber Landavensis Vita Samsonis* the hero of the story is Samson. Neither would the author of the *Vita Iltuti* have omitted the interesting details preserved by the *Vita Samsonis* if he had found them in a *Life* at Llantwit. The portrait of Iltut in the core common to the ninth and twelfth century *Lives* seems to belong to a later period than that in the *Vita Samsonis*. Iltut has become a dim and legendary figure.

But, assuming (as I think we may) that there was a Welsh *Life* of Iltut older than Wrmonoc's time, utilized both by himself and by the author of the *Vita Iltuti*, but not yet existing when the *Vita Samsonis* was written, how did Wrmonoc, writing in Léon, get to know about it? Hearsay evidence could not produce a lengthy narrative so nearly identical with that of the twelfth century writer. Why, again, is the original *Life*, as represented in this passage, so scrappy and imperfect ? Wrmonoc might have contented himself with a section from the *Life* of Iltut, omitting all that followed Paul's leaving Llantwit, but the author of the *Vita Iltuti* had no reason whatever for doing so— rather the other way. It is incredible that a Llantwit *Life* should have contained this core and nothing more—not a word about who Iltut was, his family, his conversion, founding of the monastery, career as abbot (except the construction of the sea- wall), and death. The twelfth century writer has had to invent all these to make his work even resemble a biography.

It is possible that the elements common to the *Vita Pauli* and the *Vita Iltuti* may have been contained in a *Vita Paulini* found by Wrmonoc at St.-Pol-de-Léon. A good many Breton saints seem to have had very short written or oral *Lives*, the basis of later and fuller ones, which gave the outline of their career. Thus the *Vita Brioci* tells us that the saint came from Ceredigion and the *Vita Mevenni* that Mewan came from Erging, and topographical evidence confirms these statements.[23] An ancient Léon *Life* of Paulinus may have stated that he came from Carmarthenshire and that he was a disciple of Iltut, and perhaps

---

[23] Cf. S. *Gudual* ('Cornish Saints', No. 30), pp. 19, 20, 32 and *S. Budoc* (second edition), p. 10.   *SC i 70-71, 77, iii 8-9.]

even contained some stories in which the latter figured. Iltut was, and is, greatly honoured in Léon, and the study of place-names shows that his cult there is very ancient and is associated with that of S. Paul (Paulinus). The next parish to Lampaul-Plouarzel, near Brest, is called *Lanildut* (which is the way Llantwit is spelt in the *Liber Landavensis*). The two parishes are separated by the river called *Aber-Ildut*. There was close inter-course between Léon and South Wales from the Age of the Saints down to a much later period, and Wrmonoc's own words tell us of first-hand information he had received about a Carmarthenshire monastery founded by Paulinus. This sugges-tion would solve the question of Wrmonoc's knowledge of South Wales traditions very well, and would explain why the core of legends we have been studying tells us so much about Iltut's disciples and so little about himself, but unfortunately it does not explain where the author of the *Vita Iltuti* found this 'core'. I fear we must be content with having posed the problem and wait for further researches for its solution.

A second question we are obliged to ask is : Why does neither Wrmonoc nor the author of the *Vita Iltuti* use the information about Eltut in the *Vita Samsonis,* though the former expressly mentions the *Life of S. Samson* and in c. 9 imitates a passage from it ? We shall have to consider this point so far as it concerns the *Vita Iltuti* when we come to our critical examination of the latter. Wrmonoc falls into a serious error through not following the guidance of the *Vita Samsonis.* He tells us that Iltut lived "in a certain island named Pyrus, situated in the borders of the *patria* of the Demetae". He obviously means Caldy Island, which must have been known as *Ynys Byr* as early as the ninth century—it is certainly *Demetarum patriae in finibus sita,* but in the *Life of S. Samson* the *insula fundata a presbytero Piro nomine* has nothing to do with S. Eltut, and Samson fears to offend Eltut by going there. It is very curious that the author of the *Liber Landavensis* confuses Caldy with Llantwit in the same way as Wrmonoc does; in his *Vita Dubricii* he describes an incident which, according to the *Vita Samsonis,* took place in the former monastery, as happening in the *locus* and *domus Beati Ilduti*. We observe, however, that when Wrmonoc reaches the 'core' of stories common to his own work and the *Vita Iltuti,* he

says that the miracle of the sea retiring took place at the *locus
. . . quem nunc Illuti monasterium dicunt.*

Before leaving the *Vita Pauli*, it will be well to note the fact
that the story of the connection between Paulinus (Paul) and
Iltut which it contains is supported by some very interesting
evidence supplied by the study of the topography and the local
traditions of Glamorgan and Breconshire (one of which is
recorded by Giraldus Cambrensis in the twelfth century).[24]
The study of the topography of Brittany, as we have seen, points
the same way.

One local legend about S. Iltut is even older than the
Vita Pauli. It is contained in the famous *Historia Brittonum*
of Nennius, which is not later than the eighth century. In the
section entitled 'The Marvels of Britain' (*de mirabilibus Britanniae*)
we read:[25]

> There is another marvel, in Guyr [Gower] :—an altar
> miraculously suspended in the air,[26] which is in the place that is
> called Loyngarth. It seems to me worth while relating the story[27]
> of this altar. It came to pass that [one day] while Saint Iltut[28]
> was praying in a cave that is near the sea, which washes the land
> of the aforesaid place [or monastery—*locus*]—now the mouth
> of the cave faces the sea, behold a ship sailing over the sea towards
> him, steered by two men, and the body of a holy man was with them
> in the ship and an altar was miraculously suspended over his face.
> And the man of God went forth to meet them and they took out
> of the ship the body of the holy man, and the altar still stood
> suspended over his face and never moved from its position.[29]
> And they said to Saint Iltut: 'This man of God charged us to
> bring him to thee and to bury him with thee, and that thou
> shouldest not reveal his name to anyone, for fear lest men might
> swear by him.' And they buried him, and after his burial the two
> men returned to the ship and sailed away. And the same Saint
> Iltut built[30] a church around the body of the holy man and around

---

[24] See p. 139.
[25] C. 71.
[26] *Quod nutu Dei fulcitur.*
[27] *historia*, in four MSS. *fabula.*
[28] In four MSS. *Eltudus*, in one *Eltutus*, in one *Altutus*. See the edition by
M. Ferdinand Lot, Paris, 1934.
[29] *inseparabiliter supra faciem sancti corporis stabat.*
[30] *fundavit.*

the altar, and the altar continues to be miraculously suspended there unto this very day. A certain *regulus* came one day, wishing to prove the truth of the story, with a rod in his hand, and he bent it around the altar, holding the two ends of the rod in each hand, and drew it towards himself, and thus proved the truth of what he had heard, and he died within a month. And another looked under the altar, and he lost his sight, and he too died within a month.

The origin of this interesting story is clear. The monastery of Llantwit had possessions in Gower, and S. Iltut was greatly honoured there.[31] In one of the Gower churches dedicated to him, on the southern shore of the peninsula, was the body of a saint—a bishop or priest, whose name had already been forgotten in the eighth century. Close to his shrine was his portable altar. We know that in many cases a Celtic bishop's altar was preserved as a relic. The altar of S. Leonorius was long treasured in the sacristy of the church of St.-Lunaire in Brittany, and M. Sébillot says that "throughout the Middle Ages it was believed that a false oath sworn upon this relic would lead to the death of the perjured person before the end of the year.[32] What there was about this altar that gave rise to the idea of its position being miraculous it is impossible to guess. The reason given for the name of the saint being kept secret—"lest men might swear by him"—is of special interest, since it seems to refer to a custom still common in the land to which British Christianity was so greatly indebted—Egypt :

In the Lybian desert the difficulty [of dealing with the prevailing indifference to perjury] is overcome by making the accused party take the oath at some sheikh's tomb. The Lybian desert is dotted with the tombs of sheikhs whose reputation for piety has remained long after the history of their lives has been forgotten, and such is the respect in which they are held that only the most hardened criminal will take an oath and give false evidence at a tomb.[33]

Solemn oaths used to be taken on 'S. Teilo's Tomb' in Llandaff cathedral in the Middle Ages.

[31] See pp. 140-42.
[32] The parish of *Altarnon* in Cornwall means 'The Altar of Nonna'.
[33] C. S. Jarvis, *Yesterday and To-day in Sinai*. Herodotus tells us that in his day the natives of North Africa took oaths at the tombs of holy men, and the Donatists did so at the tombs of their martyrs.

The question of the exact site of this church of S. Iltut will be discussed when we come to deal with his cult in Wales.[34]

After the *Vita Pauli Aureliani* there follows a gap of over two hundred years before Iltut is again mentioned in any hagiographical document. At the end of the twelfth century a collection of *Lives* of Welsh saints[35] (nearly all of them composed by Norman clerks during the hundred years or so preceding), intended as a South Wales legendary, was compiled— apparently at Brecon priory.

The earliest of the *Lives* it contains is the *Vita Cadoci*.[36] It was written by Lifris, who is described in the *Liber Landavensis*, in three charters granted to Bishop Herewald (died 1104), as "son of the bishop, archdeacon of Gulat Morcant and master of Saint Catoc of Lanncarvan". In his *Life of S. Cadog* (a collection of traditions and legends which had grown up in the course of six centuries) he introduces S. Iltut as a contemporary of his hero. In c. 19, which is headed '*How the earth swallowed up the robbers alive, and of the conversion of S. Iltut*', he tells the following story:

> On a certain day, while S. Cadoc was sitting in his chair teaching the people, fifty of the soldiers of Poul, surnamed Pennichen, who were out hawking, came to him demanding food, which they threatened to take by force in case of refusal. Cadoc ordered a meal to be prepared in the midst of the plain which is called Midgard [*or* Medgarth],[37] not far from the *oppidum*.[38]

The soldiers do not venture to begin to eat before the arrival of their captain,[39] named Iltut, who was absent when they made their ill-mannered request. In due course he appeared, but, before he could dismount, the earth opened and swallowed up the soldiers, as we read in the Psalms[40] that Dathan and Abiram were swallowed up. When Iltut, who is described as *dominus vel*

---

[34] See pp. 140-43.
[35] Brit. Mus. MS. Vesp. A. xiv.
[36] *Printed along with an English translation in VSBG 24-141.]
[37] Cf. *Vita Cad.*, c. 49. *Midgard* has not been identified.
[38] *Cf. VSBG 63.]
[39] *Princeps militiae*.
[40] Psalm cvi. 17.

tribunus, saw this, he "hastened to the feet of the blessed Cadoc, related to him the divine retribution which had overtaken his men in consequence of their insolence, and asked to be given the monastic habit and tonsure. Cadoc granted his request. Thus the veteran soldier entered the service of the Lord, and followed with all his might the doctrines of his teacher (*preceptor*)".[41] We observe in this story that Lifris makes the founder of the rival church a disciple of S. Cadog.

In c. 57 we have an obviously forged charter, containing a story of how a man named Euan murdered his two nephews, whereupon Cadog and Eltuth came and cursed him. Euan was obliged to come to Cadog and Eltut and confess his crimes. They said to him, "Redeem the guilt of homicide". *Catlon* and *Merchiaun*, apparently "kings who had come with" Euan, then gave respectively the *ager* of *Lanhoitlon* to Cadog and the *villa* of *Conhil*, together with three vessels, which contained six tierces of ale, to Eltut [i.e. to the monastery of Eltut].

In c. 70 (a very short chapter, which concludes the book) Iltut is, with five other well-known Welsh saints (David, Cheneder [Cynidr], Eliud, Maidoc, and Cannou), one of the "witnesses of Saint Cadoc",—a term of which the meaning is not clear.

Before we leave the *Vita Cadoci* it is important to note that in it S. Iltut appears for the first time as an ex-soldier—the *Illtud Farchog* of later Welsh tradition. It is possible that the idea may have arisen at this time owing to the fact that, under the Normans, Llantwit and a considerable stretch of territory to the north of it had become a military fief.[42] As so much ecclesiastical land in this neighbourhood was now held by military tenure, the saintly founder of Llantwit may have come to be represented, by a reverse process, as originally a knight.

The example set by the *Magister Sancti Catoci* was followed, some years later, by another Norman clerk, a member of the staff of the collegiate church which had taken the place of the monastery of S. Iltut. His *Life of Saint Iltut* is found in the same manuscript as the *Vita S. Cadoci*, and was printed, very

---

[41] *Cf. VSBG 65.]
[42] In Professor William Rees's *Map of South Wales and the Border in the 14th Century* the largest red patches are just here.

incorrectly, by W. J. Rees in 1853, with an English translation.[43]
Fortunately we have now at our disposal a much more correct
version. A proper critical edition was printed, with introduction
and notes, by the Bollandists, in the third November volume of
the *Acta Sanctorum* (pp. 219-36) in 1910. Since there is nothing
to guide us as to its date and authorship except what is derived
from internal evidence, it will be convenient to begin with a
summary of this *Life*, translating the more important passages.

INCIPIT VITA ILTUTI ABBATIS[44]

C. 1. *Of the marriage of the parents and the birth of the child.*

The wealthy and warlike province of *Letavia*, victorious
[in many battles], was originally a daughter of Britain.[45] The
princes of Britain were noble and powerful, yet were they driven
into exile. Among them was a most famous soldier named
Bicanus. He took as wife a daughter of *Anblaud*, king of Britain.
Her name in the British language was *Rieingulid*, which means in
Latin *Regina pudica* ['modest queen']. The messengers sent to
fetch her brought her back across the Channel [*Gallicum mare*] to
Gaul, where she was married.[46] She conceived and bore a son,
who was named at the font *Iltutus*, as much as to say "That child
from all evil immune" (ILLE *ab omni crimine* TUTUS), for he was
blameless in all the five ages of man's life.[47] His parents had him
instructed in the seven branches of science and art.[48] He had
such a wonderful memory that every sentence he heard his
master's lips repeat he remembered all his life. He received the
five keys of knowledge[49], and none in the whole of Gaul was so
eloquent as he. Yet he chose a military career when his education
was completed.

---

[43] *Lives of the Cambro-British Saints.* "All the Welsh Lives published by
W. J. Rees . . . have been deplorably edited" (Dom Gougaud, *Christianity
in Celtic Lands*, 55). *But now see VSBG 194-233, where the text is
accompanied by an English translation.]

[44] In margin *II idus Novembris*.

[45] For *Letavia . . . ad originem unde exierunt*, cf. the beginning of the *Vita
Paterni* in this MS.; *see VSBG 252.]

[46] Perhaps the writer's insistence on *legaliter perfectis, conjunx legitima concepit*
may be due to his having read, and been shocked by, the story of *Ebrdil* in
the *Vita Dubricii* or that of *Nonna* in the *Vita David*.

[47] See Forcellini-De Vit, *Lexicon*, Vol. i, p. 149, col. 2.

[48] The *Trivium* and *Quadrivium* of medieval scholastic theory.

[49] No explanation of this phrase has yet been found.

C. 2. *How he visited the court of King Arthur and that of Poulentus.*

Hearing of the magnificence of King Arthur his cousin, he desired to visit the court of such a famous conqueror, and leaving Further Britain,[50] as we call it, he crossed the Channel to seek the country where he would find most soldiers. He was honourably received and munificently entertained. He then departed from the court of King Arthur and visited *Poulentus*, king of the Glamorgan folk. He was accompanied by his most virtuous wife *Trynihid*. The king conceived a special affection for him and made him commander of his forces, on account of his most subtle eloquence and incomparable intellect. [The writer enlarges on this, as if learning was the principal qualification of a soldier.]

C. 3. *How the household (familia) of King Poulentus was swallowed up by the earth, and how, by the counsel of S. Cadog, Iltut resolved to abandon the military profession and take holy orders.*

One day, while he and the royal household were hunting in the territory of S. Cadog, the king's men sent an arrogant message to that famous abbot, demanding food and threatening they would take it by force if their request was refused. S. Cadog, though offended at their insolence, provided a meal for them. They sat down to partake of it, but before they could begin to eat they were punished for their behaviour. The earth opened and swallowed up the whole godless party. The captain Aeltut, however, escaped. He had not joined in their rudeness to S. Cadog, as he was away hawking at the moment. Eltut returned in time to see the fate which overtook them. It made such an impression on him that he went to S. Cadog and asked his advice for the future ordering of his life. The latter bade him resign the career of arms and devote himself to the service of the Creator. He returned to King *Poulentus* and asked for permission to leave his service, which being granted, he set off, with his wife and his squires, and finally arrived at the banks of the river *Nadauan*. It was summer time, and after constructing a temporary hut of reeds, they lay down to sleep. The horses were turned adrift to find pasture.

[50] *Ulterior Brittannia.* There seems to be no other instance of this name for Brittany.

C. 4. *How the angel came and admonished Iltut.*

While Iltut sleeps, an angel appears to him and addresses him in a long oration, bidding him return to the life of study and prayer he had led as a child.[51]   He warns him that his love for his wife is a hindrance to his vocation.

> When thou shalt arise tomorrow, hasten towards a certain wooded valley to the west, where thou shalt have an abode (*mansionem*).   For so is the will of God, seeing that the place is convenient, very fertile, and suitable for human habitation.

C. 5. *How he came to the valley of Hodnant, to live there as a hermit, and of his conversation therein.*

When Aeltut awoke, he remembered what the angel had said, and he bethought of him, too, of the Lord's words, "He that loveth father or mother . . . or wife, more than me is not worthy of me".[52]   He told his wife to get up and look after the horses. She departed to do as he said, and when Aeltut saw her coming back naked he despised her.   [The chapter ends with four hexameters expressing the feelings of a rabid celibate towards the female sex.]

C. 6. *How he first came to sojourn in the valley of Hodnant.*

Aeltut refused to allow his wife, when she returned, to get into bed again.   He handed her her clothes and dismissed her.   He then continued on his way till he came to the aforesaid valley, called *Hodnant*, which means in Latin *Vallis prospera*. It is well watered by a number of springs, from which flow brooks running into the pretty river that drains it, and was then filled with a thick forest, the haunt of wild animals.   [The writer repeats his description of the valley in four hexameters, ending: *hoc scio dicendum, pulcherrimus iste locorum*].

---

[51] *Tui parentes commendaverunt te clericali studio.*   The angel's reproach may indicate that the writer felt the difficulty of reconciling the new idea of Iltut's having been a knight with the older tradition (according to the *Vita Samsonis* he was said to have been "ordained *in his youth* by S. Germanus").

[52] Cf. Matt. x. 37; Luke xiv. 26.

C. 7. *Of the penance enjoined upon him, and of his reception of the clerical habit, of his fasting and prayer, and of the first building of the temple.*

The most blessed servant of God, Aeltut, then went to Dubricius, bishop of Llandaff, who enjoined upon him a penance for his past misdeeds, shaved off his beard, cut his long hair and gave him the tonsure. Having put on the clerical dress, he returned to the place already mentioned, and began by building there a *habitaculum*. Dubricius planned the cemetery and laid the foundations of an oratory in the midst of it, in honour of the holy and undivided Trinity.[53] Aeltut then founded there a quadrangular church of stone. A ditch enclosed the whole group of buildings. Here he lived as a hermit, fasting and praying, and distributing alms to the needy. He bathed in cold water at midnight before matins, remaining therein till he had repeated three paternosters : then he visited the church, genuflected, and prayed. Many pupils soon began to pour in, to be instructed by him in the Seven Arts.[54]

C. 8. *Of the stag tamed by S. Aeltut, and how a wonderful meal was provided for the king from a fish and water.*

King *Merchiaun*, surnamed 'the Mad' (*Vesanus*), was hunting one day and pursued a stag, which took refuge in S. Aeltut's bed-chamber, followed by barking dogs. The hounds remained outside and became silent. The king, wondering why they stopped barking, came up and saw the hermitage. He was irritated at finding that the saint had established himself there without his permission, and demanded that the stag should be delivered up to him, which the saint refused to do, though he invited the king to enter. *Merchiaun* was finally mollified and offered the saint the land, as a gift from himself.

---

[53] The words *ubi prius viderat scrophe porcellarumque anfractum* have been added in the margin. Cf. BLD 80, 81 and *Vita Pauli Aureliani*, c. 15. The same story is told of the foundation of Croyland abbey by S. Guthlac. The dedication of churches in the name of the Trinity is found in the contemporary *Vita Cungari* and several times in the BLD (pp. 80, 161, 162): "a devotion," as Mr. E. Bishop says (*Liturgica Historica*, p. 212), "which spread in the later middle ages, but was alien to the mind and feeling of those earlier times." In c. 18 our author tells us again that Llantwit church was dedicated to the Holy Trinity.

[54] Cf. p. 104, note 48.

Aeltut gratefully accepted it. This same stag, tamed by S.
Aeltut, afterwards used to draw the wagons containing timber for
building. The king was hungry and desired a meal. Aeltut
invited him to dine there, and sent his servant to the neighbouring
pond. He returned with a hugh fish, which was cooked and set
before the king, who refused to eat it without bread and salt.
Aeltut did not happen to have any, but by his prayer the flesh
of the fish was made to taste as if all manner of different kinds of
food were on the table. The king then mockingly demanded
wine or mead. Aeltut had neither, but again was able, by his
prayer, to make water from the well taste like wine and mead
and other liquors.

C. 9. *How an angel came and reproved Merchiaun.*

After this wonderful repast the king went to sleep. An
angel appeared to him in a dream and warned him, in a long
rhetorical speech, not to interfere with the saint, whose future
fame he foretells:

> None shall be more holy than he throughout the whole of Britain.
> All who oppose him shall perish. Kings and princes shall obey
> him. This valley shall be inhabited as long as the world endures.

C.10 *How the king awoke and gave leave [to Iltut] to dwell there.*

When the king awoke, he addressed Eltut in a long and
flowery harangue, offering him free possession of the *parochia*
and of the valley, at present a solitude, which he is to cultivate
and will find more fertile than Italy. The king dwells at length
on the relative merits of Italy and Glamorgan, using reminiscences of Vergil's *Georgics*. He prophesies the greatness of the
saint's *gimnasium*[55] [The whole of this passage has been added
as an afterthought. The chapter ends with a sentence :
Postquam angelus talia dixisset—obviously intended to follow
immediately after the angel's speech in c. 9].

---

[55] *Magistralis tibi cura concessa a pontifice . . . vestrum gimnasium erit vener-
abile; tributarii tibi servient et omnes indigene. Confluent multi ex diversis
partibus; erudiantur documentis liberalibus.*

C. 11 *How he began to cultivate the land and how his familia became very numerous.*

The venerable abbot Eltut was now left undisturbed. He began to plough and sow and reap. He fed the hungry, clothed the naked, and visited the prisoners. [His liberal hospitality is described, in a passage borrowed from the *Vita Cadoci.*[56]] Disciples flocked to him, among them Samson, Paulinus, Gildas, and Dewi.

C.12. *How he received holy orders and was raised to the rank of abbot.*

After receiving holy orders and being made a monk, and finally, on account of his sanctity, appointed abbot, he appointed fifty canons, who visited the church at fixed seasons and hours, each having his own prebend, that is, a *villa* with *beneficia* which were given by the people to preserve the memory of departed souls. Annual tribute was paid to the abbot and he divided it among the others. He had annual banquets prepared, to which he used to invite a multitude of poor persons, who were directed to depart immediately they had finished, for fear the supply of provisions should become exhausted.

C.13 *How the dyke was burst by the sea breaking in, and how the sea was driven back and a fountain sprang up through [the prayers of] S. Iltut.*

The waters of the sea and of the river (which was close to the cemetery) caused frequent floods. To keep them back, the saint constructed a huge dyke of mingled stones and mud, which was broken three times. In despair, Saint Eltut thought of abandoning the site altogether, but was forbidden to do so by the voice of an angel (heard in a dream the night before his intended departure), which directed him to repair next day to the sea-shore, taking with him his staff. He duly fulfilled the angelic precept and went down to the shore. The sea began to withdraw as he advanced. He struck the ground thus left bare with his

---

[56] *Centum familiares, tot operatores, clericos et pauperes centenos cotidie.* Cf. *Vita Cadoci*, c. 18 (*VSBG 62].) The expression *largiter dabat quicquid dabatur* seems a reminiscence of Caradog of Llancarfan's *Vita Gildae, quicquid dabatur ei continuo impendebat pauperibus.*

staff, and straightway a fountain began to flow.   Its water is
abundant and heals the sick, and is perfectly fresh, though so
near the sea.   The saint prayed that the sea might not return to
cover the land again, but only bring ships to the port there.
The marshy ground thus drained is very fertile, part of the land is
ploughed and part provides the clergy [of Llantwit] with all the
pasture they require.   [This detail is found in substance in the
Vita Pauli, but the verbal parallelism is very slight.[57]   The
prayer placed in the saint's mouth is quite different from that
given by Wrmonoc and is much more concise.]

C.14. *How the birds who pecked at the crops complained when they were driven away in custody.*

In autumn, as the harvest was maturing, the birds began to peck
at S. Iltut's harvest, leaving little except husks on the stalks.
Eltut was grieved at the news of the loss thus sustained and
ordered his scholars to take turns, day by day, in guarding the
crops with slings and stones.   But the disciple Samson, when his
turn came, though earnestly wishing to obey his master, failed to
prevent the birds from working havoc, though he did his best.
He sought aid and counsel from God how he might shut up the
whole flock of birds, as this seemed to him the best way of
preventing them from doing damage . . . He was enabled by
God to drive the winged creatures away from the crop as if they
were wingless.   They attempt to fly, but cannot, in spite of all
their endeavours.   The kindly Samson, seeing this, drove them on
before him as if they were quadrupeds.   They were thus forced to
go on till they came to the door of the barn.   It opened and they
entered.

[Ten hexameters follow, describing the noise made by the
birds in the barn, and how they were finally liberated by Iltut
and never did any more damage to the crops.[58]]

---

[57] In the *Vita Pauli, ipsa vero tellus, quam diximus marinis ereptam aestibus, in
opus agriculturae . . . monasterii valde fertilis permansit.* In the *Vita Iltuti,
palustris illa terra siccata ferax agricultura fuit . . . clerus . . . habundanter
habuit.* The replacement of *Monasterium* by *clerus* is characteristic of the
later writer.   His awkward use of the word *agricultura*, noted by the
Bollandists, suggests that he is carelessly imitating an older narrative.

[58] There are four different versions of this story, contained in Wrmonoc's
Vita Pauli (ninth century), the *Vita Gildae* (by Vitalis, abbot of St. Gildas-
de-Rhuis, who died c. 1067), the *Vita Iltuti*, and the short *Vita Sancti
Sansonis* in the *Liber Landavensis*.

In the first, Paul is the hero of the story, assisted by his three companions.
There are passages in the version in the *Vita Iltuti* in which we find words

C.15. Of the election of Samson as bishop, and of the springing up of the well from his tears, and how his body was miraculously brought back.

After this miracle had become known everywhere, messengers arrived from *Letavia* to elect the youthful Samson, with Eltut's permission, as bishop of Dol, the see being then vacant. He grieved at having to leave his master, and while they were conversing at a place in the upper part of the valley, he began to weep. His tears fell in a stream to the ground and a fountain sprang up from which flows a rivulet that is still called by his name. He gave commandment that, for the great love which he had for the dearly-loved teacher, his body, after his death, should be brought back to the monastery of S. Iltut and buried with him in that sweet cemetery. They then went to Dubricius, bishop of Llandaff, that Samson might receive from him the minor orders and the diaconate. While he was being ordained, there appeared to Bishop Dubricius and Abbot Iltut a dove, whiter than snow, sitting on the young man's shoulder. After this [no mention is made of his ordination to the priesthood or consecration as bishop] he sailed to *Letavia*, and was raised to the episcopal see according to Catholic usage. After his death his body was placed in a sarcophagus, which a mighty wind wafted lightly across the sea, like a wild-fowl in flight,[59] till it

and expressions identical with those used by Wrmonoc, showing that either the author is copying the *Vita Pauli*, or that both writers have copied a common source. The *Vita Iltuti* speaks of the *querelae volucrum . . . in carcere*, Wrmonoc says totus *querularum* vocum *carcer* garrit . . . *volucrum . . . . carcere*; the *Vita Iltuti* has fere *vacuatis spicis* deserere, Wrmonoc vix *vacuae spicae:* the *Vita Iltuti, agitare volatiles compulit*, Wrmonoc, *volatilium* catervas *agitantes compellunt.*

The narrative in the *Vita Gildae* is certainly based on the *Vita Pauli*, since Vitalis is known to have rewritten the latter. There is nothing worth remarking in his brief version of the story, except that only Gildas and Samson assist Paul in the miracle and that he tells us definitely that the *insula usque in hodiernum diem Lanna Hilduti vocatur.*

The writer of the *Liber Landavensis* has followed the first *Vita Samsonis*, but has added to it, very awkwardly, the story of the birds. He has turned them from sea-birds into white sparrows. In his version *segetem consummerent* seems based on Wrmonoc's *segetes* usque ad *consummationem* devorantium, and he calls the birds *volatiles*. He adds a new feature to the story by making Samson, after driving the birds to the barn, return to the field and go to sleep there. His jealous fellow-pupils find him, and mockingly ask him if he has killed all the birds with his *sling*. He informs them that he has shut them up *in carcere*. The detail of the sling is only found in these two versions.

[59] *Quasi fulica volatilis.*

came down and landed safely, like a ferry-boat, at the Gate of Iltut.[60] Some sailors, who witnessed this and observed a sweet perfume coming from the sarcophagus, announced to Iltut the marvel they had seen. The latter, remembering Samson's last charge concerning his burial, wept, and, after prayer, hastened to the sea port. The body was received and laid by the clergy with honour in the midst of stones placed four-square in the cemetery, and a stone cross was erected over it with an inscription stating that a bishop lay there, whose soul rests free from the fire that is to come.[61]

C.16. *How S. Iltut's wife visited him and how she lost her sight and recovered it by the saint's prayer.*

The blessed Iltut's former wife, named *Trinihid*, a most chaste woman, had resolved to lead a single life after her husband had separated from her. She spent her time in prayer and good works, fasting till the ninth hour, when she partook of a meal consisting of barley bread and water. The love of the Trinity, whom she loved inwardly, was her delight. She loved [too] the solitude of the mountains and chose a place there in which to dwell, constructing a cell (*habitaculum*) and building an oratory, in which she prayed. She relieved the needy and supported widows and nuns. One day she felt a desire to visit S. Iltut. On her arrival, she saw a man engaged in digging, with his face and clothes all dirty, very different from the handsome soldier she used to behold. He made no answer when she addressed him, and she lost her sight as a punishment for her uncalled-for visit. She soon recovered it, however, through his prayer, but her face became pallid like that of a fever patient.[62] She returned to her place and never visited S. Iltut again, fearing to displease him.

---

[60] *In Iltuti ostio* (corr. supra lin. *vel portu*).

[61] William of Malmesbury tells us (*De antiq. Glast. Eccl.*, c. 32) that "in the top tablet" of the taller of the two "pyramids" which stood near the old church at Glastonbury "there is an image made to represent a pontiff". Neither of the two cross-shafts at Llantwit now has any mention of a bishop or anything like the inscription recorded by our author, cf. pp. 129-30.

[62] Cf. Caradog of Llancarfan's *Vita Gildae: macies apparebat in facie, quasi quidam febricitans.*

C.17. *Of the steward Cyblim, who was melted like as wax melteth at the fire, because he had offended Iltut.*

The steward of *Meirchiaun*, king of the *Glatmorcan* folk, named *Cyblim*, a malicious man, whose name in Latin means *totus acutus*, fulfilled in his conduct what his name implied. His very disagreeable behaviour is described in vague and rhetorical language. He oppressed Iltut and his clergy and endeavoured to make him pay tribute to the royal castle. The saint forgave him, but God punished him by causing him to melt like wax in the heat of the fire.[63]

C.18. *How the man of God fled to a cave to escape the persecution of King Meirchiaun.*

King *Meirchiaun* was infuriated at the liquefaction of his sacrilegious steward, and determined to slay Iltut and destroy his *locus* and its clergy, regretting that he had ever given permission for a hermitage to be established there, preferring that it should be a haunt of wild beasts rather than the abode of God's servants, dedicated in the honour of the holy and undivided Trinity. He armed his servants and set out to attack the holy place and its *princeps* and inhabitants. To escape his rage, and also because he longed after the life of solitude and uninterrupted prayer, Iltut looked round for some secret place of retreat, where he could not be found and brought back to his post as abbot, and at length he discovered one on the bank of the river *Eugenni* (Ewenni), in a well-hidden cave, into which he entered, and abode there for a year and three days and nights, sleeping at night on a cold stone, thus fulfilling the penance imposed upon him. [The writer adds four hexameters, beginning : *Hic lapis in lecto positus sub pectore nostro.*]

C.19. *How he was fed from heaven in the cave, and of the bell sent him by Saint David, which sounded when God willed, and how he returned to the monastery (cenobium) from the cave.*

In this cave therefore the blessed Iltut prayed and fasted daily. Each day at the ninth hour there was sent him from heaven a barley loaf and a piece of fish, after eating which he went to a well

---

[63] Psalm lxviii. 2.

close by and drank water taken from it in the palms of his hands, as Paul and Antony, the first hermits,[64] used to eat and drink. He took care that nobody saw him as he returned to the cave. Meanwhile everyone, high and low, rich and poor, was grieving over his departure and searching for him everywhere. One day a traveller passed by—a messenger from Gildas the historiographer,[65] carrying a brass bell made by the same Gildas, as a present to S. Dewi the bishop, in memory of their former friendship. As he passed by the cave, which was near the public way, the bell sounded of its own accord. S. Iltut heard the sweet sound and went out to meet its bearer. He rang it three times and asked the messenger where he was carrying this beautiful object, brighter than gold. He replied, 'I am taking the bell to S. Dewi, by order of the famous Gildas.' He then continued on his journey, and, arriving at the Menevian valley, presented the bell to the bishop, who took it and rang it, but not a sound did it give forth. The bishop asked the messenger if anyone had tried to ring it on the way, and, on hearing from him what had happened, he said, 'I am sure that our master Iltut would have liked to have the bell himself, on account of its sweet sound, but would not ask for it because he heard that Gildas was giving it to me. Take it back at once to the cave and give S. Iltut what he so greatly desires.' The messenger returned to Iltut and did as he was told. Then, leaving him alone in the cave (yet not alone, because angels frequently visited him there), he went on to the monastery and related what he had seen. The monks were delighted to hear that their most religious abbot had been found. They went out to his retreat and brought him home.

The writer then gives the thanksgiving uttered by the saint's compatriots :

> Kings and princes will obey the virtuous *princeps* (abbot), this *locus* will be the chief of all throughout the country.

The cave, we are told, during Iltut's sojourn there, was unceasingly lit up by the presence of angelic visitants.

C.20. *Of the most wicked Cefygid, steward of King Meirchiaun, who was swallowed up by a marsh.*

Iltut ruled the abbey (*abbatia*)[66] in peace for some time, till

---

[64] Caradog of Llancarfan in his *Vita Gildae* (in the passage referred to on p. 109, note 56) says that Gildas fasted *ut heremita Antonius*. The author of the *Vita Cungari* (c. 8) has borrowed several expressions from this chapter.

[65] The author of the *Liber Landavensis* twice gives Gildas this title (BLD 100, 138).

[66] A term never employed in Celtic times.

fresh trouble arose with another steward of King *Meirchiaun*, named *Cefygid*,who impounded the cattle belonging to the saint and the clergy, and used to keep them for three days without feeding them till they grew lean and emaciated. Iltut was unwilling to curse him, but at last the supreme and heavenly Judge punished the evildoer by causing some marshy ground to swallow him up. This marsh may be seen to this very day in testimony of the sinner's wickedness.

C.21. *Of the rage of Meirchiaun the mad king, whom the earth swallowed up.*

King *Meirchiaun*, full of madness, hearing what had happened to his steward, was enraged, and determined to slay Iltut or expel him from his *dominium*. Arming himself, he rode hastily from his castle to the gate of the monastery (*civitas*). As he stood there, the earth swallowed him up and he was seen no more.

After some time S. Iltut resolved again to seek a retreat, in which he would be free from interruption and able to give himself entirely to prayer, so he went to the *Lingarthic* cave [i.e., cave of Llwynarth], and remained there for three years, being fed every day at the ninth hour with food brought by an angel and placed on a stone within the cave. Here he saw a great miracle.

C.22. *Of the miracle seen in the Lingarthic cave* [i.e., *cave of Llwynarth*].

[The story is abridged from Nennius's version. The men who hand over the *corpus odoriferum* to S. Iltut reveal to him the saint's name but forbid him to tell it to anyone, though without mentioning any reason. The story of the punishment of the inquisitive men is omitted, and we are simply told that "many miracles take place through his holiness."]

C.23. *Of the two robbers changed into two stones.*

One night two robbers stole S. Iltut's herd of swine, taking them from the *hara* where they were kept and driving them towards the woodlands. They lost their way and spent the whole

night wandering round aimlessly, till at dawn they found
themselves back at the place from which they had started.
[They hid themselves during the day.] The tired animals
rested till the third hour, the swineherd wondering why they
were so sleepy. At nightfall the robbers returned to the *hara*
and made a second attempt to drive the pigs off to the distant
mountain, with the same result. The patience of the King of
Heaven being now exhausted, they were turned into two stones,
which are still called after them, and the site of the *hara* still
bears the name of Iltut.[67]

C.24. *Of the three granaries, from which an abundant supply of corn
      was conveyed from Britain to Letavia, which was formerly
      called Armorica.*

The most blessed Iltut desired to visit the church of S.
Michael *in Monte Tumba,* and before setting out on his journey
gave orders that the corn stored in three barns which he possessed
should, after thrashing, be laid up in granaries against his return
from *Letavia*. He carried out his intended pilgrimage, but, as he
was about to begin the journey back, he observed that there was a
sore famine among the people of his native country and that they
would perish of starvation unless speedily succoured. Grieved
at their sufferings, he betook himself to prayer, and the corn, of
which mention has been made, was miraculously transported to a
port in *Letavia* and was found there on the shore. There proved
to be enough, not merely to satisfy the people's immediate
needs, but to provide seed corn for the next year. Iltut then
returned to Britain, though entreated by the inhabitants of
Letavia to stay with them. But, when the time drew near that
he should receive from the Lord the hundred-fold promised to
His faithful servants, he returned once more to his fatherland,
that is, *Letavia,* which we call Lesser Britain, and died there in
the city of Dol, on 6th November. [The chapter ends with a
doxology, which may have been the original conclusion of the
Life, before the addition of the last two chapters—which do not
concern S. Iltut at all, but only the history of his monastery.]

---

[67] Apparently the place meant is *Llanhari,* the church of which is dedicated
to. S. Iltut.

C.25. *How the spoil was restored and the horses appeared exactly
like each other.*

Edgar, king of the English, furious at the disobedience of
the men of *Glatmorgan*, invaded the country, violating everywhere the territories of the saints, and even their temples,[68]
and leaving no *villa* in the whole region unravaged. S. Iltut's
bell was taken from his church and carried off by a robber to
English soil. It was fastened to the neck of a horse—the finest
in the king's stable on the Golden Mount (so-called because of
the concourse of soldiers in gilt armour there). While the
spoil was being divided, the king was resting in his tent at noon,
when a terrible vision appeared to him of a soldier (seen by none
but him) who pierced his breast with a lance. Realising that he
had sinned in plundering [Glamorgan], he gave orders that all
that had been taken from God and the most holy Iltut should be
restored. Moreover he built a temple in honour of the saint, and
granted the land on which he stood to those who should serve in
that temple. Nine days after, however, he died, as a punishment
for what he had done. Meanwhile, the aforesaid horse started
off of its own accord, bearing the bell, and proceeded westwards.
It crossed the Severn, all the other horses following, guided by
musical tinkling of the bell. When the horses arrived at the
river *Tam*, the clergy [of Llantwit] heard the bell sound and
went out to meet it. They accompanied it triumphantly to the
door of the church of S. Iltut, but, as they were removing the
bell from the horse's neck, it accidentally fell upon a stone and a
piece was broken off, and to this day the fracture in the bell
testified to the miracle then wrought. A glorious psalmody
was sung in choir. Each of the innumerable canons [of Llantwit]
appropriated for himself one of the horses that had arrived, but a
contention arose as to who was to have the principal one, which
had carried the bell. The dispute continued for several hours and
nearly led to bloodshed, but this was averted by the horses next
day appearing all exactly alike. Thus for love of Iltut did
God bring back the bell and all the spoil to his most holy
temple.

[68] Cf. the expression *comburendo templa sanctorum* in the *Vita Teiliavi*
(BLD 100).

C.26. *Of the victory won by the clergy of S. Iltut over the outlaws at the castle of Meirchiaun.*

At the time when William, king of the English, was reigning throughout Britain, and the prince Robert Fitz Haimon was ruling Gulatmorcantia, the northern Britons began to offer fierce resistance to the king, and the southern Britons later made a league together and devastated and burnt villas and fortified places. Enemies came out of the woods to attack the English and Norman citizens; and, after laying waste the country, returned to the distant mountain and woods laden with booty. The Welsh raised an army of about three thousand men, on horse and foot, to lay waste Gulatmorcantia. When the news arrived, the clergy of S. Iltut, with their parishioners, threw up an earthwork by the waterside to protect their property. The enemy arrived by night— which was a mistake on their part, for, if they had come by day, they would have succeeded. In the nocturnal battle which followed, many on both sides were struck down by stones and spears; and flashes of light, indicating the presence of angels protecting the Catholic people, were seen in the air between the temple of S. Iltut and the castle of King Meirchiaun, where the fight was raging. The Refuge of God and of the most holy Iltut was violated, and in consequence a force of three thousand men was defeated near the castle by a smaller number. The defenders fought valiantly, weak women supplying the combatants with arms, and young boys helping. The enemies' shields were broken by stones hurled upon them. They uttered terrific screams, for few of them had not bloody faces. By the assistance of the mighty Iltut, they failed to scale the fortifications. There is no true strength where wickedness reigns, and this was proved when the multitude of Guynedotia fled. *Explicit.*

In order really to learn anything from a medieval *Life* of a saint, it is necessary to begin by asking, who was the author, where did he write, and when, and why, and what materials he had for his work. The questions are intimately connected with each other. Internal evidence will often point to the answers.

The first thing that strikes us as we examine the *Vita S. Iltuti* is that the anonymous author must have been a clerk of Llantwit Major. He refers no less than seven times[69] to the *clerus Sancti Iltuti*, a community (apparently) of secular clerks,

[69] Cc. 13, 15, 17, 18, 20, 25, 26.

which had taken the place of the Celtic monks of the ancient monastery of *Lan-Ildut*, a society evidently possessed of strong corporate feeling and of considerable powers of leadership (as the last chapter of the *Vita* shows), to which he was proud to belong. The writer shows an intimate knowledge of Llantwit and its surroundings. The information he gives us about Llantwit and its traditions in the period immediately following the Norman Conquest is the only really valuable part of his work, the rest being largely fiction, of no interest for the historian. He speaks with affection of the charm of the fertile valley in which Llantwit lies—he considers it "the most beautiful place in the world",[70] of the *sanctissimum templum* of S. Iltut and the saint's bell preserved therein, and its *delectabile cimiterium*—he has gazed with interest on the famous Celtic crosses the latter contains. He knows the exact situation of the holy well of S. Samson and of that of S. Iltut, and has heard, or invented, stories explaining why they are so called. He certainly possessed, in a high degree, as Duine remarks,[71] the spirit of *l'amour du clocher*. He knows the 'Refuge', the castle of King *Meirchiaun*, and the port of S. Iltut. He also knows places in the neighbourhood where there are still churches dedicated to S. Iltut, and he knows a cave associated with the saint (about which no traditions now remain) at Ewenni.

Next we observe, with some surprise, that the author's style shows a practised hand, such as we should not have expected to find in a village like Llantwit. It is much the best written of all the *Lives* in Vesp. A. xiv. He writes in a smooth and flowing manner, suitable to the work of romance he is composing, though his taste and judgment are not equal to his fluency. The repulsive stories of Iltut's treatment of his wife, which he has invented[72] and considers highly edifying, moralising on them in prose and verse, are his most serious offences against

[70] C. 6.
[71] *Mémento*, No. 111.
[72] The authors of *Lives of the British Saints* (iii. 307, 310) relate these unpleasant fictions as if they were facts—"steeled against all kindly and pitiful feelings . . . . He denied her the common kindness of a hospitable lodging, and she went away sorrowful." We have no right to blacken the character of saints of the fifth century by repeating about them the diseased fancies of twelfth century romancists as if they were undoubted truths. Iltut was probably never married.

good taste, but not the only ones. He does not see how unconvincing are the long speeches he puts in the mouths of the angel and King *Meirchiaun*. None of the stories he tells sound credible except the last. The *Life* is an elaborate and pretentious literary effort, disfigured by glaring faults of composition, one of which, however, has at any rate the merit of providing us with a clue to its authorship, since it is found in two other contemporary *Lives* of Welsh saints, the *Vita Congari* and the *Vita S. Gildae* by Caradog of Nantcarfan. It consists in a peculiar and annoying trick of style—"the frequent repetition of the same word, or the same root, in various formations". It was the late Dr. J. Armitage Robinson, dean of Wells, who first, in an article in the *Journal of Theological Studies* in October, 1921 (pp. 15-17), called attention to this "odious idiosyncracy", giving copious examples from both the *Lives* mentioned. He thought it proved that the *Vita Congari*, of which he had found a twelfth century fragment at Wells, was by Caradog of Nantcarfan. He thought, too, that it had been copied by both the *Vita Cadoci* and the *Vita Iltuti*. Here Dr. Robinson was mistaken. It is true that there has been copying, but not in the way he suggested. The *Vita Cadoci* is the oldest of these *Lives*.[73] It has been copied by them all, and by the compiler of the *Book of Llandaff*. The *Vita S. Congari*, which has not a scrap of either originality or truth, has copied the *Vita Cadoci*, the *Vita Gildae*, and the *Vita Iltuti*.

Now our author uses again and again the tiresome trick of style I have referred to, but in his work it is not so exaggerated as in the *Lives* of SS. Congar and Gildas, where its constant and senseless repetition become absolutely nauseous. A few examples will suffice :

C. 14. CONSULUIT *apud semetipsum, inspiratus divino* CONSILIO, *et invenit* CONSULENDO *quod efficere debuit.*

C. 18. *Capit celeriter* ARMA, *imperat militibus se* ARMARI; ARMATI*que pariter tendunt in sanctum locum.*

C. 19. DONANS *tali* DONO *pontificem.* DONATUS MOVIT *cimbalum; ex* MOTIONE *nullum reddidit sonum.*

---

[73] It is true that, as the Dean observes, "Vesp. A. xiv is said to have been written *c.* 1200," but this is only true of the *manuscript*. The *Lives* it contains are, as Mr. Robin Flower says, all of them older, and Lifris's work must be a century older (see p. 102).

In addition, certain identical passages are found, either verbally or in substance, in the *Vita Iltuti*, the *Vita Gildae*, and, as I have said, in the *Vita Congari*.

We have here a very difficult literary problem. On the one hand Caradog of Nantcarfan cannot be the author of the *Vita Iltuti*. He was not a clerk of Llantwit, but belonged to the rival church, from which he took his name of *Nancarbanensis*. On the other hand there are literary affinities between the *Vita Iltuti* and the *Vita Gildae*. It is possible that the explanation may be that the present version of the *Vita Iltuti* is the work of a reviser, a *littérateur* like Caradog (perhaps Caradog himself, or one of his school), who has divided it into chapters in a systematic way, and perhaps rewritten much of the text in what may be called twelfth century 'journalese'. The headings of the chapters, it may be observed, do not always correspond exactly with their contents.[74] The fact that the name of the hero is spelt in three different ways[75] may be a further indication of the hand of a reviser (unless it is due to the writer utilizing different sources). Certain passages (e.g. c. 10) have been added after the rest was written.

The last chapter of the *Vita Iltuti* gives us an approximate date for its completion in its present form (we have seen that the last two chapters may be a later addition). Robert Fitz Hamon died in 1107, and the words *Rege Anglorum Willelmo regnante . . . et Roberto principe Haimonis filio regente Gulatmorcantiam* could not have been written till after some years had elapsed. We may safely say that it was finished some time during the first half of the twelfth century (Mr. Wade-Evans thinks between 1140 and 1150), and is therefore roughly contemporary with the literary activities of Caradog of Nantcarfan, and also with the compilation of the *Liber Landavensis*.[76] Further, the *Life of S. Iltut* is also

---

[74] E.g. in the case of the heading of c. 5. A new subject is begun in the middle of c. 21. In chapters 11 and 19 we have *Dewi* in the text, but *David* in the heading to c. 19. The headings are very similar to those in the *Vita S. Congari*). The chapters are all of moderate length. *Professor C. Brooke (SEBC 233-35) thinks "that the *Life of Iltut* is the work either of Caradoc or of a disciple."]

[75] In c. 1 he is *Iltutus* and *Aeltutus*, in cc. 3-15 *Aeltutus* or *Eltutus* (as in the *Vita Samsonis*), in c. 15 to the end always *Iltutus*.

[76] Dr. Robinson seems unaware that some of the features common to the *Vita Iltuti* and the *Vita Congari* to which he calls attention are equally prominent in the *Book of Llandaff*.

roughly contemporary with the *History of the Kings of Britain* of Geoffrey of Monmouth (d. 1155). There are characteristic features common to all these writers, and until we can get beyond 'roughly' to 'precisely' we shall not be in a position to say exactly what is the relation between them. Unfortunately it is not possible at present to do so.

There does not seem to be any clue to the purpose of the author in writing, beyond the natural interest of an intelligent member of the clerical staff of a famous church in the story of the foundation of that church. Professor Tatlock thinks that this and other twelfth century *Lives* of Welsh saints were "produced at ancient religious houses in South Wales . . . threatened by the cupidity of Norman lords, with the plain purpose of defending them by exalting their early saintly founders and heroes and the antiquity of their foundations."[77]

The writer of the *Vita Iltuti* was a clerk of Llantwit Major. What materials had he at his disposal ?

We have seen that there is reason to believe that a *Life* of Iltut, written or oral, existed in the ninth century and was utilized by Wrmonoc in 884, and that the narrative in Wrmonoc's work has been inserted by our author in the centre of his own composition. It will be found at the end of c. 11 and is the basis of the whole of cc. 13 and 14.

He has also read Nennius and taken from him the story of the cave of *Loyngarth*. *Loyngarth* is Oystermouth in Gower, and Oystermouth was given by William de Londres (a contemporary of Robert Fitz Hamon) or his son Maurice to Ewenni priory about 1126. Our author knew Ewenni very well and it is tempting to explain in this way his introduction of the story of the unknown saint in the cave. But the verbal agreement between his account and that of the *Historia Brittonum* is so close that it is certain that he is paraphrasing Nennius,[78] not using a local tradition. His description of the cave is much less vivid and seems *not* to be that of an eye-witness. Like most

---

[77] In *Speculum*, 1939, p. 345.
[78] Nennius says *altare supra faciem ejus quod nutu Dei fulciebatur*. Our author writes *altare divino nutu supra faciem fulcitum*.

Celtic hagiographers of this period, our author supplements the meagre traditions at his disposal by plagiarisms from the *Lives* of other saints. He makes great use of the *Vita Cadoci* (in doing so he follows the example of the compiler of the *Liber Landavensis*). Chapters 2, 3, 8, 11, 12, 17, 19, 20, 21 and 24 all contain stories or *motifs* borrowed from this source. The theme of a saint's enemies being swallowed up by the earth, found in cc. 16 and 19 of the *Vita Cadoci*, has been worked to death by our author. The words *quem terra deglutivit* come three times in the headings of the chapters in the *Vita Iltuti*. The writer has also been attracted (as the compiler of the *Book of Llandaff*)[79] by Lifris's description of an offender "melting like wax".[80]

It is remarkable that our author does not seem to know the *Vita Samsonis*, which has inspired so many Celtic hagiographers. His chapter about Samson's relations with Iltut does indeed contain one incident found there, but in other respects is entirely independent of that famous *Life* and indeed contradicts it. He does not mention the tradition of Iltut being a disciple of Germanus and ordained by him, but tells us he was ordained by Dubricius. Is it possible that he used the abbreviated extract of the *Vita Samsonis* inserted in the *Book of Llandaff* (the work of a contemporary), supplementing it with his own fancies? This would explain the absence of the story of *Isanus* and *Atoclius*, which is *not* in that version, and the presence of the story of Samson and the birds, which is.

C. 7 has some striking parallels in cc. 5 and 6 of the *Vita S. Gundlei*[81]. Other favourite themes of the Norman hagiographers of this period (such as the dedication of churches to the Holy Trinity and the mention of *Letavia*) will be noted where they occur.

The greater part of the *Vita* is made up of local traditions of Llantwit—late, scanty, and disappointing. It is very remarkable however, that, unlike the author of the *Vita Cadoci*, the writer seems to have had no charters granted to the monastery at his disposal. It is curious that, while the *Life of S. Cadog* contains numerous charters, as well as traditions about his monastery and

---

[79] *Vita Iltuti*, c. 17; BLD 116.
[80] *Vita Cadoci*, c. 40.
[81] Another of the *Lives* contained in Vesp. A. xiv.

its lands and buildings, these buildings and the monastery itself
have entirely vanished (its very site is uncertain), while Llantwit
church shows traces of having possessed a large staff of clerks
throughout the Middle Ages and is surrounded by ruins
covering several acres.

In cc. 18 and 19 we have some interesting local traditions of
Ewenni. The situation of the cave is so precisely described as
to show that the writer must have seen it, but there seems to be
no trace of any cult of S. Iltut in the neighbourhood remaining
to-day.

Finally, the writer supplements his materials with numerous
inventions of his own (including all the *Trinihid* and *Meirchiaun*
stories), which will be found in cc. 1, 2, 4, 5, 6, 8-10, 16, 21, 24
and 25.

The *Life* begins, in a high-pitched, rhetorical way, with a
panegyric of Brittany. The Norman writers of *Lives* of Welsh
saints were interested in Brittany, and the compiler of the
Book of Llandaff and Geoffrey of Monmouth both refer to the
military prowess of the Bretons, especially in cavalry engage-
ments. Like the hero of the *Vita Paterni* and like S. Oudoceus
in the *Liber Landavensis*, S. Iltut is represented as born in
Brittany,[82] and a pedigree is constructed for him. This sudden
abundance of detailed information, appearing for the first time
in a book written seven centuries after the events described,
could hardly deceive the most simple-minded. It is obviously
all pure fiction. *Rieingulid*, like *Trynihid*, is probably a made-up
name.[83] The name *Bican* is not unlike that of a witness on p. 219
of the *Book of Llandaff—Biguan*. *Anblaud* is the same name as
Anlawdd, the father of Goleuddydd, mother of the hero of the
old Welsh story of *Culhwch and Olwen* in the *Mabinogion*.[84]

[82] Mr. Wade-Evans suggests (*Welsh Christian Origins*, 133) that the *Letavia* of
the *Vita Iltuti* (also of the *Vita Paterni*)may in reality be the Welsh, not the
Armorican, Llydaw. "There are in fact vivid traditions of St. Illtud along
the River Usk from Dyfynnog to Llanhamlach."

[83] Professor Henry Lewis says: "The form *Rieingulid* could be explained as
riein, later *rhiain*='maiden', with the adjective *gulid*, later *gwlydd*='gentle
tender'. *Rhiain* is still in use; *gwlydd* is well known in mediaeval literature.
Rhieinwlydd='Gentle Maiden' could be a genuine name composed of noun
and adjective, cf. *Branwen*. In the *Vita* the meaning 'regina pudica' gets
quite near; *rhiain* is a cognate of Old Irish *rigain*='queen'."

[84] Culhwch is also described as a "cousin of Arthur".

Iltut is a genuine Celtic name (it is the name of a witness—spelt *Illtut*, on p. 217 of the *Liber Landavensis*), though our author tries to make it mean something in Latin. The form *Eltut*, according to the late J. Loth,[85] seems to be the more authentic. The element *El* appears, as he points out, in many Welsh names of this period *El-iud*, *T-el-iau*, *El-gnou*, *El-guarui*, *El-guoret*, *El-heharn*, etc. *Iltut* is the form on the famous cross at Llantwit. Both forms, as Loth remarks, appear in Brittany: *Ildut* (with a long *i*) at Aber-ildut and Lann-ildut, *Eltut* (with short *e*) at Ploerdut. The *Vita Samsonis* and Giraldus Cambrensis have *Eltut*, Nennius and Wrmonoc have *Iltut*.

The reference to "his cousin" King Arthur in c. 2 has been differently interpreted by scholars, Some[86] regard the description of the magnificence of Arthur's court as a proof that the writer had read Geoffrey of Monmouth's *Historia*. Others [87] consider his statements about Dubricius, which are inconsistent with those of Geoffrey, as a sign that he had not. In any case there is only a passing reference to Arthur and the writer goes on quickly to the story of Iltut becoming a courtier and captain of the guard under King *Poulentus*. We have seen that all this section is copied directly from the *Vita Cadoci*. *Poulentus* is the *Poul of Penychen* of Lifris's work. Paul of Penychen (as Wrmonoc's *Vita Pauli Aureliani* shows) was a great figure in Glamorgan traditions as early as the ninth century, and Wrmonoc has made a half-hearted attempt to identify him with S. Paul of Léon[88]. Our author, however, passes over King *Poulentus* as lightly as he

---

[85] *La Vie la plus ancienne de Saint Samson* (Paris, 1923), p. 48, note 2. Professor Henry Lewis says: "There is an interesting note on the form *Illtud* by Sir John Rhys in his British Academy lecture, 'Gleanings in the Italian field of Celtic epigraphy' (read 27th May, 1914), p. 16—also found in *Proceedings of the British Academy*, Vol. vi. The Welsh form is undoubtedly *Elltud*. The corresponding Irish form would be *Iltuath*. Sir John says : 'The existence of *Iltuath* (gen. *Iltuaithe*, dat. *Iltuaith*, ac. *Iltuaith-n*) is attested by the name Lan-*yltwyt* or -*iltwyt*, for which see *The Book of Llan Dâv*, pp. 319, 325, 330, 331. This was the name of St. Illtyd's famous monastery, until it was reduced to *Lantwit*. Such instances go to prove that the Goidelic inhabitants of ancient Wales were not all driven out of the country, but rather induced in the course of time to adopt Brythonic speech.' O.W. *hil*='many' is from **pelu-s*, cognate with Gr. πολύς; **pelu-s* would regularly give Welsh **el*, which does not exist alone, but occurs in many compound names as e.g. O.W. *Eliud*, the full name of *T-el-iau*, later *Teilo*."

[86] Tatlock, op. cit., p. 355.

[87] Duine, *Mémento*, No. 111.

[88] *Paulus ... provincia quae britannicae gentis lingua ... Penn Ohen ... exortus.*

passed over King Arthur, and hastens to his elaborately worked up romance of Aeltut's separation from his wife, which is entirely his own idea as well as his own composition.

Having dismissed his wife, Iltut begins to live as a hermit in *Hodnant*. This name, a not uncommon one both in Wales and Cornwall, has puzzled commentators extremely. Rhigyfarch, in his *Life of S. David*, speaks of *Rosina Vallis, quam vulgari nomine Hodnant Brittones vocitant*,[89] and some, misled by Wrmonoc's mistaken statement that Iltut's monastery (which he calls *Insula Pyrus*) was *Demetarum patriae in finibus sita*, have supposed that Iltut's hermitage is to be placed at St. David's[90]. But a careful examination of cc. 3, 4, and 6 makes it perfectly clear that our author means Llantwit. In c. 3 Iltut sleeps on the east side of the river *Nadauan*[91] (the Thaw), and the angel tells him (in c. 4) to go next day to a wooded valley westwards. Our author explains that *Hodnant* means 'vallis prospera' and in c. 6 he gives an enthusiastic description of the valley, which is clearly the place in which he lives.[92] Consequently Iltut crosses the Thaw and proceeds to the valley indicated to him, which is "westwards", but not so far west as the *Rosina Vallis*, a place that does not at all answer to the writer's description. Why our author never mentions *Lan-Ildut* by name is a mystery, but it is quite certain that in these chapters he means Llantwit.

C. 7 shows affinities with the *Liber Landavensis*,[93] the *Vita Gundlei* (cc. 5 and 6), and Caradog's *Vita Gildae*.[94]

In c. 8 we are introduced to King *Meirchiaun*, without a word of explanation as to who he was or what had become of *Poulentus*. The reason must be that our author has now turned

---

[89] *But see now J. W. James, *Rhigyfarch's Life of St.David* (Cardiff, 1967), 9, where it is shown that these words are found only in the Vespasian manuscript.]

[90] See *Acta Sanctorum*, Nov. III, pp. 222, 223, 227. *Also Caldy Island (Ynys Bŷr); here cf. CEB 325f.; R. W. D. Fenn, 'St. Illtud and Llantwit Major' (*Province* viii. 26-30, 66-68); O. Loyer, *Les Chrétientés Celtiques* (Paris, 1965), 27.]

[91] The *Nadauan* appears in the *Vita Cadoci* (c. 62) and in the *Book of Llandaff* (pp. 148, 204, 260). *Cf. G. O. Pierce, *The Place-names of Dinas Powys Hundred* (Cardiff, 1968), 170-1.]

[92] Cf. cc. 9, 10. 15.

[93] E.g. pp. 80, 161, 162.

[94] *fluvialem aquam intrare solebat media nocte, ubi manebat donec diceretur ab ipso ter oratio dominica . . . repetebat suum oratorium; ibi exorabat genuflectendo divinam majestatem.*

from the *Vita Cadoci* for a time to the local traditions of Llantwit. In the last chapter of his book he refers incidentally to the castle of King *Meirchiaun* as situated in the village of Llantwit. He must have seen it every day. It evidently struck him, and its name has suggested to him the character of *Meirchiaun Vesanus*, whom he has made one of the chief figures of his romance—he appears in no less than seven chapters of the *Vita Iltuti* (cc. 8-10, 17, 18, 20, 21).[95]

The first story about King *Meirchiaun* closely resembles the story in the *Vita Oudocei* in the *Book of Llandaff* (p. 137). It is of course a commonplace of hagiography. The incident of the stag drawing the saint's timber may be based on a similar story in the *Vita Cadoci* (c. 9), which has been imitated in the *Life of S. Teilo* in the *Book of Llandaff*, but it is remarkable that at Llanhamlach near Brecon there was a local legend about S. Iltut and a stag, preserved for us by Giraldus Cambrensis,[96] of which our author may have heard. The meal prepared for the king by Iltut has a certain resemblance to the story of King Grallon being entertained in the hermitage of S. Corentin in the *Vita Corentini*. It may be a local legend, or it may have been invented by the author. We observe that in c. 10 the king is made to describe Llantwit as a 'parish' (*parrochia*). Its *parrochiani* are referred to in c. 26. (In the *Liber Landavensis*, *parochia* has its ancient meaning of 'diocese'.)

C. 11 continues the narrative begun in c. 7 and interrupted by the set of *Meirchiaun* stories in cc. 8-10. He lays stress on the attention paid by Iltut to agriculture.[97] He appropriates a sentence from the *Vita Cadoci* (c.15) to describe Iltut's monastery, and another from Caradog of Nantcarfan's *Vita Gildae* to describe his hospitality, and concludes the chapter with a sentence practically the same as that which concludes c. 7, with

[95] The name *Merchiaun* was an extremely common one, as a glance at the index to BLD will show: on p. 243 there is a grant made to Nantcarfan by *Merchiaun filius Riderch*. In c. 57 of the *Vita Cadoci* we find *Merchiaun* (apparently a king) granting *Conhil* to 'Eltut'. We have no other authority for *Meirchiaun Vesanus*.

[96] See p. 43.

[97] C. 24 also contains a reference to the abundance of corn in the granaries of Llantwit.

the important addition of the names of the saint's four chief disciples.[98]

The description of life in the monastery is continued in c. 12, though with anachronisms characteristic of medieval attempts at writing history. Instead of monks, we find fifty *canons*, each with a *prebend* and a *benefice*. We shall notice again[99] how clearly the *Vita* shows that the monastic tradition had long been forgotten at Llantwit. The community is always assumed to be that of the collegiate church which had taken the place of the monastery long before the Norman Conquest. This chapter, however, is imitated from the *Vita Cadoci*, cc. 45-47, so that the value of its statements is questionable. The last sentence adds a life-like touch, clearly derived from actual practice.

Cc. 13 and 14 contain the long section common to the *Vita Iltuti* and the *Vita Pauli Aureliani*. We have already attempted to deal with the problem it presents. The stories have here been retold by a practised raconteur. but he has had a written account before him. Besides the verbal agreement we have called attention to, the details of the noise made by the birds in the barn, and Iltut's permission to them to return to the shore, are common to both narratives. In our author's version the disciples do *not* join in the miracle of the sea retiring and he adds the story of the saint causing a well to flow. This is clearly a Llantwit legend which did not interest Wrmonoc.[100]

C. 15 is entirely occupied with further stories about Samson. His elevation to the see of Dol is represented as due to the fame he had acquired through the miracle related in c. 14. The story of the dove, seen both by the pontiff Dubricius, "bishop of the Church of Llandaff", and by the abbot Iltut, resting on the young man's head (*not* shoulder) at his ordination as deacon, is derived from the *Vita Samsonis*, but in other respects the account

---

[98] It is remarkable that the St. David's traditions know nothing of Dewi having been a disciple of Iltut. Rhigyfarch does not mention him.

[99] Cf. c. 25, *canonici innumerabiles*.

[100] The present vicar of Llantwit (Canon R. David) tells me that "at the Port of Illtyd, some remains of which may still be seen," is "what is now known locally as the 'pool'. This pool is a patch of sand on the beach, pretty near the land. Erosion of the soil may have changed the situation. Within the memory of an old man who spoke to me some years ago, the land reached the 'pool'. It is saturated by water—this may be due not so much to the well as to the water from the brook."

here given of Samson's relations with Iltut and his departure from Wales is entirely different. The stories about Samson in this chapter, with the exception just mentioned, have all been invented by the Llantwit writer to attempt to account for two things which have evidently struck him—the existence of a fountain called Samson's Well in the valley north of the village and the fact that the names of both Samson and Iltut are found on an ancient cross-shaft still preserved at Llantwit.

Canon David tells me :

There is no well now known as Samson's Well [at Llantwit] but there is, or rather was, a well a little to the north-east of the church, formerly known as 'Town Well', but it has been covered by the present road. There is also a well more to the north, the stream from it passes by the east end of the church. This is known by the old people of Llantwit as 'Nancy's Well'.

One can imagine that in the course of centuries 'Samson's Well' might easily be corrupted into 'Nancy's Well', and its situation and the fact that it has a stream flowing from it corresponds to our author's description of the fountain *in superiori parte vallis . . . decurrens fluxu fluviali*.

The ancient monuments now in the 'old' or western church at Llantwit have been described several times by distinguished Welsh scholars.[101] The name *Samson* appears on two of these stones, and on one of them twice. This latter is the shaft of a cross. "The head is lost, but the socket in which it was once fixed can be seen in the top of the shaft, which is seven feet high. All the surfaces have knot-work designs in panels. The stone is a laminated sandstone"[102]. Till forty years ago it stood in the churchyard on the north side of the eastern division of the church. On the front, in two panels, is the inscription + SAMSON POSUIT HANC CRUCEM + PRO ANIMA EIUS + . In four panels on the back are the names + ILTUTI SAMSONI REGIS SAMUEL + EBISAR +. The other stone, which has also lost its cross-head, bears the inscription

---

[101] Mr. J. Romilly Allen, in 'The inscribed and sculptured stones at Llantwit Major' (AC 1889, pp. 118-26), and Prof. John Rhys in 'Some Glamorgan inscriptions' (AC 1899, pp. 147-53).
[102] J. W. Rodger, *The Ecclesiastical Buildings of Llantwit Major* (Cardiff, 1906).

IN NOMINE DI SUMMI INCIPIT · CRUX · SALU-
ATORIS · QUAE PREPARAUIT SAMSONI :· APATI
PRO ANIMA SUA : ET PRO ANIMA IUTHAHELO REX
. ·. ET ARTMALI . ·. ET TECAIN +[103] (the sculptor meant,
according to Sir John Rhys, that Abbot Samson prepared the
cross for his own soul and for that of King Juthael)[104]. In view
of the frequency of the occurrence of the name *Samson* in these
inscriptions we are not surprised at our author's interest in the
connection of Samson with Llantwit, nor considering how bad
the Latin of one of them is, can we be surprised that he failed
to understand their meaning and assumed that 'Samson' must
mean the hero of the *Vita Samsonis*. None of the *Samson*s on
these stones (which, as all authorities are agreed, are later than
the sixth century) can be the bishop of Dol, nor was 'S. Samson's
Well', in all probability, called after him. But we learn one
interesting fact from the writer's reference to the Samson and
Iltut cross. The details he gives (*in medio quadrangularium
lapidum erecte insistentium*) show that originally it was the
principal feature of a monument of the well-known Celtic type
known as a *leachta*, often found in monasteries off the west coast
of Ireland. "The structure rises to a height of about three feet.
Several on Inishmurray remain in a very perfect condition,
surmounted by early crosses. These monuments were funerary,
and were apparently erected for the burial of important or holy
persons". Mr. Ralegh Radford discovered the remains of one in
the ruins of an ancient Celtic monastery at Tintagel in Cornwall.

The story of the sarcophagus, skimming through the air,
"like a wild-fowl in flight", from Dol to Llantwit, resembles
that of the sarcophagus of King *Gerennius* thrown into the sea at
Dol and crossing of its own accord to *Dingerein*, which the
author of the *Liber Landavensis* has inserted into the *Life of St.
Teilo*,[105] but which of the two writers is the plagiarist is not
easy to decide.

In c. 16 we have one more story about Iltut's wife. The

[103] *Cf. now ECMW 142-5; also CB 143, note 16.]
[104] *Samson* and *Teican* sign a charter granted by King *Ris*, son of *Iudhail*, on p.211
of the BLD. *Arthuail*, son of *Ris*, appears on p. 191. In c. 55 of the *Vita
Cadoci*, Samson, *abbas altaris S. Eltuti* and *Conigc, abbas altaris S. Cadoci*,
appear.
[105] BLD 114.

details contained in it may show us how the writer was led to invent this pathetic figure. The *montana solitudo* where she resided clearly refers to a church on a hill not far from Llantwit, associated with its founder. Now about six miles to the north-east of Llantwit is *Llantrithyd*[106], the church of which is dedicated to S. Iltut. The name may have suggested to the writer that of *Trinihid*. It is to be observed that he here states that she had a special devotion to the *Trinity—dilectio sanctae Trinitatis erat eius dulcedo* (a favourite theme with Norman writers at this period, as we have already noticed). According to Mr. Wade-Evans, "there can be little doubt that her name survives in Llantryddid, as too . . . in another form at Llanrhidian [anciently *Llandridian*] in Gower, Llandridian in St. Davids, and another Llandridian in Tremarchog near Fishguard."[107] This would explain the existence of a holy well of S. Iltut at Llanrhidian, to which we shall refer later. Perhaps a companion of Iltut has been transformed into his wife, with his name altered to make it sound like that of the Trinity.

Our author now introduces an Iltut legend he has found at Ewenni. He represents the saint's sojourn in the (then well-known) cave there as due to persecution by King *Meirchiaun*, following the divine punishment of one of the royal stewards. Two *prepositi* of *Meirchiaun* appear in the *Vita Iltuti* as oppressors of the *clerus* of Llantwit. The names of both are given—*Cyblim* and *Cefygid*, and an etymology of the first name is provided.[108] They clearly figured in Llantwit traditions

---

[106] In the fourteenth century the name is sometimes spelt *Lanryryd*, but the example of *Llanrhidian* (in 1185 *Landridian*) shows how the *t* or *d* might get dropped out. *But now see G. O. Pierce, *The Place-names of Dinas Powys Hundred* 121-4. Llantriddyd.]

[107] *Welsh Christian Origins*, 134.

[108] The author of the *Vita Iltuti* seems to have explained *Cyblim* as meaning *cwbl-lym*='completely sharp.'

Professor Henry Lewis says: "*Cyblim* is Old Welsh orthography for the modern *cyflym*, a compound of the prefix *cyf-* (from **kom-*) and the adjective *llym*='keen, sharp'. It does not contain *cwbl*. The usual meaning of *cyflym* is 'fleet, swift' (cf. the various meanings of English 'sharp'). *Cefygid* cannot be from *cy-myged*. It is far more probably to be taken as a later form of Old Welsh *cemecid* gl. lapidaria. This is *cem-ecid*, with *cem*= modern *cyf-* as in *cyflym*, and *-ecid*, in modern orthography *egydd*. The *e* is probably for an earlier *o* affected to *e* by a following *ĭ*; *oc-* is probably to be equated with Mn.W.*hogi* = 'to sharpen', in which *h* is encrescent. An O.W.*cemecid* could easily be (incorrectly) written *cefygid* by a copyist of later date, who failed to realize the proper value of the two *e*'s, giving *y* for the wrong one.

current at this period and are probably historical characters vividly remembered as having caused much trouble. It may have been our author's idea to associate them with *Meirchiaun*. (Perhaps he regarded *Cefygid* as from *cy-myged* 'respected, honoured', so he leaves it untranslated.)

At Ewenni there was evidently a now forgotten cave possessing Iltut traditions, with a holy well called after him. The cave contained a stone (probably a sarcophagus) also associated with him. The writer's words "he lay all night upon the cold stone, thus fulfilling the penance enjoined upon him" remind us of the exactly similar legend about the stone now in the church of Landeleau in Brittany, found in an entirely independent source—the *Vie de St. Yves*, by a seventeenth century writer, Albert Le Grand.[109] The story of the bell is modelled on that in the *Vita Cadoci* (c. 27). The other details in this section are either commonplaces derived from our author's reading, or his own invention, though there may have been a local legend about the angelic illumination of S. Iltut's cave. The chapter ends with yet another instance of the writer's devotion to the place in which he lives.

After describing the punishment of King *Meirchiaun*, our author thinks this will be a convenient place to insert the famous story of the saint's cave in Gower recorded by Nennius.[110] He introduces it with several very inartistic repetitions from his own account in Iltut's life in the Ewenni cave, using the same phraseology. He considers the cave so well known that there is no need for him to tell us where it is—*adivit Lingarthicam speluncam*. Unfortunately the cave is no longer well known and its exact site is a matter of conjecture, though it must have been somewhere on the sea-shore near Oystermouth in the peninsula

He should have 'modernised' it to *cyfegyd*, a correct Ml.W. spelling of *cyfegydd*. The original meaning of the word therefore seems to be 'the entirely sharp one'. It is seen therefore that these two characters in the legend are aptly named. They were both 'sharpers'."

[109] "A voice told him that the saint was lying on the cold stone . . . found Saint Yves in the stone in which Saint Elleaw had done his penance."

[110] The authors of *Lives of the British Saints* (iii, p. 310) have confused it with the Ewenni cave.

of Gower.[111] It is described in greater detail by Nennius, who tells us that "the mouth of the cave looked towards the sea" and that a church was built over the altar and body of the saint. Oxwich church is dedicated to S. Iltut, and its site answers exactly to the requirements of Nennius's story, [112] though it is ten miles from Oystermouth.

In c. 23 we are suddenly transported back to Llantwit, without any attempt being made to take the saint with us, and a topographic legend about two stones in the neighbourhood is given.[113] Mr. Wade-Evans has made the excellent suggestion that by the *hara Iltuti* is meant *Llanharan*, nine miles north of Llantwit, "where to our own time survived a place called Llecha, 'Stones'."[114] It is possible, however, that our author is thinking of *Llanhari*, just south of Llanharan. It is dedicated to S. Iltut, and Llanharan is not.

C. 24 brings us back to one of the most difficult problems our subject presents.

The writer may have known that there was a cult of S. Iltut, with relics, in Brittany. On the other hand, the vagueness of his language, and his choice of Dol as the place where the saint died shows that he was ignorant of the correct geographical distribution of his cult.[115] It is difficult to understand why in this chapter he brings Iltut back from Brittany to Wales only to send him back immediately to die there.[116]

The saint's death is briefly referred to in a single sentence,

---

[111] In the Peniarth MS. 147 (written *c.* 1566), in a list in Welsh of the parishes of Wales, under *Tir Gwyr* [=Gowerland] appears "ll[an]ystum llwynarth." Ystum Llwynarth = 'The Bend of Llwynarth'. The name was later corrupted into *Ystumarth*, now Oystermouth. It has nothing to do with the oyster-beds there.

[112] Cf. pp. 140-41.

[113] A story about robbers of Nantcarfan appears in c. 16 of the *Vita Cadoci* (in c. 30 wolves are turned into stones).   *See VSBG 59, 93.]

[114] Op. cit., p. 135.

[115] La Borderie's suggestion that St. Ideuc near Dol was originally called after S. Iltut is very unconvincing. The earliest form of the name (eleventh century) is *Sancti Idoci (Pouillé de Rennes*, vi, p. 79). Duine remarks that the wealthy and pious Baderon family, established at Monmouth since the Conquest, came from Dol, and that their influence may explain the frequent recurrence of Dol in the hagiographical documents of South Wales at this period.

[116] Our author's language in this chapter is half-hearted and hesitating. It looks as if, when he wrote c. 15, he thought that Samson and Iltut were both buried at Llantwit.

the language of which is pure 'common form'. We have seen
that in the seventh century there was a detailed story of his last
hours and that the author of the *Vita Samsonis*, himself a monk
of Dol, clearly supposes him to have died at Llantwit—the story,
he says, was related to him "by catholic brethren *who were in that
place*". The Breton writer's narrative shows no sign of Iltut's
being a character known at Dol when it was written. On the
other hand, another church in Brittany *does* claim to possess
relics of S. Iltut, while no reference whatever to any relics
of the founder of Llantwit existing in his own monastery is
found in any document which has come down to us. The
difficulty is increased by the fact that two other places claim
to be his place of burial—Defynnog in Brecon [117] and Glastonbury,—in an interpolated passage in William of Malmesbury's
De Antiquitate Glaston. Eccl. (c. 22), containing a list of saints
buried at Glastonbury, we find the statement "There, too, is
Iltut *inter Walenses famosissimus*".[118]

A visit to S. Michael *in Monte Gargano* is found in *Lives*
of the thirteenth century, such as the *Vita Petroci* of the newly
discovered Gotha MS., but a pilgrimage to Mont-St.-Michel
seems unique in Celtic hagiography. It is to be observed,
however, that the *Annales Cambriae* record in 718 the consecration of the abbey church there—*Consecratio Michaelis
Archangeli ecclesiae* (the alternative reading of MS B—*Sancti
Michaelis in monte Gargano*—shows the vagueness of the
information on the subject in Wales at this period). Needless to
say, S. Iltut's pilgrimage to the Mount, which was not dedicated
to the archangel till two hundred years after his death, is not
historical. Largillière says that "the cult of S. Michael in
Brittany does not seem to be older than the eleventh century".

[117] See p. 140.
[118] John of Glastonbury (p. 19 of Hearne's edition of his *Chronica*, printed in
1726) says that the relics of *S. Iltwithe* were given by 'Duke Ethelstan" :
*Ibi eciam quiescit Sanctus Iltwithe, inter Walenses famosissimus, de dono
Ethelstani ducis*. A little further down on this page the same donor is said to
have given "the bones of the blessed virgins Wenta and Mamilla." It will be
observed that we are *not* told that Iltut came to Glastonbury, as we are
assured that Patrick, Benignus, Indract and David did (the last is said to have
returned to Menevia to die). Hearne printed at the end of his edition of
Joh. Glast. a long list of the *Reliquiae sacrae Glastoniensis Ecclesiae*, from a
manuscript in the library of Trinity College, Cambridge. Towards the end
(p. 454) we find the statement: *Sunt eciam de antiquis reliquiis, duo dentes
Sancti* ILWIT.

The incident of the granaries seems to be based on a story in the *Vita Cadoci*, c. 11.

The doxology at the end of the chapter suggests that the *Life* originally ended here, and the addition of the last two chapters may be an afterthought.

The saint's bell, which was still at Llantwit in our author's time, had a piece broken off it, and the first of the two stories in c. 25 was invented to account for this fact, and also, perhaps, to be, at the same time, like the *Meirchiaun* stories, a warning to robbers of churches. Duine remarks that the writer takes care not to offend the Normans, so the culprit here chastised is stated to be an Anglo-Saxon monarch—Edgar. This king seems to have been better remembered in Welsh tradition than any other pre-Conquest ruler of England. He is mentioned four times in the *Book of Llandaff*. The *Aureus Mons* may be a (now lost) Somerset[119] place-name known to the writer. The second of this pair of stories was probably not intended originally to be taken seriously, and both have an unreal look, which shows they are deliberate fictions. We note again the mention of *canons*, not monks, at Llantwit.

The author of the *Vita Congari* has imitated this chapter.

The final chapter is the only part of the whole *Life* which can be regarded as historical. It is a life-like and obviously true description by an eye-witness of a recent event, and gives us an interesting picture of life in Glamorgan in the early years of the twelfth century. It shows how the sympathies of the inhabitants, who are called 'the parishioners', of Llantwit had ceased to be pro-Welsh. The exact site of the skirmish is given. The defeat of the attacking force is stated to be due to their violation of the saint's sanctuary.

---

[119] The *Vita S. Carantoci* shows personal knowledge of S. Carantoc's church of Carhampton and of Somerset legends about him. It is possible that there may have been a tradition, perhaps genuine, of a church of S. Iltut in Somerset, the coast of which is covered with dedications to Celtic saints, including S. Dubricius. The problems connected with the *Vita Congari*, which is divided into two sections, dealing respectively with Somerset and Glamorgan, need to be considered separately.

It will be seen that the *Vita Iltuti*, except for the glimpses it gives us of the church of Llantwit at the beginning of the twelfth century and in the period immediately preceding, is of no historical value. Two other writers of the twelfth century contain references to S. Iltut, which exhaust our supply of early documentary evidence about the saint and his cult.

The compiler of the *Book of Llandaff*, in the section entitled *De primo statu Landavensis ecclesiae* which forms the introduction to his work and which consists of a short sketch of the early ecclesiastical history of Britain and South Wales, intended to prepare the reader for the claims to the antiquity and pre-eminence of the see of Llandaff which the rest of the book will give in detail, states that Dubricius completed the organization of the diocese by "appointing *Ildut* as abbot at the *podum* called after him *Lannildut*", which is thus represented as the chief monastery of Glamorgan, none other being mentioned. Later, he inserts into the *Vita Dubricii* a passage containing an analysis of cc. 33-36 of the *Vita Samsonis*, in which he represents the incidents there stated to have happened at the *Insula Pironis* as taking place at the *locus et domus Beati Ilduti*. (Wrmonoc also confused the two places, as we have seen.)

Giraldus Cambrensis, in his *Itinerary through Wales*, the record of a journey made in 1188, records a local legend, which he says is "derived from ancient and authentic writings of those parts, [to the effect that] during the time when S. Eltut was living the life of a hermit at Lanhamelach, the mare that used to carry his provisions was covered by a stag and gave birth to an animal of wondrous speed, resembling a horse before and a stag behind".[120] Once again we remark how frequently in tradition Iltut appears as a hermit.

It remains to examine what traces the cult of S. Iltut has left in the topography of Wales and Brittany.[121] The study of topography and of hagiography must go on side by side if we are to discover what was really happening there during the Age of the Saints, but the celebrated saying of the late M. Joseph Loth

[120] Lib. i, c. 2.
[121] *For the general distribution of the saint's cult, see Bowen SCSW 42-45.]

is certainly true in this particular case, as in so many others :
"In these countries it is not the *Lives* of the saints that tell us
most about the existence of the saints and the national organization of religion, but the *names of places*."[122]   The tabulating of
places dedicated to Celtic saints, or bearing their names,
sometimes confirms the statements of ancient hagiographers, but
sometimes it also reveals facts about their work of evangelization
and about the history of the churches they founded of which
their written *Lives* give us no hint whatever.[123]

Llantwit Major was of course the chief centre of the cult of
S. Iltut, and in many cases the reason why a place in Wales is
dedicated to him is because it belonged to Llantwit.   In the
Liber Landavensis it is called 'Ilduti' twenty-nine times,
'Lannildut' three times, and 'Lanniltut' once; 'Sancti Ilduti'
four times, 'Ecclesia S. Ilduti' three times, and 'Podum S.
Ilduti' once.   In the later parts of the book, written in the
fourteenth century, it is spelt 'Lanyltwyt'.   In the *Vita S. Gildae*
it is 'Lanna Hilduti'.   In a charter of Nicholas, bishop of Llandaff
(d. 1183), it is spelt 'Landiltuit', and in the *Annals of Tewkesbury*
(1230), 'Llandirwit'.   The *Book of Llandaff* contains many casual
references to the monastery, which throw interesting light on its
history.   It mentions many of its abbots.   It describes a solemn
agreement made there, with an oath made upon the altar of
S. Ildut, between King *Morcant* and his uncle *Frioc*, followed by
the murder of the latter and the excommunication of the king.
Before he was absolved *Morcant* had to remit to the church
of S. Ildut the annual tribute of a bottle of honey and an iron
cauldron hitherto paid to the king by the monastery.   An
intensive critical study of the *Book of Llandaff* may one day shed
further light on the history of 'Lannildut'.   Before the Norman
Conquest it had become (under circumstances unknown to us) a
collegiate church, with canons.   It was appropriated by Robert
Fitz Hamon to the abbey of Tewkesbury, which he had
refounded, and became an ordinary parish, with a vicar appointed
by the abbot.   But the cult of the saint remained undiminished

---

[122] *Les Noms des saints bretons*, 1.
[123] Doble, *Dedications to Celtic Saints in Normandy*.

and he has never been forgotten at Llantwit. The pre-Reformation bell now hanging in the Town Hall bears the inscription *Sancte Iltute, ora pro nobis*, and the name has continued to be a favourite Christian name.[124] Leland in the sixteenth century records a tradition that the *Locus S. Iltuti* had the privilege, due to the prayers of the saint, that no adder was able to live anywhere in the parish.[125]

Near Llantwit are two places the churches of which are dedicated to S. Iltut and which (as I have said) are apparently referred to in his *Life*—Llantrithyd and Llanhari. Newcastle (Bridgend) is also an Iltut church, and it will be observed that it is near Ewenni, which is mentioned in his *Vita* (c. 18).

Besides Llantwit Major, there were two other great centres of the cult of S. Iltut in South Wales, one in Brecon and the north of Glamorgan, the other in Gower.

Looking north from Llantwit towards the former of these, we find, in the mountainous district of Glamorgan, *Llantrisant*, i.e. 'The Llan of the Three Saints', who, according to Browne Willis and Rice Rees, are Illtud, Gwynno, and Tyfodwg.[126] Close by, to the north-east, is Llantwit Vardre (Faerdre), formerly one of the five chapels of the huge parish of Llantrisant. The second of the saints of Llantrisant, Gwynno, is the eponym of Llanwynno (Llanwonno), on a mountain a considerable distance to the north (though once in the parish of Llantrisant), north-west of Pontypridd and south of Merthyr Tudful, where,

---

[124] The fourth bell in the church tower, dated 1722, has the inscription 'Iltyd Nichols, clark' (he was one of the churchwardens). *On the evidence for Llantwit as an important religious centre from the ninth century and earlier, cf. W. H. Davies, CB 131, 139. See also J. E. Lloyd, HW 144; Nash-Williams, 'The Medieval Settlement at Llantwit Major, Glamorgan' (BBCS xiv. 313-33), ECMW, No. 223.]

[125] An exactly similar legend is recorded by a ninth century writer, Wrdisten, in his *Vita Winwaloei*, of Breona, near Paimpol in Brittany. Curiously enough, it comes in a serpent story copied from a Llantwit story in the *Vita Samsonis*. (Unfortunately the legend in Leland is partly unintelligible, owing to a misprint which cannot now be corrected.)

[126] Samuel Lewis says the three saints are Dyvnog, Iddog, and Menw. It is a pity these writers have not given their authorities. It looks as if there has been some guess-work here.

besides the holy well of S. Gwynno, there is a Ffynnon Illtud.[127]
It may be observed that Llantrisant is not far from Llanishen,
where the eponym may be the abbot *Isanus* mentioned in the
story of Iltut's death (see p. 92).

There are two parishes in Breconshire where the popular
cult of S. Iltut has survived down to the present day.

One is Llanhamlach, four miles east of the town of Brecon.
We have seen that Giraldus Cambrensis found a local legend
about S. Eltut here, which he said was derived from *"written
records—ex antiquis et authenticis partium istarum scriptis
colligitur"*—perhaps a now-lost *Life* read in the church of
Llanhamlach, which, according to Rice Rees, is dedicated to
SS. Peter and Illtud.[128] In this parish, "on a farm called Mannest
. . . are the remains of a kistvaen, under an aged yew tree,
and surrounded with stones apparently from a dispersed cairn . . .
It consists of three upright stones [supporting a capstone] . . .
the whole height does not exceed three feet from the ground . . .
it is usually designated *Ty Illtyd* [i.e. 'Illtyd's House']".[129] (A
dolmen in the parish of Landeleau in Brittany is similarly called
Ty Sant Heleau.) "There are several small incised crosses
carved on the slabs.[130] There formerly stood within a few paces
of it a stone called Maen Illtyd, and a little distance off is
Ffynnon Illtyd, the stream of which divides the parish from
Llansantffraid".[131] In view of the tradition recorded in the
Vita Iltuti that Paulinus was one of his chief disciples, it is
particularly interesting to find that the next parish is Llan-gors,
where the church is dedicated to S. Paulinus and there is also a
chapel of *Llanbeulin*, and a holy well, called in the *Book of
Llandaff*[132] "Finnaun Doudecseint", clearly in memory of his
"twelve presbyters", referred to several times in Wrmonoc's
Vita Pauli Aureliani.

---

[127] LBS, iii, 316.   The name of the eponym of Merthyr Tudful is sometimes
spelt *Tutuil* and *Tudeuel*. These forms closely resemble the Breton *Tudual*.
It may be remarked that *Llan-ynys-Tudwal*, now Llanstadwel, in Pembs., is
near St. Ishmael's (*Lann Isan*).   Cf. p. 145.

[128] Lewis and Browne Willis only name S. Peter.

[129] Lewis's *Topographical Dictionary of Wales* (1833).

[130] Westwood, *Lapidarium Walliae*, p. 67; AC, 1867, 347-55; 1903, p. 173;
Theo. Jones, *Breconshire*, p. 452.

[131] LBS, iii, 316.

[132] P. 146.

West of the town of Brecon, in the ancient parish of
Defynnog, is the church of Llanilltud (sometimes called *Capel
Illtud*, or simply *Illtud*), on a mountain known as Mynydd Illtud.
Near this church is another megalithic monument associated with
S. Iltut, where he was honoured until comparatively recently
by the practice, dear to the Catholic Welsh, of 'watching' (vigil)
before his festival. It is known as the *Bedd* or Grave of Illtud's
Festival, a very unusual type of name, showing the prominence
of the liturgical observance of the saint's *depositio* in the traditions
of the locality. Lewis[133] describes it as follows :

> On an adjoining eminence, near a pool, are two large stones,
> placed six feet asunder, at each end of a small tumulus, which is
> called Bedd Gwyl Illtyd, . . . from the ancient practice of
> watching there on the eve of the festival of that saint, who was
> supposed to have been buried here.

It lies within a ruined rectangular enclosure.

The church of Llanhilleth, on the top of a mountain in the
west of Monmouthshire, is said to be dedicated to S. Iltut, but
it is called "Il. hyledd vorwyn", i.e 'Llan Hyledd the virgin', in
the *Report on MSS. in Welsh* (i, 920). The local pronunciation
is *Llanhiddel*.

There is another cluster of Iltut dedications in Gower.
He is the patron of *Ilston* (contracted from *Iltwitston*), which
was formerly called *Llanilltud Gwyr*, and of *Oxwich*. In the
parish of Llanrhidian on the north coast of Gower there was a
holy well of S. Iltut, referred to in the *Annals of Margam* in 1185:

> In the same year [as the siege of Neath], about the Feast of the
> Nativity of John the Baptist, an extraordinary thing happened not far
> from the said castle [of Neath]. In the district known as Gower,
> in the *villa* called Landridian, on Wednesday, there was a copious
> flow of milk, lasting for three hours, from a certain fountain, which
> the inhabitants of the place called the Fountain of S. Iltut. Several
> persons who were there state that they saw with wonder the well
> continue to pour forth milk, while butter was forming on the edge
> of the spring.

For this reason Lewis and Owen thought that the true patron
of Llanrhidian was Iltut. The former describes a holy well on
Cefn Bryn mountain, "to which, in former times, miraculous

---

[133] Op. cit., under *Glyn*.

efficacy was attributed",[134] but a writer in *Archaeologia Cambrensis*[135] says that the well of S. Iltut "is at the bottom of a garden, on the other side of the road, to the north of the church-yard".[136] Somewhere, too, in Gower, was the famous cave of *Loyngarth.* We have seen that Oystermouth is a corruption of *Ystum Llwynarth.* There seems, however, to be no sign of a cave at Oystermouth, nor any traditions of S. Iltut there.[137] As Ystum Llwynarth means 'the Bend of Llwynarth', the name *Loyngarth* may have been that of a considerable district, stretching as far as Oxwich, where there is a church of S. Iltut in a situation exactly answering to Nennius's description. The late Rev. J. D. Davies says :

> The position of the church is peculiar, standing isolated on the verge of the cliff and almost overhanging the sea at high water. The church was built in the twelfth century, probably on the site of a much older one . . . Mr. Waller, the diocesan architect of Gloucester, after a close inspection in 1891, thinks that it was originally a cell, and the abutting portion of the walls shows the original proportion of the cell. When it became a parish church, it was lengthened and a tower added.[138]

It is to be observed, as explaining the number of Iltut dedications in this neighbourhood, that the *Liber Landavensis* shows that the monastery of Llantwit owned a good deal of property in Gower. In the charter of *Lann Cingualan* (or *Cella Cyngualan*) *in patria Guhyr* we are told that "a great dispute arose between Bishop Oudoceus and Biuon, abbot of Ildut, who said that the *ager* was his". The exact site of the place in question has not yet been identified, though its bounds and those of *Lann Gemei*, which adjoined it, are given in detail on pp. 145 and 140. It is significant that Gower and Breconshire

---

[134] "It was generally frequented on Sunday evenings during the summer season by numbers of persons, who drank the water, and according to an ancient custom, threw in a pin as a tribute of their gratitude."

[135] 1920, p. 313.

[136] It is just possible that the chronicler, whose language is rather confused here, may really mean 'S. Illtud's Brook' at Llantwit-juxta-Neath, which would be *"non procul a memorato castello."*

[137] Oystermouth church is dedicated to All Saints.

[138] *West Gower*, Part iv (1894). He says, "The chancel arch is round, the opening very narrow, by far the narrowest of all the Gower churches, so much so as to present the appearance of a mere doorway. Mr. Freeman remarks on the narrowness of the opening as giving a strange, dark, and cavern-like appearance to the chancel, most extraordinary and unusual".

are, with Llantwit, the three districts where traditions and legends of our saint are abundant.

In addition to the three groups we have described, there are some scattered Iltut dedications in Wales.

Between Llantwit and Gower lies *Llanilltud Fach*, or Llantwit-juxta-Neath.[139]

Facing the north of Gower, on the coast of Carmarthenshire, is Pen-bre, whose church is dedicated to S. Iltut. Richard Fitzwilliam, in an undated charter, gave to Sherborne abbey the churches of St. Ishmael at Pennalt, of All Saints at Kidwelly, and of St. *Elthut* at Penbray, *cum capellis, terris, decimis et omnibus earum adjacentiis*.[140] In a bull of Alexander III and a charter of Maurice of London to Sherborne[141] the name is spelt *Eltwyci*. A brief reference to Pen-bre in the *Book of Llandaff*[142] shows that it once belonged to the monastery of Llantwit Major and thereby provides a valuable clue to its early history: "In Pennbre Catmor, the son of Mor, was priest (*celebravit*), after him Gurhi, son of Silli—the *Doctor* of Lanniltut, and afterwards Sed".

Llantood (Llantwyd) in the north of Pembrokeshire has been claimed as an Iltut church, because it appears as *Llantwyd* in the *Valor Ecclesiasticus* of 1535, but the Royal Commission of Ancient Monuments in Wales points out, in their inventory of the county, that the early forms of the name make this unlikely. In the *Taxatio* of 1291 it is 'Langetot', in the *Ep. Reg.* in 1513 'Langettod'. The local pronunciation is *Llantyd*.

Iltut is the patron of Llanelltud, close to Dolgellau in Merioneth. The chalice belonging to the church, dated 1591-2, bears on it 'Llanilltid'. The name of the parish in the *Record of Carnarvon* is 'Llanulltud' and 'Llaunulldit'. Edward Lhuyd (in his notes on the parish) wrote in 1699 : "Of Elltyd they have no more to say than that he was Elldyd Farchog".

It is perhaps worth observing that there is a *Llanfrynach* near Llantwit Major and another in Brecon adjoining Llan-hamlach, while in Pembrokeshire Llantood is near both

---

[139] For 'S. Illtud's Brook' see Birch, *Neath Abbey*, p. 250.
[140] Dugdale, *Monasticon*, iv, p. 65.
[141] Dugdale, *Monasticon*, i, p. 339.
[142] P. 279.

Llanfyrnach and S. Brynach's church of Nevern.   This may
point to a connection between the two saints.

Rev. A. W. Wade-Evans regards the mysterious *Saint
Aldate*, patron of a parish church in Gloucester and of another
in Oxford, as identical with S. Eltut.   Geoffrey of Monmouth
spells the name *Eldad*, makes him a bishop of Gloucester, and
introduces him into Lib. vi, c. 15, and Lib. viii, cc.7 and 8, of
his romance.   Unfortunately we have no very early documents
for the history of either of these churches, nor ancient forms
of the name of the saint.

There seems to be no dedication to S. Iltut in Cornwall.
The chapel at Halton in St. Dominic is called *St. Ildreith* in 1362,
St. Etheldrid in 1405, and *Saint Ildract* in 1419, and in 1445 the
parish feast was moved to 9th May, the day after the feast of
S. Indract.

The study of Breton dedications is specially illuminating
for the cult of S. Iltut, as for that of S. Teilo.
The liturgical cult of S. Ildut is confined to the ancient
dioceses of Léon, Tréguier, and Vannes, and it is to be noted
that no dedications to our saint are found outside those three
dioceses.[143]   The feast of *S. Ilduti* is found, with nine lessons,
on 7th November in the printed Léon breviary of 1516, on the
same day in the fifteenth century breviary of Tréguier (*Ilduti*),
and on 5th November in the fifteenth century breviary of
Vannes (*Ylduti*).   *Iltut* is invoked in the tenth century litany in
the Salisbury psalter (Chapter MSS. No. 180), which is of
Breton origin.   Many of the saints there invoked are specially
honoured in Léon.   Iltut's name follows that of S. Columbanus

---

[143] The name of *Iltut* has been inserted on 16th November in the 1775
Supplementum Missalis ad normam Lectionarii Dolensis, because of his
connection with S. Samson, but he had no cult in the diocese.   Dom
Lobineau does not mention St. -Ydeuc, and the identification of the eponym
of this parish with S. Iltut, now officially accepted, appears to be not older
than the nineteenth century, and to be due to a guess of La Borderie.   The
name *Idocus* (found in the twelfth century) does, however, remind us of
one of the saints of Llantrisant (see p. 138, note 126).

and precedes those of *S. Catoc* and *S. Brangualadr*. He is thus
placed (as Duine observes) in a little group of Celtic abbots who
were famous teachers and legislators. His name does not appear
in the Rheims, Limoges, or St.-Vougay litanies.

There have been exceptionally strong Welsh influences in
Léon. M. Longnon[144] has pointed out that in the whole of
France there are only three place-names beginning with the
common Welsh prefix *Aber*, and they are all close together in
the west of Léon[145]—Aber-Vrach, Aber-Benoit, and Aber-Ildut.
On the mouth of the latter is situated the parish of *Lanildut*.
In the same deanery, at the mouth of the Aber-Benoit, is the
parish of Saint-Pabu (the church is dedicated to S. Tudual),
which contains a chapel of *Sant-Illtut* (also one of St. Hillio,
who is identified by Loth with S. Teilo). In the south-east of
Léon, in the parish of Sizun, is a place called *Loc-Ildut*('Saint
Ildut' in the *carte Taride*), where there is a chapel of our saint,
containing his statue—the figure holds a book in its hands.
It may be observed that on the opposite side of the Aber-Benoit
to St. Pabu is *Lanillis*, which appears to be the same name as
Llanilid[146] in Glamorgan. There must have been very considerable immigrations from Glamorgan to Léon, and Lanildut is
almost certainly a daughter house of Llantwit.

In the diocese of Tréguier the parish church of *Coadout*
(south of Guingamp) is dedicated to S. Ildut; and so was that of
Troguery (south of Tréguier) originally (it is now dedicated to
the Trinity). It still possesses a statue of our saint. "At
Coadout is a dolmen, destroyed in 1863, except for three stones,
one of which is much polished. On this, according to local
tradition, S. Iltud and S. Brioc were wont to meet and pray
together, and it contains holes supposed to have been worn by his
knees".[147] A *kantik Sant Iltud, patron Coadout*, is sung at the
pardon.[148] Coadout was an enclave of Dol before the French

---

[144] *Noms de lieu de la France* (Paris, 1920), p. 323.
[145] There is also in Léon a stream called simply Aber.
[146] In Wales *Llanharan* (the next parish to Llanilid) must have the same eponym
as *Lanharan* in the western part of the diocese of Tréguier—a St. Haran
whose name appears in several places in that neighbourhood.
[147] LBS iii, 317. It is curious that both in Wales and Brittany a dolmen is
associated with our saint.
[148] Duine. *Inventaire liturgique de l'hag. bret.*, p. 269.

Revolution, and therefore connected with S. Samson. The church of Landebaeron (north of Guingamp), which is dedicated to S. Maudez,[149] has a statue of S. Ildut, and more important still, possesses a silver reliquary containing his skull. The latter is mentioned in the parish inventory of 1683. The relics of S. Ildut and S. Maudez were verified before witnesses on 25th September, 1828.[150] In addition, there was formerly a chapel of S. Iltud (now destroyed) in *Plouguiel* (north of Tréguier). In this parish the chapel of N. D. de Kélo-Mad has a statue of our saint. There is also a statue of him in the chapel of N. D. de Kerhir in the parish of *Plounevez-Quintin*.[151] (It will be observed that the places where there is a cult of S. Ildut in the diocese of S. Tudual are on a line running due north and south through Tréguier.)

Finally, there is a parish of *Ploerdut* (thus spelt in 1285) in the north-western portion of the diocese of Vannes, near Guémené. It contains a chapel of *S. Iltut* (pronounced *Zand-Illut*), written *Sant-Yllud* in 1449.[152] The next parish is that of *Saint-Tugdual*.[153]

A very remarkable fact we have discovered in our examination of the cult of S. Ildut in Brittany is that it is in almost every case found in proximity with that of S. Tudual. We have noticed that in Wales S. Tudwal's Island is not far from Llanelltud. The association of the cult of two (or more) saints together is one of the most characteristic features of Celtic hagiography and there are abundant examples of it in Wales, Cornwall, and Brittany.[154]

---

[149] Not to S. Iltud, as stated in LBS.
[150] *Acta Sanctorum*, Nov. III, p. 223, note 11.
[151] The information in this and the two preceding sentences was communicated to me by M. Couffon, who has made a careful inventory of the parishes of the Côtes-du-Nord and their works of art.
[152] Both the parish church and the chapel are described in Duhem's *Églises du Morbihan*.
[153] In this part of the diocese of Vannes there is a chapel of S. Tugdual in the parish of Quistinic and a village called after him in Guiscriff.
[154] SS. Gwinear and Meriadoc, David and Nonna, Winnoc and Nectan, Mewan and Austol, Brioc and Marcan, Kea and Fili are constantly associated with each other and have chapels dedicated to them in close proximity in many places.

SAINT PAULINUS OF WALES[1]

EVERYONE knows that the little city of St-Pol-de-Léon, near Roscoff, with its granite cathedral and the marvellous spire of the Kreisker, is one of the most beautiful and interesting places in Brittany. It has generally been assumed, though hitherto without any definite proof, that the saint who gave his name to St-Pol-de-Léon was the founder and eponym of Paul, near Penzance, in Cornwall. I hope here to offer some reasons for concluding that this assumption is justified, based on a fresh examination of the ancient *Life* of the saint, which has enabled some interesting discoveries about him to be made, showing a connection, unsuspected before, with Carmarthenshire and Breconshire.

The *Life* to which I refer was written in 884—it is almost the only *Life* of a Celtic saint of which we know the exact date of its composition.[2] Its author tells us that he was called Wrmonoc, that he had been a monk in the abbey of Lendévennec in Brittany under Wrdisten, and that it had been the example of Wrdisten in writing a *Life* of the founder of Landévennec[3] which had given him the idea of writing a *Life* of the founder of the see of Léon.

Wrmonoc divides his work into two books, the first describing Paul's life in his native country and the second his work in Brittany. Here I shall deal only with the first. In it he has utilized a certain number of traditions brought from Wales, and some (probably) from Cornwall. He twice mentions *transmarini* from whom he has heard them, and it is on their

[1] *Published in 1942, Billing and Sons, Ltd., Printers, Guildford and Esher.]
[2] I have recently published a critical edition of this very important *Vita* (in No. 46 of my 'Cornish Saints' series-*S. Paul of Léon, with a History of the Parish of Paul in Cornwall*. *Now see SC i. 10-60]). The *Vita Pauli Aureliani* was printed, with a very few brief notes, by Cuissard in the *Revue celtique* in 1883 and by Dom Plaine in *Analecta Bollandiana* in 1882. It has never before been printed in English.
[3] I have dealt with the *Vita Winwaloei* in No. 4 of my 'Cornish Saints' series, 2nd edition. *Now see SC ii. 59-108.]

146

authority that he tells us that Paul's first monastery (at Llan-ddeusant) "now contains numerous buildings" (*quod nunc multis decoratum aedificiis dicunt*). Some of the Welsh traditions reappear in the *Lives* of Glamorgan saints contained in the famous collection in the British Museum (MS. Vesp. A. xiv.), made at Brecon priory at the end of the twelfth century and printed by Rees in *Lives of the Cambro-British Saints* in 1853.[4] As Wrmonoc's work is thus at least three hundred years earlier,it affords valuable evidence for the antiquity of these traditions. It will be instructive to see what use he has made of them.

In chapter 1, entitled 'Of the Origin of Saint Paul', he tells us :

> The same Saint Paul, surnamed Aurelian, the son of a certain count named Perphirius, who held a position of high rank in the world, came from a province which in the language of the British race is called *Penn Ohen*.

After a fanciful explanation of this name, and a few common-places about Paul's childhood, he makes a fresh start, and continues :

> Now we read that this man, who sprang from a family most noble in the eyes of the world, had eight brothers, who all lived in the *regio* which in their language is called *Brehant Dincat*, but in Latin *Guttur receptaculi pugnae*, so that, with him, they made up the sacred order of nine, after the pattern of the nine orders of angels. He had also three sisters, in imitation of the Three Persons of the Holy Trinity. One of the brothers was called Notolius, another Potolius, and one of the sisters Sitofolla. The names of the others have been lost, owing to the enormous space of time which has elapsed since then, and also to the distance from us of the land where they lived.

In chapters 2 and 3 Wrmonoc says that Paul was sent to the monastic school of the celebrated Iltut, at *Lan-Iltut*, now Llantwit Major on the coast of Glamorgan :

> Iltut had many young men distinguished for piety and learning among his disciples, but four of them far outshone the others and by the command of the master were placed in a position of authority over them. These were : first, Saint Paul, of whose life and mighty works in the northern part of the country of Domnonia this book deals; Saint Dewi (Devius) . . . also Samson, the holy bishop . . . and lastly Saint Gildas.

[4] *More recently by A. W. Wade-Evans in VSBG.]

Wrmonoc next proceeds to describe a miracle worked by
Iltut in which his four chief disciples join—the master, after
prayer, causes the sea to retire, and so enlarges the monastery
land; and another, worked by Paul alone—he drives the seagulls who had devoured the newly sown seed into a barn, as if
they were sheep. Paul then resolved to leave *Lan-Iltut* and live in
solitude, "serving God in the uninterrupted life of contemplation". In chapter 7, which is entitled 'Of his Life as a Hermit',
he tells us:

> Having received his master's blessing and kiss of peace, and leave
> to depart, he went forth and sought the seclusion of a certain
> desert place which adjoined his father's possessions. There he
> built some cells and a little oratory, which, they say, is now a
> monastic settlement containing numerous buildings bearing the
> names of his two brothers already mentioned. Here he received
> from the bishop [his name and see are not mentioned] the dignity
> of the priesthood, and lived for some time with twelve presbyters
> who desired to obey his precepts in everything relating to the
> monastic life.

The statement that Paul was born in the province of
Penn Ohen seems clearly borrowed from a tradition referred to
three times in the *Life of S. Cadog* contained in the British
Museum MS. Vesp. A. xiv. Its author begins with a preface in
which he tells us that after the death of King Glywys his
domains were divided up among his ten children, and the third,
called *Poul* (an old Welsh form of *Paul*), obtained, as his share,
the province of *Penychen*. In chapter 8 a swineherd who has
become blind is counselled by Cadog to go to his master,
"Poul Penychen", whom he finds "in the court which in the
British language is called Nant Poul", and is healed by him.
In chapter 24 the inhabitants of *Penychen* submit to King *Run*.

The *Vita Catoci* thus points us to the origin of Wrmonoc's
statement that Paul came from the province of *Penn Ohen*.
An older book, the celebrated *Historia Brittonum* of Nennius,
will supply us with a promising explanation for his further
statement that Paul's surname was *Aurelian*. The hero of the
British resistance to the Anglo-Saxon invasion of the fifth
century was, as Gildas tells us in the *De Excidio Britanniae* (the
passage is quoted by Bede, *Eccl. Hist.*, Lib. i, c. 16), "Ambrosius
Aurelianus, a modest man, who, of all the Roman nation, was

then alone, in the confusion of this troubled period, left alive".
Nennius has a story of how the messengers of King *Guorthigirn*
find two boys, one of whom is *Ambrosius Aurelianus*, playing at a
place called *Campus Elleti*, "which is in the region which is
called Gleguissing"—the ancient kingdom of Glywys, of which
(as we have seen) the province of *Penychen* formed part.

Now the reader will have noted the very awkward way in
which Wrmonoc begins his story by telling us that S. Paul,
surnamed Aurelian, belonged to a noble family in the province of
Penn Ohen, and then begins all over again, almost in the same
words, and says that he came of a noble family established in the
region of *Brehant Dincat*. We shall see the reason for this if we
carefully examine chapters 3, 4 and 7.

Chapters 3 and 4 contain three *Lan-Iltut* traditions which
all reappear in the *Vita Iltuti* in Vesp. A. xiv. The stories of the
sea retiring and of the predatory birds need not detain us, but
the list of Iltut's four chief disciples is of capital importance for
the solution of our problem. Wrmonoc's list is the same as that
given in the *Life of S. Iltut*, except that Wrmonoc has *Paul*,
while the *Vita Iltuti* has *Paulinus*. Paul and Paulinus are
clearly the same person.[5] Now in Brittany the founder of
St-Pol-de-Léon is very often called *Paulinus* in official and
liturgical documents of early date. In Bili's *Vita S. Machutis* (or
Maclovius, *Malo*), written c. 869, the city is called *oppidum
Sancti Pauliniani*. Bishop Mabbon signs a charter in 954 as
pauliniani episcopus, while Bishop Omnes signs one in 1081 as
presul sancti Pauliniani. In the tenth-century kalendar of
Landévennec the *Depositio sancti Paulinennani* is entered on
March 12. The cartulary of Quimperlé speaks of "the relics of
Paulennanus". In the litany of St-Vougay in Léon (late eleventh
century) S. Paul is invoked as *Paulinnanus*. At St-Pol-de-Léon
the feast of S. Paulinus on October 10 was observed as a

---

[5] We have an interesting parallel to this at Llansadwrn in Anglesey. The
eponym is *Sadwrn*, and there is an inscribed stone on which the name is
written SATURNINUS. M. le Comte de Calan was the first to suspect
that this was the case with the saint of Léon. "It seems remarkable," he
says, "that while either *Paul* or *Paulininnus* is invoked in all the ancient
Breton Litanies, the two names never appear together, and that *Paul* is
not invoked in the Léon Litany of St.-Vougay, while *Paulininnus* is" (*Mél. hist.*,
Vannes, 1908, p. 90). In a copy of the *Achau'r Saint* of 1527 (Cardiff MS. 5)
we even find a "Pawl vab pawl-polinus". *See also Bartrum, EWGT 71.]

secondary festival of 'S. Paul, bishop of Léon'. In Breton place-names, however, at least in their vernacular form, we always find *Paul*. In Cornwall, in the same way, the parish dedicated to him is always called *Paul*, while in Latin documents the church is at first called *Ecclesia S. Paulini*[6] though *Pauli* early appears as a variant (Mr. J. C. Cox is quite wrong in saying, in his *Cornish Churches*, that "the church was re-dedicated to S. Paulinus of York in 1336"), and the parish feast is on October 10.

Wrmonoc chooses to call his hero *Paul*, and he tells us that at the age of sixteen[7] he went, with his brothers *Potolius* and *Notolius*, to live as a hermit in a solitary place near his father's patrimony (which we have already learnt was called *Brehant Dincat*) and that this hermitage developed into a considerable monastery, which in the ninth century was called after the saint's two brothers. Up to the present nobody seems to have made any attempt to identify this place, and attempts which *have* been made to identify *Brehant Dincat* have not been very successful. I hope, however, to prove to the reader's satisfaction that *Brehant Dincat* is Llandovery in Carmarthenshire and that the unnamed monastery near it is Llanddeusant, seven and a half miles to the south-east, in a lonely situation on the slope of the Mynydd Du.

Wrmonoc attempts to explain *Brehant Dincat* as if it were one word. *Brehant* he considers to be the Welsh *breuant*— 'throat' or 'wind-pipe'.[8] *Dincat* he translates, not quite correctly, as meaning in Latin *receptaculum pugnae* (in reality it is, as J. Loth pointed out, "undoubtedly composed of *duno*—

---

[6] I have given in my *S. Paul of Léon* the different titles which the church bears in the episcopal registers. The fact that originally Paul was usually called 'the Church of Saint Paulinus' may explain the existence in Cornwall of the not uncommon personal name *Pawlyn*.

[7] This must be a reminiscence of Palladius's *History of Mar Paule* (with which Wrmonoc was familiar), where Paul, the first hermit, begins to live in the desert in Egypt "when sixteen years of age".

[8] The authors of *Lives of the British Saints* (iv. 76) try to explain *Brehant = Guttur* by a reference to a natural wonder in the province of Gwent, described by Nennius among the 'Marvels of Britain'—"a pit from which the wind blows at all times without intermission." Nennius, however, expressly tells us that the British name for this wonder was *Chwyth Gwynt*. The name *Brehant* seems now to be lost, but there are several names in the valley of the Tywi which might be corruptions of it. Near Llandeilo are a *Breynant* and a *Brenaye* Forest, and apparently (according to Professor W. Rees) a *Bryngton*.

'citadel' and *cat*—'combat' "). But what he entirely fails to see
is that *Dincat* from being a place-name, had become a personal
name. A *Dunocat* is commemorated on a sixth-century
inscribed stone at Glan Usk Park in Breconshire. A saint
called *Dincat*, one of the 'children of Brychan',[9] is the eponym
and patron of the parish church of Llandingad on the Tywi in
Carmarthenshire, the parish which contains the town of
Llandovery.

Now it is surely very significant that the neighbourhood of
Llandovery is full of traces of the cult of S. Paulinus. In the
ancient parish of Llandingad are two chapels dedicated to him,
one at Capel Peulin and the other at Nant y Bai, and a holy well
called Ffynnon Beulin. Close by, in a situation exactly corresponding to that of Paulinus's monastery as described by
Wrmonoc in chapter 7 (*cujusdam loci deserti qui paternis finibus
adhaerebat . . . quaedam habitacula et parvum oratorium quod
nunc sub nomine suorum fratrum multis decoratum aedificiis dicunt*),
is Llanddeusant—the 'Llan of the Two Saints'. At Llanddeusant, Mr. Wade-Evans says,[10] "the annual fair was held
on the 10th of October, which marks the festival of an obscure
pair of saints. The two saints of Llanddeusant are commonly
said to be Simon and Jude, perhaps as being the only pair of
red-letter saints in October". October 10 is the festival of
S. Paulinus, and after what has been said I think we may regard
it as certain that "the obscure pair of saints" are his brothers

---

[9] The 'Children of Brychan' are found closely associated with places where
Paulinus is honoured, both in Wales and in Brittany. Wrmonoc refers to a
(now lost) place-name in St-Pol-de-Léon—*Brochana pars*, which Loth
(*Chrestomathie bretonne*) considered to be a reminiscence of the Brychan
tradition. Seven miles west of Llanddeusant is a place called *Llys Brychan*.
The whole neighbourhood is full of Brychan dedications. *Dingad* (father of
Tyfriog = S. Brioc) at Llandingad, *Tud(w)ystl*, patron of Capel Tudyst
(south of Llangadog), *Cyn(h)eiddon*, patron of Capel Cyneiddon (south of
Carmarthen), *Cynog* at Llansteffan, *Cein* at Llanceinwyry, *Tybie* of Llan-
dybie, *Lluan* at Llanlluan, and *Clydai* (eponym of the parish of that name in
Pembrokeshire) are all found in the lists of Children of Brychan.
At Llandyfaelog is a Ffynnon *Berwyn*. There is a *Berven* in Léon, and a
little to the west of Dinan in East Brittany is a parish of *Landebia*, where
there is a holy well of S. David. Another child of Brychan, *Ilud*, eponym of
Llanilid in Glamorgan, is also eponym of Llanilis and Bodilis in Léon.
A clerk called *Dincat* signs a charter in the *Book of Llandaff*, p. 203. *Cf.
further EWGT 14-19, 43, 81-84.]
[10] *Parochiale Wallicanum*, 1911, p. 32.

S. Potolius and *S. Notolius*, and that Llanddeusant owes its name
to them.[11]

We have now, I think, succeeded in identifying Wrmonoc's
Brehant Dincat and have found the site of the monastery near it
which he describes but does not name. But this is not all.
There is one (and only one) other place in South Wales dedicated
to S. Paulinus—the parish of Llan-gors, east of Brecon, which is
called in the cartulary of Brecon priory "the church of S. Paulinus
of Lancors" and "the Church of S. Peulinus de Mara", while in
the parish list in Peniarth MS. 146 (c. 1566) it is *Llangors Peylyn
Sant*. It is a lonely place among the mountains, like Llanddeusant, and suitable for the life of contemplation. Not only
is the parish church dedicated to S. Paulinus, but there is also a
chapel there called *Llanbeulin*.[12] Further, there is at Llan-gors a
holy well, called in the charter in the *Book of Llandaff*[13] by which
Agustus, king of *Brecheinniauc*, grants *Lann Cors* to Oudoceus,
bishop of Landavia, "the Well of the Twelve Saints (*Finnaun y
Doudecseint*) on lake Syuadon". Not far away was a chapel, also
mentioned in the *Book of Llandaff*,[14] called "the Llan of the
Twelve Saints." Now the reader will remember that Wrmonoc
tells us in chapter 7 that Paul had under him at Llanddeusant
"twelve presbyters", whom he took with him to the court of
King Mark (chapter 8) and who accompanied him to Brittany
(chapters 11 and 19). These are clearly the 'Twelve Saints' of
Llan-gors. Llan-gors adjoins Llanhamlach, where the patron
saint is S. Iltut, and where there is a very ancient legend about
Paulinus's master, referred to both by Giraldus Cambrensis
(*Itin.*, Lib. i., c. 2) and by the author of the *Vita Iltuti* (chapter 8).
The coincidences between Wrmonoc's statements and the

---

[11] No explanation of these two names has yet been offered, but it is worth
noting that M. Loth has suggested (*Les Noms des saints bretons*, p. 104),
that Lambezellec near Brest, very near several places called after saints
mentioned by Wrmonoc, may owe its name to a monk of the name of
Petheloc. The father of S. Leonorius (eponym of St-Lunaire near St-Malo)
was called *Beteloc*. *Potolius* might well be a misreading of this name. The
Martyrology of Tallaght has on July 31 *Sancti Natali i Cill Manach*. This
might be *Notolius* (*Notalius* in the Paris MS. of the *Vita Pauli*).

[12] Wade-Evans, op. cit., p. 18.

[13] P. 146 in the 1893 edition. This holy well seems to be the same as that now
called 'All Saints' Well', near Penllanafel.

[14] P. 255 (*seith* is an obsolete word for 'saint'), cf. p. 276 (Welsh Bicknor).
Wade-Evans, op. cit., p. 18.

information derived from Welsh topography are thus most striking and cannot be fortuitous.

I think we can now explain the curious dislocation at the beginning of Wrmonoc's work. It comes from his utilizing two different sources. He has heard of a *Paul* of *Penychen*, and he has also heard of a famous saint in Carmarthenshire called *Paulinus*, and he knows (though he does not say so) that the Breton Paul was sometimes known as *Paulinus*. He cannot make up his mind between the two, whether he shall identify his hero with the Glamorgan Paul or the Carmarthenshire Paulinus, and attempts to amalgamate them, and in giving the list of Iltut's disciples alters *Paulinus* to *Paul* and states, in a suspiciously sententious way, that this disciple is the hero of his story. But while Wrmonoc cannot resist the temptation to equate Paul of Léon with the once well-known Paul of Penychen, he has not attempted to appropriate any stories about the latter, while he has drawn considerably on the legend of S. Paulinus. The authors of *Lives of the British Saints* (iv. 72) thought that "it was much to be regretted that no *Life* of this famous teacher of Saints has come down to us". Some such *Life* once, I think, existed, and Wrmonoc must either have read it or (more probably) have had anecdotes from it related to him. Paulinus must have played a very conspicuous part in the monastic movement in Wales and traditions about him abounded there as late as the eleventh century. Rhigyfarch introduces him twice into his *Life of S. David*. After his ordination to the priesthood the youthful David "went to Paulinus the scribe, a disciple of S. Germanus the bishop, [15] who in a certain island [or monastery] was leading a life pleasing to God, and who taught him in the three parts of reading till he was a scribe. And Saint David tarried there many years, reading and fulfilling what he read". Rhigyfarch goes on to relate a miracle worked by David who, when his master becomes blind "by reason of an intense pain in his eyes", restores his sight by touching them, "and Paulinus blessed holy David with all the blessings which are written in the Old Testament and in the New". Later, in describing the

---

[15] The Welsh *Life* of S. David, printed in *Lives of the Cambro-British Saints* (p. 104), says that Paulinus had been "disciple to a holy bishop in Rome". *See also D. S. Evans, *Buched Dewi* (2nd ed. Caerdydd, 1965), 5.]

Synod of Brefi, Rhigyfarch says that "one of the bishops, called Paulinus, with whom the pontiff Saint David had formerly read, rises and says, 'There is one who has not yet appeared at our synod, an eloquent man, approved in religion . . . My advice, therefore, is that you invite him'," which is done.[16] So too the *Life of S. Teilo* (whose chief monastery, it is to be observed, was in Carmarthenshire, at Llandeilo Fawr, quite close to Llandingad) states that Teilo, "having heard of the fame of a certain wise man named Poulinus, went to him and abode with him for some time, so that whatever secrets of the Scriptures were previously hidden from them they were now able, by studying together, to understand. And there he became an associate of Saint David, a man of most perfect life".[17]

The fame of this great Welsh saint has been obscured owing to there being a much better known saint of the same name, about whom Bede has told us a great deal—Paulinus, bishop of York and afterwards of Rochester. Now an examination of the liturgical cult of S. Paul of Léon in Brittany and France reveals one remarkable fact—viz., that the festival of the saint who baptized Edwin of Northumbria has been very widely appropriated as a second festival for S. Paul of Léon, precisely because the latter was also called Paulinus. There are innumerable examples of this phenomenon. Turn to any hagiographical dictionary, and where you find a large number of saints of the same name you will frequently find that many of them are honoured on the same day. It is incredible that they shall all have died on the same day, and the obvious explanation is that all have eventually come to be commemorated on the day when the best known saint of that name is honoured. This has happened in the case before us. Paulinus of York died on October 10, 644, and his festival appears in a very large number of kalendars. It is easy to see how continental clerks, ignorant

[16] *Life of S. David*, ed. Wade-Evans, pp. 7 and 25. *Cf. J. W. James, Rhigyfarch's Life of St. David* (Cardiff, 1967), 32-33, 44.]

[17] *Vita Teliavi*, in *Lib. Land.*, p. 99. The statements in both these *Lives*, it will be observed, are quite inconsistent with the Glamorgan traditions preserved by Wrmonoc, which reminds us that we must not go to any of the *Lives* of Welsh saints for accurate history. They contain only dim reminiscences of once-famous names and traditions about them, the exact chronology of which has been lost.

of English ecclesiastical history, should assume that the *Paulinus*, *episcopus*, honoured on October 10, was the Paulinus or Paul of Léon. Exactly the same thing happened in Cornwall, where the saint was also called by both names, and in Carmarthenshire, where only the form *Paulinus* was used. In these two countries he came to be honoured on October 10[18] only, and the festival in March is unknown. The natural result was that he came to be confused, on this side of the Channel, with the saint of York and forgotten by hagiographers. Only one Welsh kalendar—the Demetian—commemorates him (Cwrtmawr MS. 44, of the sixteenth century). It has, on November 22, *Gwyl Polin*, *Escob*. I suppose this *may* represent the original Welsh tradition.

Whether the Paul or Paulinus of Léon is really the same as the Carmarthenshire saint is a question not easily answered. It is possible that the latter may never have left Wales. An inscribed stone (date *c.* 500) has been discovered in a field called Pant-y-polion at Maes Llanwrthwl in the parish of Caeo (north-west of Llandovery) with the words :

SERVATVR (=SERVATOR) FIDAEI PATRIAEQUE SEMPER AMATOR HIC PAVLINVS IACIT CVLTOR PIENTISIMVS AEQVI,

which Archbishop Benson rendered :

> Guard of the Faith, and Lover of his Land,
> Liegeman of Justice, here Paulinus lies.[19]

But it does not necessarily follow that this stone commemorates our saint, as the authors of *Lives of the British Saints* suppose. The inscription does not seem to me quite what one would expect on the grave of an abbot who was regarded as a saint, and sounds more like the epitaph of a virtuous and pious layman. The *patriae amator* may have been a chieftain, who gave his name to the *Cwmwd Pellinog* or *Peulinog* in this part of Carmarthenshire. The name was a common one, and is found on three other inscribed stones in South Wales—at Caerwent, at

---

18 The Roman Martyrology commemorates yet another Paulinus on October 10' a bishop of Capua.

19 *Cf. now ECMW 107 : 'Preserver of the Faith, constant lover of his country, here lies Paulinus, the devoted champion of righteousness."]

Port Talbot, and at Llandysilio in Pembrokeshire. It seems probable that some of the Welsh saints *did* visit Brittany. S. Cadog appears to have founded Pleucadeuc[20] near Redon (the whole neighbourhood is full of dedications to Glamorgan saints), and the cult of St. Iltut (associated in more than one instance with that of S. Paulinus of Léon)[21] and the cult of S. Teilo are so extensive in Brittany and so firmly localized there that it can hardly be supposed that they were imported through literary channels. But, though the subject still remains in partial obscurity, one thing has become clear. The monasteries of the Tywi valley had played their part in the evangelization of northern Brittany, and they had not been forgotten there in the ninth century. Wrmonoc had seen someone who had given him the very definite information about Llanddeusant and its monastery which he has inserted in the *Vita Pauli*, and he decided to identify Paul of Léon with its founder Paulinus.

The section of the *Vita* which deals with Paul's life in the country of his birth ends with two incidents of very great interest, based on insular British traditions, for which we have no other evidence outside Wrmonoc's work.

For the existence of King *Mark* we have indeed other evidence (though he does not appear in the *Life* of any saint except Paul), and it is interesting to find that it entirely confirms what Wrmonoc tells us about him. Everyone knows that Mark, king of Cornwall, the husband of Iseult, is one of the most prominent figures in the Arthurian romances. In their later versions he is made to reside at Tintagel, but the late M. Joseph Loth showed, in his fascinating *Romans de la table ronde*, that the earliest romances place him at Lantyan, which is a manor in the parish of St. Samson, Golant, on the estuary of the Fowey. Close by is a very important earthwork called Castle Dore, partly excavated by Mr. Ralegh Radford in 1938, which is the

---

[20] See *S. Cadoc in Cornwall and Brittany* (No. 41 in my 'Cornish Saints' series), pp. 25-28.

[21] There is a *Lanildut* and an *Aberildut* in Léon, near Lampaul-Ploudalmezeau, which seems to confirm the tradition of a connection with our saint. There was a very considerable cult of S. Ildut in the north of Brittany, and Landebaeron claimed to possess his head.

original site of the inscribed stone which now stands on the road to Fowey a little distance to the south. On it are the words CIRUSINIUS FILI CUNOMORI.[22] There are several place-names in the neighbourhood containing the name of King Mark,[23] and (apparently) another personal name familiar in Arthurian legend—Gorlois. We have thus several mutually independent sources of evidence for Mark being a Cornish king, and one of them provides a full and entire justification for Wrmonoc's statement that "Marc is also called Quonomorius (*quem alio nomine Quonomorium vocant*)".[24]

Scholars have not, however, been, up to the present, so fortunate in their endeavours to discover the site of *Caer Bannhed*. There is no need to go, with the authors of *Lives of the British Saints*, to Bannockburn in Scotland to look for it. It is probably a lost place-name in Devon or Cornwall—perhaps the original name of Castle Dore.[25] It is to be hoped that further research may eventually trace it, for the statement that it is the place "where now the bones of the same king rest awaiting the day of judgment" seems to be based on a genuine contemporary tradition and likely to afford a valuable clue to Cornish history in the sixth century.

On the other hand, the statement that King Mark "ruled over four races, each speaking a different language", is not likely to add to our knowledge of the early history of the insular Domnonia, since it appears to be a citation from Bede (*Eccl. Hist.* iii. 6).

The story of the bell is not unparalleled in Celtic hagiography, for the *Vita Cadoci* has a somewhat similar story of

---

[22] *See *Journal of the Royal Institution of Cornwall*, new series (1951), 117-9, emending CIIC 487: DRUSTANUS HIC IACIT CUNOMORI FILIUS Cf. J.Morris, *Past and Present* 11 (1957), 15-16; *Britain and Rome* (1965), 184.]

[23] *Kilmarth (Kylmerth,* 1327), in the parish of Tywardreath, is less than a mile from Castle Dore.

[24] As *march* = 'a horse' in Cornish, the late Professor J. Rhys suggested that "*Quonomorius* should be regarded as originally in Goidelic *Quonomorcius*, or, better still, *Quenna-morcius*, an epithet meaning 'having a horse's head'." (AC, 1895, p. 300, note 1.) *Cf. R. Bromwich, SEBH 122-3.]

[25] *Ban* in Cornish = 'height'. The *New Cornish-English Dictionary*, by R. Morton Nance, says that "in place-names it becomes *ben*". The same authority says that *heth* = 'stag, or red-deer', and is *hedhas* in the plural. I have consulted Mr. Nance. He writes: "*ban hydd* has a special meaning in Welsh—'stag's horn'. The final *d* might stand for Welsh *dd*, but if so *ban hedd* = 'height of peace' is nearer to the spelling."

Cadog asking Gildas to give him a bell and meeting with a refusal, but at last obtaining it through the intervention of the Pope. The incident of S. Paul's bell being afterwards found inside a fish is of course based on one of the most familiar themes of the world's folklore, but it may have been suggested to Wrmonoc by the worn condition of the handle, which he supposed must have been gnawed by the denizens of the great deep.

The story of Paul's visit to his sister Sitofolla and her monastery on the seashore contains some problems not easy of solution.

The name *Sitofolla* is a Celtic name.   The second element, in the opinion of the late M. Loth, is the *fol* which enters into place-names in Brittany like *Folgoat* and personal names like the *Follaethou* who appears in the cartulary of Quimper as a witness to a charter in 1031.[26] *Sito*, he says, "is more difficult, but can be explained."   Sir John Rhys[27] points out that one of Paul's companions has a name with the same beginning—*Siteredus*, and that there is an Irish personal name *Sithridh*.

It has been suggested that Paul's sister Sitofolla may be the same person as the Exeter saint *Sativola*, who is patron of a church in the suburbs, and it has been pointed out that one of the churches in the British quarter of Exeter is dedicated to S. Paul, who (it is suggested) may be S. Paul Aurelian, Sitofolla's brother.

The question is a thorny one.

The Exeter saint has two forms of her name, a Latin (*Sativola*) and an English one (*Sidwell*).   The first reference to her is in the Leofric missal (mid-eleventh century), where *Reliquiae sanctae satiuolae uirginis* occur in the list of relics Bishop Leofric gave to the cathedral of Exeter, and among the alienated property which he regained for the minster was *Sidefullan hiwisc*—'S. Sidwell's fee'.   From *Sidefulla* developed the later *Sidwell*. Professor Max Förster[28] regards *Sidefulle* as an English, not a Celtic, name (meaning 'full of purity' or 'perfect in

---

[26] Pp. 139 and 148, printed edition.
[27] Op. cit., p. 301.
[28] *Devon and Cornwall Notes and Queries*, April, 1933 (this and the July number had a series of articles on S. Sidwell).

behaviour'), and *Sativola* as "an early monkish attempt at translating the meaning of the English name into some form of Latin."

There is a *Vita S. Sativolae* in Bishop Grandisson's *Legenda Sanctorum*. It is purely legendary, but evidently represents the Exeter tradition about S. Sativola in the Middle Ages. It tells us that her father was *Benia* or *Benna*. The Exeter martyrology commemorates on July 13 the *translatio Sanctae Juthuarae virginis* : *sororis sanctae Satiuuolae virginis* and *Nova Legenda Angliae* has a *Life* of S. Juthwara, which tells us that she had a brother named *Bana*, and three sisters—*Eadwara*, *Wilgitha*, and *Sidewlla* (sic.). The medieval traditions about S. Sidwell are thus quite inconsistent with her being identical with the *Sitofolla* of the *Vita Pauli*. The names of her sisters are, like her own name, typically English, her father is not *Perphirius*, and Paul Aurelian is not mentioned in her legend and is unknown to Exeter tradition.[29] Fr. Grosjean points out[30] in addition that the church of S. Sidwell is in the English, not the British, side of Exeter.

What Wrmonoc tells us about *Sitofolla*'s residence also seems inconsistent with her being an Exeter saint. He says, "she lived in the extreme limits of that country, that is, on the shore of the British Sea" (the English Channel), and Exeter certainly could not be thus described. True, Sativola is not honoured only in Exeter. She is the patron of a parish in Cornwall—Laneast,[31] near Launceston, but this place, again, does not answer to Wrmonoc's description. It is neither on the British Sea (being as far from the sea as any place in Cornwall can be), nor is it "in the extreme limits of that country." It seems then impossible to identify Sitofolla with Sativola, and places connected with the latter seem ruled out as the site of Sitofolla's convent. Where, then, was it ? It can hardly have been in Wales, which is not on the British Sea, nor on the way from King Mark's country to Brittany. It is tempting to place it near Paul in Penwith. The name *Penwith* seems to mean

---

[29] He is not in the Exeter martyrology, and the church of S. Paul is nowhere stated to be dedicated to the Breton saint.

[30] AB 1935, p. 362, note 7.

[31] The dedication of Laneast to Sativola is not mentioned before 1436, and Mr. Henderson says, "St. Michael was possibly the oldest patron."

something very like '*extrema terrae*',[32] and there must be some reason for the dedication of Paul church to S. Paulinus. Our saint may well have visited this neighbourhood, and Mount's Bay would be an ideal place to sail from to Ushant. The miracle of the sea permanently withdrawing to its low-tide level might well be located here, as there has been much coast erosion in Mount's Bay even in historic times. Baring-Gould[33] boldly suggests Gulval parish as the site, on the ground that "his sister Wulvella had a settlement there". S. Wolvela is, it is true, the eponym of Gulval, but Baring-Gould is entirely unjustified in asserting that the Celtic *Wolvela* is the same name as the Saxon *Wilgitha*, the sister of *Sativola*, and therefore (in his opinion) the sister of Paul. There seem to be no place-names in any of the Mount's Bay parishes which contain any name remotely resembling *Sitofolla*. The exact site of her monastery cannot therefore at present be identified. This is a pity, as the story Wrmonoc relates about 'Paul's path'[34] is an extremely interesting one. She asks him to enlarge the monastic land. They go down to the shore at dead low tide. Paul tells her to fill her hands with pebbles, which she is to place in two rows along the low-water mark. The pebbles grow into longstones, and the avenue is still called by the *transmarini* 'Paul's Path'. The story is, of course, a legend, but Wrmonoc has not invented every detail of it. It is a 'topographic legend', and a topographic legend necessarily requires a place about which the story has grown up to explain its name or some remarkable feature it possesses. Now there are several submerged 'boulder-hedges' on Samson Flats (between the islands of Samson and Tresco) and elsewhere in the Isles of Scilly, uncovered at low tide, which were described, with photographs, by Mr. O. G. S. Crawford in an article (entitled 'Lyonesse') in *Antiquity*, vol. i., pp. 5-14. When such hedges are made in Wales or Cornwall, he says "a wide double row of

---

[32] Mr. R. Morton Nance suggests that *Penwith* is from *pen* and *gweth*, like the Cornish word *finweth* = 'an end' (from *fin* and *gweth*). In Breton this word has given us *Finistère* (for *Finvez-tyr* = 'The end of the land'). Mr. Henderson has adopted this explanation.

[33] LBS iv. 78.

[34] Albert Le Grand tells us the path was called *Hent-Sant-Paul*, and this is what *Semita Pauli* would be in Cornish. Mr. Henderson found a *Hent Selevan* in the parish of St. Levan (see No. 19 in this series). *See now SC i. 3-9.]

upright stones is set up, and the space between—often as much as
six feet—is gradually filled in with smaller stones," which soon
fall out, if the hedge is neglected, leaving only the uprights.
Scilly is certainly *semotus a consortio mundialium hominum* (in
Sitofolla's words), and was full of monasteries and hermitages in
the Age of the Saints.

I think, then, we may conclude that S. Paul of Léon sailed
to Brittany either from Scilly or from Mount's Bay, and by a very
curious coincidence the last bishop of Léon (Mgr. de la Marche),
driven out of his diocese by the French Revolution and compelled
to take refuge in England, landed in Mount's Bay on March 3,
1791.

SAINT TEILO[1]

THE earliest and most trustworthy evidence which we possess about the cult of S. Teilo is derived from the *Book of Saint Chad*.

This famous manuscript is a gospel-book containing the whole of the Gospels of St. Matthew and St. Mark and part of that of St. Luke, apparently written in Ireland before the year 700.[2] It became the property of a church of S. Teilo, and while there a certain number of entries of considerable historical value were made on the margins of its pages. One of these entries tells us how it was given to this church and gives the name of the donor, but unfortunately does not tell us the date of the gift. It afterwards passed into the possession of the cathedral church of St. Chad at Lichfield, where it still is—hence its name, but in this case we know neither how nor when, except that it must have been after the middle of the ninth century, because it contains the names of Bishop Nobis and other persons mentioned in the *Annales Cambriae* as living about that time, and not later than the latter half of the tenth century, since the name of Bishop Wynsi (974-992) is found on the margin of p. 1.

The *Book of St. Chad* is a document absolutely sincere and reliable, not doctored to suit later ideas and claims, like the *Book of Llandaff*. Unfortunately its Welsh entries are few.

The first marginal entry tells us that the book was given to God by being offered "on the altar of Teilo" (*sancti Teliaui super altare*). The second records the composition of an ancient feud, and *Teliau* is the first witness. Then come the names of three important personages followed by "the whole family of Teilo" (*tota familia Teliaui*), i.e. the monks of the monastery bearing

---

[1] *Published in 1942, Caxton Hall Printing Company, Lampeter, in the 'Welsh Saints' series, No. 3.]

[2] *The influence of Irish calligraphic tradition can certainly be traced in it: nevertheless its place of origin could have been Welsh. Cf. Edward Swansea and Brecon, 'The Gospels of St. Chad' (NLWJ iv. 46-49.)]

his name. The third entry records a gift "to God and to Saint Eliud" (another name for Teilo). God is the first witness. Then come the names of four clerical witnesses (the second being *Nobis*), the rest being laymen. The next entry describes a transaction in which the first clerical witness is *Nobis episcopus Teiliav* and the second *Saturnguid sacerdos Teiliav*.

It will be seen that the *Book of Saint Chad* does not tell us anything whatever about S. Teilo himself. But the entries show that in the ninth century, long after his death, he was venerated in South Wales as the founder of a monastery in which the altar is called the Altar of *Teliau*[3] and the monks of which are the *familia Teliavi*, governed by an abbot-bishop called the 'Bishop of Teiliau'.[4] The saint is represented as being, with God, a witness to a gift to the monastery, which is described as "offered to God and to saint Eliud", and also as a witness to a solemn agreement made in the monastic church. The gospel-book belongs to the saint and the curse of God and of S. Teilo[5] is invoked on those who violate agreements recorded in it. The site of the monastery is not mentioned. Till recently it was supposed to be Llandaff, but it is now generally accepted that this is a mistake and that the Altar of *Teliau* was at Llandeilo Fawr in Carmarthenshire. The name of this church of course implies that it was the most important of several others called after Teilo, and the *Liber Landavensis* mentions no less than twenty-one places named *Lann Teliau*, all or most of which were probably once connected in some way with 'Great Llandeilo'. But, while it is clear that the 'Bishop of *Teiliau*' did not rule at Llandaff, it is equally clear that the traditions of his monastery and most of its property and rights were eventually transferred to Llandaff, and the 'Book of Llandaff' is described by its author as *Gref Teliau*.[6]

Our next source of evidence for the cult of S. Teilo, the *Liber Landavensis*, is about three hundred years later than the

---

[3] The monastery of Nantcarfan is called *Altare Catoci* both in the *Vita Catoci* (c. 61) and the *Book of Llandaff* (p. 180).

[4] It looks as if, in Bishop Nobis's time, the office had become hereditary, as a clerical witness is called *Cuhelin filius episcopis* (sic).

[5] *Sit maledictus a Deo et a Teiliav in cujus evangelio scriptum est.*

[6] *sicut in isto gref Teliau reperitur* (p. 248). On p. 258 *Ruid*, apparently a priest of Llandaff, is called *presbyter sancti Teliavi*.

Book of St. Chad. S. Teilo has a very important role in this great
plaidoyer in favour of the claims put forward by the see of
Llandaff as recently re-organized by the Normans.   It is
impossible not to admire the enthusiasm, patience and literary
skill shown by its author in his re-arrangement of old documents
and insertion of new matter derived from his reading and his
travels, though it has resulted in a huge series of falsifications of
history—it will take a very long time before they are all detected.

The *Book of Llandaff* contains a long and elaborate *Life* of
S. Teilo.   A very able critical edition of this *Life* by the late
M. Joseph Loth, of which full use will be made here, appeared in
the *Annales de Bretagne* in 1893,[7] but a great deal of fresh
material for the study of the Celtic saints of Wales, Cornwall and
Brittany has since been discovered, and the criticism of the
Life of S. Teilo can now be carried much further.

To understand the *Vita Teliavi* it is essential to bear in
mind the fact that there is another recension of it, in the British
Museum MS. Vesp. A. xiv, which is identical with the version in
the *Book of Llandaff* except for certain important differences,
consisting mainly of a number of significant omissions.   A
complete list of these omissions and of every variant reading was
given by the late Mr. J. Gwenogvryn Evans on pp. 360-2 of his
admirable edition of the *Liber Landavensis*.

The version in Vesp. A. xiv. begins by telling us that it was
written by Geoffrey, brother of Urban, bishop of Llandaff
(d. 1133), and over the name Geoffrey has been interlined
"i.e. Stephen".[8]

It has been assumed by many scholars that Geoffrey was
the author of the longer version of the *Life of S. Teilo* in the
Liber Landavensis and also of most of the rest of the book, and
that the version in Vesp. A. xiv. is an abridgement of his work.
It seems possible, however, that Geoffrey may have written a
little before the compilation of the *Book of Llandaff* and that the
writer of the latter may have been another Norman clerk of
Llandaff, more thorough-going than Geoffrey, who included
Geoffrey's work in his own, but inserted into it some passages

---

[7] Tom. ix. pp. 81-85, 278-86, 438-46. Tom. x. pp. 66-77.
[8] INCIPIT VITA SANCTI TELIAVI EPISCOPI. A MAGISTRO GALFRIDO [i. *Stephano*
interlined above] FRATRE URBANI LANDAVENSIS ECCLESIAE EPISCOPI DICTATA.

(including one of great length) containing several of his favourite ideas—the insertions have remarkable parallels in the *Vita Oudocei* and in the charters of the *Liber Landavensis*. This is the view which will be taken in the following pages.[9]

---

[9] It is strange that those who have hitherto dealt with the *Liber Landavensis* do not seem to have observed that the question of these passages is of vital importance for the solution of the problem of the authorship of the book. *Note now the references in p. 12, n. 70.]

Are these passages omissions made by a reviser abbreviating a longer original, or insertions made by someone expanding the original ?

It seems impossible reasonably to maintain that the *Life* in Vesp. A. xiv. (which we will call V) is an abridgement of the longer *Life* in the *Lib. Land.* (which we will call L). Internal evidence is all against it.

First, L is much too long to be read in church, yet it has the homiletic exordium with which V begins and the homiletic comments which come further on. V therefore must be the original, of which L is an expanded form.

Again, L omits certain words which are found in V. Now these are all important words, the omission of which makes nonsense of the text, e.g. on p. 98, 1. 8, V rightly reads *corda*. L has carelessly written *doctrinam*; on p. 99, 1. 6, L has accidentally omitted *nullo*; on p. 101, 1. 14, L has omitted the verb *discuterent*; on p. 102, 1. 28, L reads *uouerunt*, while V has rightly *uouerent*; on p. 103, 1. 8, L has carelessly omitted *parvum* before *curriculum*. It is much more likely that these mistakes have been made by the writer of the *Liber Landavensis* copying another document than that they were in the original.

Further, what object could the author of V have in omitting the passages contained in L ? It could not have been to shorten the *Vita Teliavi*, for he has copied the whole of the much longer *Vita Cadoci*. It might be suggested, in favour of those who regard the passages in question as having been purposely omitted by V, that the scribe who wrote Vesp. A xiv was not a Llandaff but a Brecon writer, who lived in the diocese of St. David's, had included Rhigyfarch's *Vita David* in his collection, and was free from the prejudices of the author of the *Lib. Land.* Yet he has, in his version of the *Vita Teiliavi*, copied the whole of the Jerusalem story (except six words), with its glorification of S. Teilo at the expense of David and Padarn, and in another part of his MS. he has given the whole of the *De primo statu Landavensis ecclesiae* in the *Lib. Land.*, with the Dubrician charters and the *Vita Dubricii* which follow. (It is remarkable that in this case the differences between the two versions are mostly insignificant.)

It seems to me certain that the passages not in V are additions to V, not omissions made by V. But I do not regard the suggestion I have made that they were added to Geoffrey's *Vita Teiliavi* by a later writer as by any means certain. I only offer it tentatively as a working hypothesis. The question of the authorship and composition of the *Lib. Land.* is one of the most difficult in the whole sphere of historical criticism. Urban died in 1133 and Geoffrey cannot have died very long before, which does not leave much time for another writer of the same school to revise his work, for after Urban's death it would have been useless to continue the contest for Erging and Carmarthenshire. It is possible that Geoffrey himself may have revised his own work and made the additions in question when writing the *Lib. Land.* It may also be possible that the writer of Vesp. A xiv is mistaken in asserting that Geoffrey was the author of the shorter version. The latter may have been written by an earlier writer. The Brecon scribe may have had a copy of it and assumed it was by Geoffrey, who in this case would be the author of the *Lib. Land.* The copy the Brecon scribe used was not the same as that

DE VITA SANCTI TEILIAVI LANDAVENSIS ECCLESIAE

ARCHIEPISCOPI

The opening sentences of the *Vita* show that it is a sermon composed to be read on the saint's festival in Llandaff cathedral. He begins *Sanctus iste, fratres karissimi,* and the first page is in the typical homiletic vein. We observe that Geoffrey simply remarks that Teilo was "born of noble parents". The *Vita Oudocei* in the *Book of Llandaff* adds considerably to this statement, giving us a long story of his father *Ensic* and his mother *Guenhaf* and introducing *Budic,* prince of *Cornugallia,* who married Teilo's sister *Anauued* and became the father of *Ismael, Tyfei* (who "lies in Pennalun") and *Oudoceus. Budic, Ismael, Tyfhei* and *Oudoceus,* it is to be observed, all appear in the passages inserted into Geoffrey's work by the author of the *Book of Llandaff.* Further, Geoffrey does not tell us where S. Teilo was born, but in the *Book of Llandaff* we are twice[10] told that he was born at *Eccluis Gunniau,* which is near Penally, and a passage inserted further on into the *Vita Teliavi* by the author of the *Liber Landavensis* says that at his death *Pennalun* claimed his body "on the ground of the sepulture of his fathers being there and of his hereditary rights in the place".[11]

Geoffrey then informs us that the saint, whose name he has not yet mentioned, "was, because of his virtue and wisdom, called by the wise HELIOS,[12] which in Greek means the sun", but he sorrowfully admits that "illiterate men have corrupted the last syllable into *ud.*" Like the author of the *Vita Iltuti,*[13] Geoffrey finds a classical explanation for a Celtic name. The saint's original name was *Eliud.* It was quite a common name at the time. The son of a king of *Brecheinniauc* mentioned in the *Book of Llandaff*[14] was called *Eliud,* and an *Eliud filius Guerith* (a layman) signs a charter a little further on (he may be the *Eliudus*

---

used by the latter, since V omits a part of a sentence given by L, and which was obviously in the original form of V,—*frequentate . . . pauperibus* on p. 117,11. 22-23. A scribe has been misled by the *ate* in which *frequentate* and *erogate* both end—a clear case of homoioteleuton.

[10] *Eccluis Gunniau ubi natus est sanctus Teliaus.*
[11] p. 116.
[12] In the BLD (p. 98) ELIOS.
[13] *videlicet* ILLE *ab omni crimine* TUTUS.
[14] p. 146.

who signs a charter in the *Vita Cadoci*[15]). The name, as M. Loth has shown, is made up of two elements: *el* (found in such names as *El-ci, El-cu, El-gnou, El-guarui, El-haern*, etc.) and *iud* (found in *Margetiud*—later *Maredudd*; *Grip-iud*—later *Gruffudd*; *Iud-hail*—later *Ithael, Ithel*, in Breton *Iuthael*; *Iudguallaun*, etc.). *Eliau* is derived from the first element with the suffix *-avo*, and is found in the *Book of Llandaff* both as a personal name and as a place-name.[16] *Teliau* is a hypocoristic form of the same (*Teliavos*), like *Ty-suliau*. Usually the hypocoristic name is derived from the first element, with suffix *aco*, like *To-wed-oc*,— here a different suffix is employed.[17] Both forms of our saint's name, as we have seen, appear in the *Book of St. Chad* (*Eliud* twice and *Teliau* and *Teiliau* each three times) and both are found in Rhigyfarch's *Vita David*.[18]

Geoffrey then begins the story of *Eliud*'s life by saying that he was a pupil of S. Dubricius :

> We read that as a child he was taught the Holy Scripture by Saint Dubricius the archbishop (*archipresul*), whose immediate successor he afterwards became.

The word *legimus* brings us at once to the question of the materials which Geoffrey had at his disposal for writing a *Life* of S. Teilo. Does it mean that he had an older *Life* of the saint before him ? It is not an easy question to answer. The reader cannot fail to be struck by the fact that the great part of his *Vita Teiliavi* consists of, or is based on, extracts (often very lengthy ones) from the *Life* of another Welsh saint, and the author of the *Book of Llandaff* has added an extremely long story, the idea of which he had obtained from the *Life* of a Breton saint. It is true that in a further insertion by the later author another claim to follow written records is made, as we shall see, but only to introduce some exceedingly brief references to five traditional miracles of S. Teilo in Carmarthenshire and Pembrokeshire, two of which are prefaced by the word *dicunt*, showing that they

---

[15] c. 65.
[16] BLD 227, 255-7.
[17] *El* with the suffix *aco* is found in the names *Elioc, Eloc* and *Eluc* (BLD 178, 202, 205).
[18] In the list of St. David's disciples he is called *Eliud*. In the story of the journey to Jerusalem he is "Eliud, who is now commonly called Teliau."

are oral legends. If there was an older *Life* of Teilo, it must have been a very short and imperfect one, or very little of it has survived in Geoffrey's work—nothing in fact except perhaps the vague traditions of Teilo's relations with Paulinus and David, the story of the Yellow Plague and of the emigration to which it led and the legend about the multiplication of the saint's body after his death.[19]

In a previous study of S. Dubricius we have seen the reason why those who were labouring in the twelfth century to build up the see of Llandaff were so anxious to claim S. Teilo as his pupil. The author of the *Liber Landavensis* names Teilo first among the disciples of Dubricius at *Hennlann*, and in the charter purporting to grant *Penn Alun* to Dubricius Llandeilo Fawr is referred to as the place "where Teiliaus the *alumnus* and disciple of Saint Dubricius lived". He repeats the assertion that Teilo and Samson were both disciples of Dubricius in his long addition to the *Vita Teiliavi* (p. 109). Geoffrey does not say *where* Teilo studied under Dubricius, but he tells us that he was such a promising pupil that :

> Dubricius not only recognised him as his own equal, but saw that, guided by the Holy Ghost, he could unravel the mysteries of the Scriptures by himself better than if any human teacher were to instruct him, and consequently made up his mind that he should be his successor in the *magisterium*. But such grace was upon him and so much was he on fire with the love of sacred learning that he who could have been master decided to place himself under the guidance of another. Therefore,[20] having heard of the fame of a certain wise man named Poulinus, he went to him and stayed with him for some time. Thus whatever secrets of the Scriptures had hitherto been hidden from him [the two saints] by discussion together now understood perfectly.

[19] It seems just possible that the very long story on pp. 127-9 of the BLD comes from a Llandeilo Fawr *Life* of Teilo. It certainly cannot have been in any charter. But it may be a local legend of Llanddowror.

[20] It looks as if the sentences between *intelligere* on p.98 and *audita sibi Poulini* on p. 99 were an insertion, as they interrupt the thread of the story. Before *audita* Vesp. A. xiv reads *Beatus Theliauus*, which the author of BLD has changed to *Deinde* because he sees how awkward the insertion makes the sentence which goes on with the story. It is possible that the reference to *stultorum philosophorum* may be, like that to *figmenta poetarum* two pages later, a sly hit at the literary tastes of the contemporary bishop of St. David's—Bernard.

Poulinus is an old Welsh form of *Paulinus*, a saint who plays an important part in the *Vita David*. It is possible that, in making Teilo a disciple of Paulinus, Geoffrey may be simply imitating the *Life of S. David*, which he certainly has before him, as we shall see. On the other hand there are reasons for thinking that the story of Teilo studying with Paulinus may really have been part of the original legend of Teilo (whether written or oral). Paulinus was a great figure in Welsh tradition. Wrmonoc, writing in Brittany the *Vita Pauli Aureliani* in 884, identifies him with the founder of the see of Léon, and seems to quote a lost *Life* of Paulinus, which represented him as belonging to a noble family established at *Brehant Dincat*, and, after studying under the famous *Iltut*, founding in a lonely spot near his home a monastery, which in the ninth century bore the name of his two brothers, *Notolius* and *Potolius*. *Brehant Dincat* is clearly Llandingad, now usually called Llandovery, and the unnamed monastery must be Llanddeusant ("the Llan of the Two Saints"), seven and a half miles to the south-east of Llandovery and nine miles north-east of Llandeilo Fawr.[21] This is surely very significant. It is not impossible that both the *Vita David* and the *Vita Teiliavi* may have been following independent and perhaps genuine traditions in making their heroes disciples of Paulinus, though in that case the Glamorgan tradition, followed by Wrmonoc, which made Dewi and Paulinus disciples of Iltut, would have to be abandoned. Rhigyfarch says that Paulinus was a disciple of S. Germanus, and this may prove to be the truth. Neither Rhigyfarch nor Geoffrey say where their respective heroes studied under Paulinus (Rhigyfarch states vaguely that it was "in a certain island", which may mean 'monastery'), but Wrmonoc has given us a clue, which has, I think, enabled us to solve the problem. It was evidently at Llanddeusant.

On the whole, the connection between the two Carmarthen-shire saints, Paulinus and Teilo (who are both, as we shall see, honoured in Brittany close to other saints of Carmarthenshire), seems better supported than the story of Teilo having been a pupil of Dubricius, and Geoffrey's not very convincing account of

---

[21] I have given the evidence which proves this in *S. Paul of Léon* ('Cornish Saints' series. No. 46) and in *S. Paulinus of Wales*. *See now SC i. 10-60, especially pp. 33-34, and pp. 146-61 of this volume.]

his having studied under both may be merely an attempt to reconcile two traditions by combining them.[22] This would not necessarily be inconsistent with the traditional connection between Teilo and Dubricius. The statement of the writer of the *Book of Llandaff* (p. 69) that Dubricius was appointed *summus doctor* and bishop by S. Germanus may prove, after all, not to be all pure fiction, and if (as Rhigyfarch says) Paulinus was a disciple of Germanus, it would not be impossible for Teilo to have been the 'successor' of Dubricius and rightly associated with him in Welsh tradition.[23]

Geoffrey says little about Teilo's sojourn with Paulinus, but he tells us that while "there [he does not say *where*] he associated with himself David, a man of most perfect life." He proceeds to make a long series of plagiarisms from the *Life of S. David*, which make up altogether about a third of the *Vita Teiliavi*.

This *Life* is known to us in two versions—Rhigyfarch's *Vita David* (written about 1090) and a *Life* in Welsh, *Buchedd Dewi Sant*, written (or copied) in the fourteenth century.[24] It would seem that Geoffrey did not copy Rhigyfarch, but an older *Life* containing substantially the same material, since every story he relates differs in detail from Rhigyfarch's account even where there could be no motive for altering it.[25]

The portions of the *Life of S. David* utilized by Geoffrey are, first, the traditions of David's connections both with Paulinus and with Teilo, the story of *Baia* and his wife, followed by one about David's disciple (or associate) *Maidoc* and another about wells which ran wine, and finally the legend of the journey of David, Teilo and Padarn to Jerusalem. In each of these the

---

[22] Just in the same way Wrmonoc combines two traditions by identifying S. Paul of Léon both with Paul of Penychen and with Paulinus.

[23] The list of the churches of Erging, compiled early in the eleventh century (BLD 275), mentions an oratory called *Teliau ha Dibric* in the cemetery of *Lann Guern* (Llanwarne), and states that *Hennlann Dibric* and *Lann Teliau* were "in one cemetery" (at Hentland). It seems impossible that the writer should have invented these names.

[24] *Lives of the Cambro-British Saints*, 102-43. *Also D. S. Evans, *Buched Dewi* (2nd ed. Caerdydd, 1965)].

[25] *Here cf. now J. W. James, *Rhigyfarch's Life of St. David* (Cardiff, 1967), in which is printed the text of the twelfth century B.M. MS. Nero E 1. The basic text is accompanied by an introduction, critical apparatus and translation; note especially the section of the introduction entitled 'The Vespasian Recension' (xxxiii-xxxvii). Cf. also N. K. Chadwick, SEBC 149.]

Vita Teiliavi, as we have said, differs in greater or less degree from the account given in the *Lives* of S. David which have come down to us. In the first case Rhigyfarch's version differs not only from Geoffrey's but from the much older *Vita Pauli Aureliani*. There David and Paul are fellow-disciples of Iltut. In the *Vita David* Paulinus is David's master, not his fellow-pupil, and *Eliud* is "one of the three most faithful disciples of David". In the *Vita Teiliavi* Teilo has already been the disciple of Dubricius and of Paulinus before living with David in Carmarthenshire and Menevia. Geoffrey of course wished to represent his hero as David's equal, not his inferior. Rhigyfarch is naturally just as anxious to make David the leader of the group of famous South Wales saints whom he is going to introduce into his story. Geoffrey here contents himself with telling us in three rhetorical sentences that Teilo and David had *idem velle et non velle*.[26]

The passage about the Picts which follows is intended as a preface to the story of *Baia*. Rhigyfarch tells us that *Baia* was *Scottus* (i.e. an Irishman). Geoffrey regards the Picts and Scots as identical. He draws on his reminiscences of several historical works he has read to describe them—he refers the reader to "the History of Gildas, the historiographer of the Britons", but does not tell us that he has also used Bede, from whom he has copied the information that the Picts came "from Scythia", and Isidore of Seville.[27] He then relates how "a certain leader of that wicked race [he means *Baia*, but does not name him[28]] had disembarked at the *civitas Minuensis* to slaughter the wretched inhabitants and burn their houses and the temples of the saints, and had there constructed a palace for himself." The story of the method employed by *Baia* and his wife to drive

---

[26] A reminiscence of Sallust's *Catilina*, c. 20.

[27] M. Loth has pointed out that the expression used by Geoffrey, *oculorum stigmata*, should read *aculeorum stigmata*. Isidore of Seville who also confounds the Scots with the Picts, says *Scotti propria lingua nomen habent a picto corpore, eo quod* ACULEIS *ferreis cum stramento variarum figurarum* STIGMATA *annotentur*. Loth says that this legend is a dim remembrance of the fact that the Scots had made settlements both in North and South Wales.

[28] To tell a story and omit the name of the person concerned is frequently a sign that a writer is making a plagiarism from some well-known source.

away David's monks[29] is considerably shortened, and Geoffrey adds a detail not found in Rhigyfarch—the slave-girls go mad as a punishment for their conduct, and this leads to the conversion of "the aforesaid persecutor and all his house," on which Geoffrey enlarges in his usual rhetorical manner.

Geoffrey now passes abruptly to another incident borrowed from the *Life of S. David*, which he represents as happening not long after that just described :

> For when the blessed Teliaus and Maidocus [were reading[30]] in the *atrium* of the monastery, not the figments of the poets nor the histories of the men of old,[31] but rather the Lamentations of Jeremiah, that they might be enkindled with love of the heavenly country, a certain servant came saying that there was no fuel to prepare the supper for the brethren.

They set out at once to the woods, anxious because of the short notice they had received, yet hoping to find a supply sufficient to leave them free for a considerable time to devote themselves to prayer and study. Two stags appear and offer to carry the faggots, and without needing to be driven, follow Teilo and Maidoc to the monastery, while the natives of the place look on in amazement. After this the stags continue to fetch the wood day after day, so that the monks' prayers are not interrupted. Geoffrey adds some pious reflections, and continues the story :

> Meanwhile S. David, coming out from his tabernacle, finds a book, which the brethren had inadvertently left open just outside the door, perfectly dry in spite of heavy rain which had come on.

Geoffrey introduces Maidoc without telling us who he was, which is a sure mark of literary larceny. When a writer is telling his own story, he explains who the characters in it are, but, if he is copying another book, he often forgets that his reader is not

---

[29] In the *Revue celtique* for 1929 M. Vendryes suggested another explanation of this incident. He observed that among the Gauls a procession of naked women was regarded as having a magical effect and quotes Caesar's story of its being employed at the siege of Gergovia.

[30] The author of the *Book of Llandaff* in copying Geoffrey has accidentally omitted the important word *discuterent*.

[31] Again, as Duine points out (*Mémento*, No. 117), in all probability a covert gibe at Bernard, the bishop of St. David's, with whom Geoffrey's brother was engaged in litigation. Giraldus Cambrensis tells us that Bernard was *facetus*, as well as *copiose litteratus*, and so not likely to be specially fond of the Lamentations of Jeremiah.

(like himself) familiar with the context in the original. Maidoc plays an important part in the legend of S. David. Rhigyfarch tells us that his hero arrives at "Vallis Rosina, which the Britons commonly called Hodnant", accompanied by a band of disciples, the three chief of whom are *Aidan, Eliud* and *Ysmael*,[32] Later on he tells us a number of stories about the first of these. He does *not* tell us that he came from Ireland, but he says that when his training under David had been completed he went to Ireland and constructed a monastery at Ferns. One of these stories is about *Aidan* being sent by the *prepositus* to fetch wood.[33] He takes a couple of oxen to carry the wood, but he goes alone— no mention being made of *Eliud* or of any other companion. On his return he finds the book he had left open uninjured by the rain. Further on Rhigyfarch refers to this disciple again and calls him "Maidoc, who also from infancy is Aidanus".[34] The late Dr. Plummer, in his *Vitae Sanctorum Hiberniae*,[35] printed a *Vita Sancti Edani siue Maodhog, ep. et conf.*, which states that *Sanctus Edanus, qui vulgo appellatur Maodhog*,[36] was born in Ireland. In c. 11 we are told that Saint *Moedhog* sailed to Britain, to blessed David, bishop of the city which is called *Ceall Muni*, and remained there with him a long time. In c. 12 the miracles of the two "untamed oxen" and of the book are related, with details differing from both Rhigyfarch's and Geoffrey's accounts. The Brecon compiler of Vesp. A xiv added to his legendary an abbreviated version of this *Vita*, headed *Vita S. Aidui episcopi. ii Kal. Mart.*[37] which Plummer[38] considered an earlier recension. John of Tynemouth saw a copy of

---

[32] LCBS 124. *James, op. cit. 9.]

[33] Ib. pp. 130-1. *James, op. cit. 15.]

[34] Ib. 133, *ubi fuit Maidoc, qui et Aidanus ab infantia* (everywhere else he calls him *Aidanus*). *But see James, op. cit. 18, where it is stated that c. 42 which contains these words is found only in Vespasian A xiv and derived MSS.]

[35] Oxford, 1910, vol. ii, pp. 141-63.

[36] In the rest of the *Vita* he is invariably called *Moedhog*. Other MSS. give *Moedoc* and *Medocius*. The *Vita* was written at Ferns.

[37] This statement has puzzled scholars considerably, as the Irish versions of the *Life* say that the saint died ii Kal.Feb. It is repeated, however, at the end of the *Vita Aidui*, where we are told that "the day of the Festival of S. Aidus is ii Kal. Mart" (28 Feb.). The kalendar in Vesp. A. xiv, which internal evidence shows to have been composed at Monmouth priory (a little-known Saumur saint is given on 8 July), has *Sci. Maidoci epi. et conf.* on 28 Feb.

[38] op. cit., I. lxxv. In II. 295-311, he has given a new edition of this *Vita*, an immense improvement on the poor edition in LCBS.

this *Vita* at St. David's in the fourteenth century and analyzed it. At the end of his version, printed in *Nova Legenda Angliae*[39] he observes that "this saint is called *Aidanus* in the Life of S. David, but *Aidus* in his own Life, and at Menevia in the church of St. David [i.e. the cathedral] he is called *Moedok*, which is Irish, and there his festival is observed with great honour".

It is possible that these *Lives* of *Aidus*, *Aidan* or *Moedhog* are really a contamination of two different legends, one Welsh, the other Irish. So far, modern scholars have not questioned the identification of the two saints, which was already accepted in the eleventh century, and have regarded the *Maidoc* of the *Vita David* and the *Vita Teiliavi* and the kalendar in Vesp. A. xiv as a form of *Mo-aed-oc*, the Irish hypocoristic form of *Aidus* or *Aidan*, anxiously warning us that it is necessary carefully to distinguish this saint from the *Madoc* who is honoured at Llanmadog in Gower and elsewhere in South Wales. Nevertheless the number of dedications to Madoc in Pembrokeshire would seem to point to there being a Welsh saint of this name who was associated with S. David in the evangelisation of South Wales, and who afterwards visited Cornwall and (perhaps) Brittany.[40] It is not likely that a bishop of Ferns, who is represented as being in his youth a pupil of S. David, should have churches dedicated to him in Wales. The idea that the name *Madoc*, spelt *Maidoc*, might be a hypocoristic form of *Aidan* led to his identification by some early hagiographer with the well-known saint of Ferns, a monastery with which St. David's was closely connected,[41] and to the insertion of Menevian traditions about

---

[39] I. 22 (Oxford 1901).

[40] In Pembrokeshire *S. Madoc* is patron of Nolton (where there is also a *Madoc's Haven*) and Haroldston West in the deanery of Rhos. There is a *S. Madoc's Well* at Rudbaxton in the deanery of Dougleddy (Daugleddyf), and a *Ffynnon Fadog* (Mr. Wade Evans says it is now *Faeddog*) between St. David's and Porth Mawr. There is a *Carn Madog* in Llanllawer. The church of St. Twinnel's in the deanery of Castlemartin is dedicated to S. Winnoc, and it is remarkable that in the *Vita Winnoci* S. Madoc and S. Connoc (who are honoured together in Brecon and who have dedications in Cornwall not far from St. Winnoc) are given as his companions (see Doble, 'Cornish Saints' series No. 44, pp. 16, 17, 32, 58 and 60). *Maidocus* appears in the *Vita Cadoci* as a companion of S. Keneder (Cynidr), another Brecon saint. (There were chapels of S. Cadog and S. Cynog in the parish of Llawhaden in Pembs., where the church is dedicated to S. Aidan).

[41] In the Irish *Vita S. Edani* already referred to, S. David is made to say to Moedhog : *firmissima fraternitas in celo et in terra inter me et te, et inter posteros nostros semper sit.* (Plummer, op. cit., ii. 153).

Madoc into the *Life* of the Irish saint, where they have all the appearance of excrescences.

We have seen that the story about *Maidoc* utilized by Geoffrey differs in its details from the version of the same story in Rhigyfarch's *Vita David* and that that version differs in turn from the one in the *Vita Edani*. It is remarkable that Geoffrey's version resembles much more closely a similar story in the *Vita Cadoci*, though there the personages are all different. Two saints (*Finian* and *Macmoil*) instead of one are sent to fetch the timber, and there are stags instead of oxen. Moreover there are some striking verbal parallels between the stories in the *Vita Cadoci* and the *Vita Teiliavi*. In the former we have *pergentes prae magna festinatione . . . suae ferocitatis obliti mansuetius colla jugo submittunt . . . Vir Dei librum a pluvia penitus illesum*[42] *nimis admiratus invenit*. In the *Vita Teiliavi* we read *nimia festinatione perrexerunt . . . colla prebentes ad subjugandum . . . exuit nobis ferocitatem nostram et fecit nos mansueta pecora . . . Sanctus David librum invenit a pluvia prorsus immunem . . . Quod admirans . . . librum eorum illesum ab imbribus*. It would seem that Geoffrey is copying the *Vita Cadoci*. The word *mansuetus* has taken his fancy and he repeats it no less than four times. The story, however, is essentially the same in all these different versions, especially the part about the open book. We have here a very curious literary problem.

Geoffrey next inserts a story which, he says, was a local tradition he had collected on the spot (i.e. at St. David's),[43] about some holy wells near the monastery, which ran sweet wine. In reality it is taken from the *Life of S. David*. Rhigyfarch places the story before the one we have just been considering. In his version the fountain (he only speaks of one) is due to the prayers of S. David, who had been asked by the brethren to procure them a better water supply, and it provides wine for the sacrament of the Lord's body and blood. But afterwards, he says, the disciples imitate their master and cause other sweet waters to flow. This detail is much more explicit in the Welsh

---

[42] So in Vesp. A. xiv. The author of the *Book of Llandaff* has omitted *illesum*, which was in Geoffrey's version, and has altered *seruauerat* to *liberauerat*.

[43] *ut a veteribus illius loci incolis accepimus*.

Life, which says that "afterwards Bishop Gweslan [i.e. Guis-tilian[44]], brother in the faith to David, and a disciple to David who was called Eliud . . . obtained from God two fountains, which are called to this day Ffynnawn Gweslan and Ffynnawn Eliud". This seems to prove conclusively that Geoffrey did not use Rhigyfarch's edition of the *Life of S. David,* but some other version of it.

Geoffrey concludes his series of plagiarisms from the *Life of S. David* with a lengthy version of the story of the visit of Teilo, David and Padarn to Jerusalem.

The reason for the invention of this famous legend seems clear : it was no doubt due to the wish of the Welsh churches to find an answer to the claims of Canterbury,[45] the need for which had become more urgent since the Norman Conquest, while the first Crusade had made the *motif* of a journey to Jerusalem a frequent theme in Celtic hagiography at this period.[46] But the fact that there are three different versions of it, inspired by the conflicting interests of the three principal churches of South Wales, represented by David, Teilo and Padarn, reveals the weakness of the Welsh church, which suffered from the dis-union that has so often been fatal to the independence of the Celtic peoples. They could not agree as to which church should have the primacy, and Llandaff was already in friendly relations with Canterbury.

The story must have been invented at St. David's. It cannot have formed part of the original *Vita Paterni,* although Rhigyfarch, in introducing Padarn into his narrative, refers to that *Life* as already existing.[47] The story as we have it now in the *Life of S. Padarn* must be later than the *Life of S. David.* It is written from the point of view of David instead of from that of Padarn, and indeed seems to be partly copied from Rhigyfarch. Writing at Llandaff about forty years later, Geoffrey could not deny the legend, which was already accredited, but he takes care

---

[44] For this saint see Wade-Evans, *Life of St. David,* 9, 84-5, 101. He is found in the kalendar in Vesp. A. xiv on 2 March, *Sci. Gistliani, epi. et conf.*
[45] LBS iv. 45.
[46] Duine has called attention to this, see *La Métropole de Bretagne,* p. 59. A pilgrimage to Jerusalem appears in the *Lives* of SS. Cadog, Cyngar and Cybi in Wales, Budoc and Tudual in Brittany, and Petroc in Cornwall.
[47] *cujus conversatio atque virtutes in sua continentur hystoria.*

to insert into his version of it a number of details which will show that throughout Teilo was accorded the pre-eminence among the three pilgrims.

According to Rhigyfarch, an angel appears to David and commands him to undertake the journey, accompanied by Eliud and Padarn. Rhigyfarch says that their pilgrimage was on terms of equality, but he gives us plainly to understand that David is the leader. It is he who, when they reach Gaul, is endowed with the apostolic gift of tongues to help them on their journey. The patriarch of Jerusalem, informed of their approach by an angel in a dream, prepares three honourable seats for them and places them therein when they arrive. He then promotes Saint David to the archiepiscopate. The three saints preach to the inhabitants of Jerusalem, and at their departure David is presented with four gifts by the Patriarch,—an altar, a bell, a staff and a tunic wrought of gold. The Patriarch arranges that these gifts shall be sent after them. The story here shows signs of having been afterwards altered by Rhigyfarch. He first says that all four gifts are made to David, but a few lines further on the three saints "receive their gifts in their respective monasteries," David receiving his at Llangyfelach. This must have been the original story, but Rhigyfarch has clumsily inserted a correction in the interests of the see of Menevia.

The reviser of the *Vita Paterni*, who is anxious to get the former episcopal see of Llanbadarn restored, tells the story shortly, following the version in the *Vita David*, but he takes care to state that while gifts were bestowed on all three saints, Padarn received a double gift, viz., a staff and a tunic, and he does not mention what the other gifts were. The significance of his receiving the staff, the sign of episcopal jurisdiction, is obvious.

Geoffrey has given the most elaborate version of all. He retells the story in flowery language, using the rhetorical amplifications characteristic of his style, adding suitable texts from Scripture and a story of robbers being converted by the saints' patience and disinterestedness, which he seems to have borrowed from Palladius's *Paradise of the Fathers*[48] (though it may have been suggested by the notorious dangers of the passage

[48] e.g. vol. ii. p. 42, No. 187 (ed. Budge).

of the Alps at this period), and pointing out that the number of
the pilgrims recalls the mystery of the Trinity. The divine
command through the angel to set out is addressed not to David
in the first place, but to [all three of] 'the saints'. On their
arrival at the Holy City, instead of reposing, after their fatigues,
on soft beds, they pass three days prostrate on the bare pavement
of the Temple in prayer. The story of the seats is greatly
elaborated. Using a well-known folklore theme, Geoffrey says
that two of the chairs were of magnificently worked metal
while the third was of plain cedar, and that it had been previously
decided that the choice of the latter should be the test to
indicate which of the three pilgrims they were to regard as the
leader (*quem illorum ceteris prelatum constituerent*). Eliud's
humility in choosing the least ornamented of the three proves his
superior sanctity, and all present prostrate themselves before
him, saying :

> *Salve, sancte Dei Teliave*, may thy prayers prevail for us before the
> Lord, for today thou art exalted above thy fellows and dost sit in
> the chair from which our Lord Jesus Christ preached to our
> fathers the kingdom of God.

Teilo in turn prostrates himself, repeating a suitable text from
the Psalms (Ps. i. 1) and pointing out that the chair was composed
of the same material as the Cross. He preaches to the people,
and all present hear him speaking in their own tongue. Then,
at his suggestion, David and Padarn are invited also to speak.
After this they are all three, by the choice of the whole assembly
(*ab universa plebe electi*) raised to the episcopate, and, to increase
still further the impression we are to feel of the special honour
accorded to S. Teilo, the author of the *Book of Llandaff* heightens
the effect by inserting a statement that "Teliaus is regarded as
the successor of Peter and David of James." In the story of the
gifts David receives only the altar, Padarn being represented with
the staff and "choral cope in recognition of his excellent
singing", and Teilo with a bell. The description of the bell is
long and detailed in the *Vita Teiliavi* (in the *Vita David* it is
dismissed in a short phrase) and no doubt contains genuine
traditions about the bell which Teilo, like other Celtic saints,
must have possessed, and which was probably at Llandaff when
Geoffrey wrote. It was not large nor handsome, but was

sweet-sounding and was greatly venerated.[49] It condemned the perjured (i.e., those who took a false oath upon it) and healed the sick, and at one time it used of its own accord to sound the hours of the day, till, touched by polluted hands, it ceased to perform this useful function. Geoffrey in his usual way finds it an edifying likeness to Teilo's preaching powers.

The intention of a large number of Geoffrey's improvements on the story as told by Rhigyfarch to increase the prestige of the church of Llandaff is obvious.

Geoffrey finishes the story of the Jerusalem pilgrimage by saying that "they returned happily to their own country, but they could not stay there very long, owing to a pestilence, which nearly destroyed the entire nation". The author of the *Liber Landavensis*, while copying this, realized the existence of a most serious omission in Geoffrey's work—he had actually written a *Life* of Teilo without anywhere stating that he ever became bishop of Llandaff. It was of vital importance to remedy this, so the reviser inserted into the middle of the sentence, after the words "to their own country," the following statement :

> and S. Teliaus received the pastoral care of the church of Landavia, to which he was consecrated, together with all the diocese (*parrochia*) adjoining it, which had been that of Dubricius his predecessor.

At the same time he altered, in the second part of the original sentence, the words "they could not" to "he could not". With this short addition, the *Life* now contained in essence what the author of the *Book of Llandaff* wished the world to believe about Teilo, but the mere fact that the addition had to be made shows how different the original Teilo tradition must have been.

Geoffrey describes the famous plague as follows :

> It was called the Yellow Pestilence, because it made everyone it attacked yellow and bloodless. It appeared to men in the form of a column, consisting of a watery cloud passing over the whole region. Everything living that it touched with its pestilential breath either died straightway or became sick unto death.

[49] *magis famosum quam sit magnum, magis pretiosum quam pulchrum.*

The author of the *Book of Llandaff* here inserts a statement that "it attacked Mailcon, king of Guenedotia, and destroyed his country," which he borrowed from the *Annales Cambriae*[50], a book with which he was well acquainted, as we have observed when dealing with his statements about S. Dubricius.[51] Teilo, Geoffrey says, pleaded with the Lord in fasting and prayer[52] and the violence of the plague abated for a time, but, warned from heaven, he took the survivors and, with them "departed into distant regions". The reviser supplemented this statement by adding a short passage saying that "some went to Ireland and some, under his guidance, to France (*in Franciam*)," but, on second thoughts, he determined to enlarge on this yet further and introduced a much longer passage (it covers seven pages in the printed edition of the *Book of Llandaff*), consisting of a romantic story of a visit to Brittany. It is much the longest, most original and most characteristic episode in the whole book.

He begins by expanding Geoffrey's *celitus ammonitus* into an angelic vision, and then says:

> S. Teliaus arose, taking with him certain of his suffragan bishops and clergy of different ranks, with many others, both men and women, and went first to the region of Cornwall (*ad Cornubiensem regionem*), and was well received by Gerennius, the king of that country, who treated him and all his party with every mark of honour. And while they were enjoying his hospitality, King Gerennius spoke in homely fashion to S. Teliaus the bishop, saying: 'Father and Lord, I pray you to receive my confession and to be my confessor in the Lord.' And the pontiff consented, and received his confession, and made him a solemn promise . . . that he should not see death till he had first received the Body of the Lord consecrated by himself. After this the saint continued his journey, with his companions, and coming to the peoples of Armorica was well received by them. And when Samson, archbishop of the church of Dol, heard of the arrival of his old associate (*confratris sui*) in the country, he went to meet him rejoicing. For they had been born in the same region and were men of the same language, and had been instructed together

---

[50] A.D. 547. *Mortalitas magna fuit in Britannia in qua pausat Mailcun rex G[u]enedotae.*

[51] Misled by the *Ann. Camb.*, he says that Dubricius died in 612.

[52] His prayer is based on Joel ii. 17 (*perditionem* instead of *opprobrium*), together with a reminiscence of the second prayer at the benediction of the Ashes on Ash Wednesday.

under[53] the blessed Archbishop Dubricius, by the imposition of whose hands Saint Samson had been consecrated bishop, as we learn from his Life. And he asked S. Teilus to live with him. And Teliaus consented and abode with him for a long time and left there certain benefits due to his sanctity (*patrocinia suae sanctitatis*), namely the health-giving fountain called Cai, which his merits obtained from the Lord. And not only do many sick persons receive from it healing, in the name of God and of Teliavus, but a further striking manifestation of his miraculous power continues to be shown forth there even to this present day. For the Armorican sailors, when they are waiting for a favourable wind, are accustomed to clean out that health-giving fountain, and in this way constantly obtained from the Lord, by the intercession of the holy pontiff, the wind they desire. He also left in that country yet another benefit, which still reminds men of his sojourn there. For he and the aforesaid S. Samson planted a great grove of fruit-bearing trees, three miles long, reaching from Dol to Cai, and it is still called after them 'The orchard of Teliavus and Samson'. And ever since that time the prestige of the bishopric of Dol has been greatly increased among the Armorican Britons through the reverence paid to S. Teliavus.

Meanwhile the Yellow Pestilence had, by the mercy of Christ, ceased everywhere in the island of Britain. When the news of this arrived, the faithful leader Teliaus was exceeding glad and sent messengers to gather together the scattered exiles in France and Italy and wherever they had gone, in order that they might all return home, and he prepared three very large ships to transport them across the Channel.

The saint then proceeded to "the maritime port" (the name of which is not mentioned), amid the tears and lamentations of the Bretons.

The writer here inserts a long story, of a purely legendary character, which has all the appearance of an afterthought, clumsily added to a narrative previously completed. While Teilo is waiting at the port for a favourable wind, "behold, the king of the country, Budic by name, comes to meet him with a great army of Amoricans." They all kneel before him and beseech him to save their land from a huge viper, which has almost destroyed a third part of the kingdom. Encouraged by an angel, the saint then proceeds to deal with the viper in the

---

[53] *simul cum beato Dubricio.* The language in this section is affected and obscure.

traditional way and with his stole fastens him to a rock in the midst of the sea. The Armoricans then ask "the pontifex Samson" to persuade Teilo to remain with them, for fear the viper may renew its ravages. Teilo is unwilling to do so, but the angel again appears and bids him stay, telling him he will next day be offered the bishopric of Dol. He gives him a long and highly coloured account of what will happen (some of the details look as if they were borrowed from a fairy tale). The pontifex and the king and a great multitude of people will come to lead him to the episcopal see. He is to accept the offer and to remain at Dol for a time until the whole party of exiles is complete. The Armoricans will offer him a noble horse to ride on, but he is to refuse, for the angel himself will bring a magnificent horse from heaven, on which he is to ride to the bishopric of Dol. All this duly comes to pass on the following day. After his enthronement Teilo presents the celestial horse to the king and prays that the Armorican soldiers may always excel all others when mounted on horseback, and in this manner defeat their enemies and protect their native land. And this privilege, granted by S. Teilo, has, the author says, endured right down to the present day, as the writings of all their chroniclers testify. For the Armoricans are seven times more successful when mounted on horses than if they were fighting on foot.

The writer then comes back very awkwardly to the story of the return to Wales, which he begins all over again. One day the bishop S. *Teliaus* called to him his family, that is, the people (*plebem*) of his country, and reminding them of his promise to King *Gerennius* on the way to Brittany, said to them :

> Know ye, my children, that our king Gerennius is grievously afflicted with a painful disease . . . and will shortly depart from this life . . . Therefore prepare for us our ship

(the writer seems to have forgotten that *three* very large ships (*maximas*) had previously been prepared, which, it might be assumed, were still available). A large bark having accordingly been prepared, S. *Telius* entered into it, exactly seven years and seven months after his first coming to Armorica, accompanied by many learned teachers and certain other bishops, by whose labours the British nation might be renewed in holiness after the pestilence. They were much surprised when Teilo commanded them to bring with them a huge sarcophagus, which ten yoke of oxen could scarcely move, wherein to place *Gerennius*'s body. It was, however, by his direction cast into the sea before the prow of their ship and floated in front of them.

> As they were sailing and were half-way across the sea, another ship met them, and as the sailors of one were conversing with those of the other, a bishop sent by Gerennius announced that the king was dying but was awaiting the coming of S. Teliavus and the fulfilment of his promise. The two ships, sailing on together, arrived at the port called Dingerein [King *Gerennius*'s capital had not been named before]: and lo! the aforesaid stone, which had been cast into the sea, appeared between them. S.Teliavus went straight to where the king lay, and found him still alive. Having received the Lord's Body from his hand, the king departed unto the Lord. His body was carefully placed by his blessed confessor in the aforesaid sarcophagus, and commended to God. After this the holy man, accompanied by the clergy and people in great numbers, made his way back to his episcopal see[54], and abode there unto the end of his life.

The source of the story about King *Gerennius*, which plays such an important part in the *Vita Teiliavi*, has only recently been revealed, thanks to the discovery in 1912 by the late M. l'abbé Duine of a long-lost *Life of S. Turiau*, sixth bishop of Dol, in the public library of Clermont in Auvergne.[55] This manuscript is a thirteenth century copy of a *Vita Turiavi* which must originally have been composed at Dol in the second half of the ninth century. The forms of the personal names and place-names it contains are very archaic and it shows every sign of an early date. It contains a great deal of material not found in any other *Life* of the saint, including a story about a friend of *S. Turiau*, called *Geren*. In c. 9 we read :

> Now it came to pass that a certain friend of his, named Geren, whom he had beyond the sea, who rested after a spiritual manner in his love (*qui in ejus spiritaliter requiescebat visceribus*), had departed this life; and [one day] when the blessed Turiavus was, with the clergy and people, carrying crosses [in a procession], the saint

---

[54] Here ends the very long passage inserted by the reviser into the *Book of Llandaff*, which began on p. 108.
[55] He printed it in the *Bull. de la société arch. d'Ille-et-Vilaine* in that year (pp. 1-48).

lifted up his eyes and saw his soul being borne by angels, who were surrounded by malignant spirits. Calling for silence, he said: 'Pray, all of you, to the Lord for my friend, because I see him being borne by angels, and enemies following him.' And when they had all prayed . . . the demons were driven away from that soul. Then they launched a vessel in the sea, with the aid of sailors, to find out the truth about the miracle, and in the middle of the sea they met men who brought the news of the death of the friend of the man of God.

Now it is clear, I think, that we have here the origin of the similar story which we read in the *Life of S. Teilo*. The form of the name, *Geren*, latinized by the author of the *Book of Llandaff* as *Gerennius*, is precisely the same in both documents and seems to be found nowhere else. The meeting of the two ships in mid-channel is related in almost exactly the same words in the *Life of S. Teilo* and in the *Life of S. Turiau*. The author of the *Liber Landavensis* was obviously specially interested in Dol. He must have paid the little city a prolonged visit. He had seen the holy well at *Cai* (Carfantain[56]) and learned on the spot about the superstitious practices in use there to obtain favourable winds, and on the way he had observed the orchards which stretch up the valley from Dol to Carfantain. At Dol he had seen the *Vita Samsonis*, to which he refers in the *Vita Teiliavi* and of which he has made good use in his *Vita Dubricii*.[57] At Dol he must also have seen the *Vita Turiavi*. He has taken from it the incident of the death of *Turiau*'s friend *Geren*, and skilfully adapted it for his *Life of S. Teilo*. In the *Vita Turiavi* it is just a scrappy anecdote, badly introduced and badly told. In the *Vita Teliavi* it has been worked up into a coherent and attractive story. The phrase *qui in ejus spiritaliter requiescebat visceribus* is developed into an account of the relations between King *Gerennius* and the confessor S. Teilo.

Unfortunately the identity of this *Geren*, and the exact nature of the relations between him and *S. Turiau* are not at all clear. It is not even stated in the *Vita Turiavi* that he was a

---

[56] La Borderie suggested that *Cai* was *Lairgué*, which till the seventeenth century was spelt *Ergai* and *Argai*, near Carfantain, in a valley full of apple trees.

[57] Another hand has copied into the *Lib. Land.* his extracts from the *Vita Samsonis*.

king.[58] There was a chapel of *Saint Geran* in Dol cathedral and there is a parish of *Saint-Gerand* in Brittany between Loudéac and Pontivy, but no traditions about the saint have survived either there or at Dol. There is a parish called *Gerrans* on the south coast of Cornwall, where the eponym is a *S. Gerendus*,[59] whom tradition in the eleventh century described as a king.[60] It is probable that the author of the *Book of Llandaff* identified this Cornish *Gerent* with the Geruntius, king of Domnonia, to whom Aldhelm's famous letter was addressed in 705. He may have visited Gerrans and seen a large sarcophagus there. He says that the residence of King *Gerennius* was called *Dingerein*. No such place, however, can be found at Gerrans or anywhere else in Cornwall,[61] but it can be found in Wales, at the mouth of the Teifi, below the town of Cardigan (near which is a place called *Cilgerran*). It is possible that our author may have come across some tradition of Teilo and a Welsh king called *Geraint*. Having read the *Vita Turiavi* and visited, or heard of, Gerrans, he may have turned the Welsh king into a Cornish one.

The discovery we have made as to the source of the story told by the author of the *Liber Landavensis* about Teilo and *Gerennius* will throw light on other details in his account of Telio's visit to Brittany. It explains the otherwise amazing statement that Teilo became bishop of Dol. A further examination of the *Vita Turiavi* shows that *S. Turiau* was associated with the holy well mentioned in the *Life of S. Teilo*. This is the *Fontaine Saint-Samson*, north-east of the church of Carfantain.[62] Near it, standing by the side of the ancient way leading to the bishop of Dol's palace at Les Ormes, was a chapel of *S. Turiau*.[63]

---

[58] The author was familiar with Cornish traditions. He has an interesting reference to Constantine, king of Cornwall.

[59] *Gerendus* 1302, 1322, 1327, *Seynt Gerent* 1360.

[60] The Exeter martyrology says that a *filius regis Gerenti* was "healed by the merits of S. Berriona," the eponym of Veryan (the next parish to Gerrans). See Doble, *The Original Exeter Martyrology*, in *Ord. Exon.* (Henry Bradshaw Society, 1941), vol. iv, pp. 10, 34, 41, 42.

[61] See Doble, *S. Gerent* ('Cornish Saints' series, No. 41), pp. 17-19. *SC iii 86-88.] The name *Dingerein* now printed in the Ordnance Survey Map of Cornwall as that of a barrow in Gerrans is due to the influence of nineteenth century antiquarians misled by Dr. Whitaker.

[62] Banéat, *Le Département d'Ille-et-Vilaine* (Rennes, 1927), I. 518. The village of course owes its name to the fountain.

[63] ib. 519.

In c. 8 of the *Vita Turiavi* there is a story of how the saint went
by night to "a certain chapel by the well of the blessed Samson"
—clearly the same chapel. The author of the *Book of Llandaff*
had seen these places and he had found Samson and *Turiau*
honoured there together. He had also read at Dol the *Vita
Turiavi* with its story of *Geren*. The difference between the
names *Turiau* of Dol and *Teliau* of Wales is not very great, and
he jumped to the conclusion that they were the same saint.
He was not the only person who thought so. Geoffrey of
Monmouth, who was writing his *History of the Kings of Britain*
at this very time, tells us (Lib. ix. c. 15) that "in the place of the
holy Samson, archbishop of Dol, was appointed Theliau,[64] an
illustrious priest of Llandaff". Hitherto this statement has been
regarded as a purely gratuitous invention, no less ridiculous than
shameless. We see now how the idea arose. Whether it first
occurred to Geoffrey of Monmouth or to the writer of the
Liber Landavensis (as seems more probable) it is impossible to
say. But we can see why it was welcomed by the latter. It was,
as M. Loth has pointed out (op. cit., p. 74), "an answer to a
legend which the chapter of St. David's were trying to get
accredited. In a letter addressed to Pope Honorius (1125-1130)
they asserted, as we learn from Giraldus Cambrensis,[65] that
S. Samson had been archbishop of Menevia and had taken the
pallium of S. David with him to Dol." It is clear that our
author was much perplexed by the difficulties presented by his
story. He has invented the detail of Teilo's temporary
acceptance of the see of Dol in order to try to gloss over the
patent absurdity of his being bishop there in the lifetime of
S. Samson, though nobody will agree that he has succeeded in
his object. The incidents in this section are, indeed, so unconvincing that one wonders if they were really intended to be
taken seriously.

It is remarkable that Breton topography, as we shall see,
indicates the existence of an association of S. Teilo with
S. Turiau which can hardly be due entirely to the influence of the
Vita Teliavi.

---

[64] Mis-spelt *Chelian* in the English translation.
[65] *De Invect.* (*Opera*, iii. 59, 60). Geoffrey of Monmouth has a story of a
plague in Britain causing an emigration to Armorica (Bk. xii. cc. 15, 16).

Budic is not mentioned in the *Vita Turiavi*. This *Budic rex terrae* is not an historical character, but the name was a common one, especially in Brittany. Three counts of Cornouaille are said to have been called *Budic*. Our author was aware of this, and he begins his *Vita Oudocei* with a story of a Budic *natus de Cornugallia*—he seems to have taken him from the *Cartulary of Landévennec*. It is significant that there are several dedications both to Teilo and to Turiau in Cornouaille, and that the cult of S. Teilo is more deeply rooted there than anywhere else in Brittany, as we shall see.

The reference to the prowess of the Breton cavalry is one more proof of our author's knowledge of, and interest in, Brittany. He seems to refer to the decisive effect it exercised in the defeat of Charles the Bald at the battle of Ballon in 845.[66]

In conclusion, the use of the word *plebs* to describe Teilo's party of ecclesiastics and laity—both men and women, is interesting because of the light it seems to throw on the vexed question of the origin of the Breton *plous*. True, the *Vita Teiliavi*, as M. Largillière says,[67] is much too late for us to base on it an argument as to the circumstances of the Breton immigration six hundred years before. Still, this picture of a party of exiles, under the guidance of their clergy, crossing the Channel to find a new home in Armorica may possibly correspond to the facts. Plédeliau near Dinan certainly seems to be at any rate the settlement of a little Christian community from Carmarthenshire led by its priest.

"After this the holy man returned to his episcopal see [Geoffrey says "his native soil"], and remained there to the end of his life". The reviser here (at the words "remained there"[68]) returns to the text he is copying.

Geoffrey passes over the rest of the *Life* of S. Teilo very rapidly. He says that the saint "held dominion over all the

---

[66] Geoffrey of Monmouth also speaks of the efficiency of the Armorican cavalry and the author of *Vita Iltuti* begins his work with a panegyric on Brittany,—*provincia victoriosa, potens in armis*, etc.

[67] *Les Saints et l'org. chrét. prim. dans l'Arm. bret*, pp. 198-9.

[68] Geoffrey, instead of the long story we have dealt with, simply has a couple of sentences in which he says that "by God's mercy Eliud, the faithful leader, collecting the remnants of his nation, returned from exile to his native soil," etc.

churches of the whole of Southern Britain according to the tradition of the fathers who had consecrated him at Jerusalem. The nation, decimated by the pestilence, very quickly increased in numbers, because implicit obedience was rendered to all the saint's commands, and the holy church, so long dispersed, was, by the intervention of Teliavus, the most holy of the saints, exalted". He then hurriedly concludes his narrative. He does not mention the saint's death, but passes at once to the story of the dispute which followed it. The author of the *Liber Landavensis* has felt how awkward this abrupt transition is and has made a fresh long insertion, covering a whole page.

He tells us, first, that on his return he was joined by the former disciples of the blessed Dubricius, viz., *Iunapeius, Gurmaet, Cynmur, Toulidauc, Juhil, Fidelis, Hismael, Tyfhei, Oudoceus* and many others. Of these he consecrated *Hismael* bishop and placed him in charge of the church of Menevia, for S. David had since departed to the Lord (this is a final shot at the claims of Menevia to the primacy). He also made others bishops and assigned dioceses to them.

It is remarkable that none of these "disciples of Dubricius", except the first (and perhaps, the third), appear in the list of his disciples in the *Vita Dubricii*.

Gurmaet is the eponym of *Lann Guruaet, quae antea fuerat in primo tempore sanctorum Dubricii et Teliavi,* granted, with all its territory, by *August,* king of *Brecheniauc,* to S. Oudoceus.[69] It is mentioned again in the list of Teilo churches on p. 255 of the *Book of Llandaff.* It is now Llandeilo'r-Fân, west of Brecon. He must also be the patron of the *Ecclesia de Sancto Wormeto* which appears in the *Liber Landavensis* among the churches of the deanery of Nether Went paying annually *synodalia seu cathedratica* (p. 323), now Howick, near Itton (north-west of Chepstow).

Cynmur may be the eponym of the church of Bishopston in Gower, called in the *Book of Llandaff Ecclesia Cyngur Trosgardi* (p. 145) and *Monasterium Sancti Cinuuri* (p. 239), also of Llangynnwr, adjoining Carmarthen, and of Capel Cynnor in Pen-bre. (The next name, it is to be observed, is of a saint honoured in the town of Carmarthen.)

[69] BLD 154.

Toulidauc is the eponym of the *Lan Toulidauc ig Cair Mirdin*[70]
mentioned in the list of churches in the bull of Pope Innocent II
copied on p. 62 of the *Book of Llandaff* (all of them, except one,
being near Carmarthen).[71] The Augustinian priory of S. John
in the town of Carmarthen, which replaced this ancient Celtic
monastery, is called in its cartulary the 'Priory of S. John the
Evangelist and of S. Theulacus'.[72] The original monastery
(Llan *Teulydawc*) was one of the more important of the "seven
bishop-houses in Dyfed" mentioned in the Laws of Howel the
Good—its abbot had to be "graduated in literary degrees."

Juhil and *Fidelis* reappear in the charter in the *Book of
Llandaff* (p. 126) which grants *Tref Carn* and *Laith ti Teiliau* to
S. Teilo. The clerical witnesses to this charter are "Saint
Teliaus, Iouil and Fidelis his disciple". In the next charter
(*Cil Tutuc* and *Penn Clecir*) the clerical witnesses are again
Teliaus cum suis discipulis, Iouguil et Fidelis (this charter describes
the murder of *Typhei*, who is the next but one in this list of
"disciples of Dubricius and Teilo"). Nothing is known of either
of these two saints and neither has left any trace in Welsh
topography.

The names of *Hismael*, *Tyfhei* and *Oudoceus*, which
conclude the list, are a further proof that the additions to
Geoffrey's *Life* of S. Teilo are by the author of the *Book of Llandaff*.
They are all taken from his *Vita Beati Oudocei*, which was
clearly written after Geoffrey's *Vita S. Teiliavi* since it quotes
several pages from it verbatim. In the *Life of S. Oudoceus*
"Ismael and Tyfei, the martyr who lies at Pennalun", are the
children of *Budic*, count of Cornouaille, born during his exile in
Wales, while *Oudoceus* is their brother, born after *Budic*'s return
to Brittany. They are nephews of S. Teilo, their mother
Anaumed being Teilo's sister.

Hismael or *Ismael* (an older form would be *Osmail*) must
once have been a prominent figure in Welsh hagiography.

---

[70] Other forms of the full name will be found on pp. 124, 254, 287.

[71] Among the churches in this list is *Lann Isann* (also mentioned on pp. 56, 124
and 255), which is probably the *Eglwys Ysmael* found in the list of seven
bishop-houses in Dyfed, again as one of the more important. It will be
observed that *Hismael* follows closely in our author's list of disciples of
Dubricius and Teilo.

[72] LBS iv. 252.

He may have had a *Life*, which is now lost, and the entry *Sci. Ismaelis epi. et conf'* is found in the kalendar in Vesp. A. xiv on 16 June. We have already seen how he appears in the *Life of S. David* as one of the three chief disciples of that saint. He is patron of several churches in Carmarthenshire and Pembrokeshire; viz. Llan Ishmael near Cydweli; St. Ishmael's in Rhos, on the north side of Milford Haven (the *Eglwys Ysmael* of the "seven bishop-houses in Dyfed" already referred to); Camros and Rosemarket (also in the deanery of Rhos); and of Uzmaston, near Haverford (close to the last three parishes). It has been thought that he may have been the original patron of Haroldston St. Issels (adjoining Uzmaston).

Tyfhei is also taken, as we have seen, from the *Life of S. Oudoceus*. In the charter of *Cil Tutuc* (near Tenby), on p. 127 of the *Book of Llandaff*, there is a story of how "a certain infant named Typhei, the nephew of Saint Teliavus" was murdered by a "rich man" named *Tutuc*. This would of course make it impossible for *Tyfhei* to have been a disciple of S. Dubricius. No doubt it is a pure legend. *Tyfhei* is the eponym of Lamphey (formerly *Llandyfei*) between Tenby and Pembroke, and of Llandyfeisant in Dynevor Park, west of Llandeilo Fawr. The position of both these churches supports the tradition of their eponym being connected with Teilo. There was also formerly a chapel at Lampha in Ewenni (Glamorgan), called *Lan Tiuei* in the *Book of Llandaff* (p. 212).[73]

The writer then adds five stories of miracles worked by S. Teilo, "which we have learnt from written records".[74] Each is summarized in a single sentence. Three of them are stated to have happened at places in Carmarthenshire or Pembrokeshire whose names are given. In the case of the other two no names of persons or places are mentioned.

He had three beasts of burden, and they used to go to the forest without anyone to drive them, and, after being loaded by the woodcutters, they used to return in the same way of their own accord, and thus they served the brethren daily. For they say

[73] LBS iv. 290. Martletwy in Pembrokeshire (pronounced locally *Martel Twai*)=Merthyr Tyfai.

[74] *Nunc quae scripto cognovimus facta per eum miracula ea litteris et memoriae commendemus.*

that he raised to life by the river Couin[75] a dead man called
Distinnic. And they say that a paralytic was healed by him one
Sunday before all the people in the church of Radh,[76] and the sick
were cured of whatsoever disease they had by the imposition of his
hands. But those who were guilty of disrespect towards him
either died straightway, like the rash woman who sinned against
him and was liquefied before all the people, [the rest of the
sentence is missing].

Also a certain nobleman (*regulus*), named Guaidan, violated his
sanctuary (*refugium*) in a certain church of his, commonly called
Lanteliau Bechan,[77] and in consequence went raving mad and
died immediately a shameful death in the cemetery of the same
[church]. But those who acknowledged their fault forthwith
recovered health and pardon by his prayers.

It has been suggested that these stories came from a *Life*
of S. Teilo kept at the monastery of Llandeilo Fawr. This
might conceivably be true of the first. It is to be observed that
it contains a repetition of a theme already utilized in the story
of the two stags.[78] The two following are introduced by the
word *dicunt*. The fourth story is only referred to in the vaguest
language—the writer seems to have borrowed the expression
liquefacta est from the *Life of S. Cadog*.[79] The last is a local
legend, like the stories about *Distinnic* and the paralytic healed
in the church of Radh, and all three seem to belong to the class
of verbal traditions picked up by the author of the *Book of
Llandaff* in his travels through South Wales, of which we shall
have many examples in the charters dealing with Teilo churches
which will be examined later.

The *Vita* ends with the famous story of the multiplication
of the saint's body to satisfy the claims of three churches
connected with him. It was in Geoffrey's version, but the
author of the *Book of Llandaff* has added to and embellished

---

[75] R. Cywyn in Carmarthenshire.
[76] Amroth in Pembrokeshire, cf. BLD 124, 255, *Lan Rath et Lann Cronnguern
cum tribus territoriis Amrath*.
[77] *Lann Teliau Bechan in Difrin Teiui* is mentioned twice in the *Book of Llandaff*
(pp. 124 and 254). But Mr. J. G. Evans and Professor William Rees think
that Llandeilo Abercywyn is meant. There is a *Llanfechan* in Llanwenog
(Cardiganshire).
[78] BLD 102, *multo tempore post . . . ligna eis amministrabant*.
[79] c. 40, *conspectu totius exercitus liquefactus est, prout cera ante faciem ignis*.
The author of the *Vita Iltuti* has also copied this expression (c. 17), and so
has the writer of the *Vita Congari* (*Nova Legenda Angliae*, I. 253).

it, inserting several of his favourite ideas.   Numerous *Lives*
of Celtic saints contain stories of disputes following the death of
their heroes and of methods adopted for settling them—the
commonest being to place the body on a cart drawn by oxen
and leave them to take the direction they chose.   The claim to
possess the *whole* body reminds us, as M. Largillière has pointed
out,[80] that it was not the custom of the Celtic Christians to
disperse the bones of saints among different churches.   A similar
story was related by popular tradition of another Welsh saint.[81]
It is possible that there may have been more than one primitive
saint of Wales named *Eliud* or *Teilo* and that they were afterwards
amalgamated by hagiographers.   Our author tells us in his
Life of S. Oudoceus that that saint removed from *Lan Teliaumaur*
"some of the relics of the disciples of his uncle Teliau", and that
his action was resented by the natives.[82]   It is certain that
Llandeilo Fawr was robbed in more ways than one to benefit
Llandaff.   A possible explanation of the fact that Penally claimed
to possess the body of S. Teilo will be considered when we come
to deal with the saint's cult there.

   Teilo's death is not described.   The author of the *Liber
Landavensis* tells us, in the longer of the two passages he has
inserted here in Geoffrey's work, that it took place *super ripam
Tyui*,[83] i.e. at or near Llandeilo Fawr.   He also tells us, what
Geoffrey had omitted to specify, which were the three churches
whose clergy claimed his body, the first being *Penn Alun*, the
second Llandeilo Fawr (though he has accidentally omitted the
name, while giving the grounds for its claim), and the third
Llandaff, for five reasons which he proceeds to state.   Later on
he cannot refrain from inserting, after the story of how each party
carried home a body of S. Teilo, to the satisfaction of all
concerned, a definite assertion that "miracles proved that Teilo's
body was undoubtedly brought to Llandaff".   Geoffrey had
merely said that "at his tomb [he does not say *which*, but must

---

[80] op. cit., p. 143, (Note 24).
[81] *Lives of the British Saints*, i. 220 and iv. 237.
[82] BLD 135. *Also pp 217-9 of this volume.]
[83] *ibi vitam gloriose finierat*.   It is worth noting that someone has written in the
   margin of the *Book of Llandaff*, where *Finis territorii Lann Teiliau Maur*
   begins on p. 78, the words *ubi corpus Sancti Thelyai sepultum fuit*.

have meant that at Llandaff] the sick are frequently healed of all their diseases, the blind receive their sight and the deaf hear".

The *Life* then ends in the usual homiletic style.

The author of the *Book of Llandaff* has omitted the EXPLICIT VITA VENERABILIS *confessoris* THELIAWI with which Geoffrey had finished his work, and instead has inserted a sentence stating that in Teilo's time the church of Llandaff not only increased in holiness but was enriched by gifts from Welsh kings who were his contemporaries—he names seven.   This serves as a transition from the Life to the Charters which are to follow, several of the kings mentioned (*Idon* and *Aircol*) being the donors who sign them.   But first he inserts, in Latin and Welsh, "the Privilege of S.Teilo, which the aforesaid kings have granted to his church of Llandaff".   The Welsh of this document, says M. Loth is "a mixture of Old Welsh and Middle Welsh",[84] and "cannot be older than the end of the eleventh century or the first half of the twelfth".   As it stands, it obviously cannot have been granted by kings of Dyfed and Gwynedd to a Llandaff which probably did not exist in their time.   In fact it deals largely with the relations between "the king of Morgannwg", i.e. Glamorgan, and "the church of Llandaff and its bishops", and so presumes a political situation not very much older than the Norman Conquest.   But the point to notice for our present purpose is that throughout it identifies the cathedral and see of Llandaff with S. Teilo, as being *par excellence* the Llandaff saint, no other saint being mentioned in it.   It speaks of the "bishop of S. Teilo", "the lands of S. Teilo", "the people of S. Teilo" and "the *gundy* of Teilo at Llan Dav".

The author of the *Liber Landavensis* had placed the charters purporting to grant lands to Dubricius before his *Life* of that saint.   He has arranged the Teilo charters, however, after the *Vita Teiliavi*.   Unlike the Dubricius charters, a great number of them contain biographical details about the saint, handed down by local tradition,—often whole stories (one being of considerable length).

He begins with three charters dealing with Teilo churches in Monmouthshire.

---

[84] He says, "c'est une langue de transition, au point de vue orthographique".

The first relates how *Idon*, son of *Ynyr*, king of Gwent, granted "to the church of S. Peter of Llandaff and Archbishop Teilo" one of his houses, viz. *Lanngarth* [Llanarth], which had formerly belonged to S. Dubricius the archbishop, with all its territory and its sanctuary (*refugium*). The king, carrying on his back the gospel-book and accompanied by the clergy, bearing crosses in their hands and sprinkling holy water and dust from the pavement of the church and of the sepulchre (we are not told *whose* sepulchre), perambulated the boundaries. Four of the clerical witnesses appear in the list of the disciples of S. Dubricius in the *Vita Dubricii*.

In the next charter the same king grants *Lann Maur, id est Lann Teliau Porth Halauc*, "where Biuan with his four companions lie" with its sanctuary. Three of the clerical witnesses are the same as in the first charter.

The third is also a grant by King *Idon* and contains a story of how he defeated a Saxon invasion, thanks to the prayers of S. Teilo. He went to the saint, who was then abiding in his *podum* (monastery) of *Langarth*, with his clerks, and asked the aid of his prayers. Teilo came with him to a mountain in the middle of *Crissinic* by *Trodi* (the river Trothy), where he stood and prayed to Almighty God for His people who had been spoiled, and God gave them the victory. In gratitude the king granted to the saint the land surrounding the *cumulus* on which he had stood.

The writer here adds, without any introduction, a list of Teilo churches and estates. They are all in Carmarthenshire and Pembrokeshire. As Llandeilo Fawr is not mentioned among them, it looks as if the original list had been written there. After eight Carmarthenshire churches (all, except *Lann Toulidauc*, being called *Lann Teliau*), comes the heading *I Pennbro*, followed by the names of twelve churches in that district, including "Eccluis Gunniau, where S. Teliaus was born". After the heading *In Ros* come four churches, including *Lann Issan*.

The charter of *Mainaur Brunus* (Llandeilo Rwnws in Llanegwad, Carmarthenshire) relates how "Margetud, son of Rein, king of Dyfed, in a fit of passion slew Gufrir, a man of S. Teliau, in the saint's refuge, before his altar", and, in order to obtain pardon, gave to God and to *S. Teliau Mainaur Brunus*, with its church, fish and woods, together with *Telichclouman* and *Tref Canus*—all places near Llandeilo Fawr. It may have been copied from a document at Llandeilo Fawr resembling the *Book of St. Chad*. *Margetud* seems to be an historical character,[85] and the incident related may well be historical.

The remaining three sections belong to a different category. They are not really charters at all, but local legends, two of them about places near Penally and Tenby and one about Llanddowror, and are closely connected with the *Vita Oudocei* which follows. In all three of them *Aircol Lauhir*, son of *Tryfun*, king of Demetia, appears. We have met with him already in the list of royal benefactors of Llandaff, and shall find him again in the *Life of S. Oudoceus*. Unlike *Margetud*, he is not mentioned in the *Annales Cambriae*, but only in a Welsh pedigree of the tenth century.[86] He looks like a legendary figure of the type of *Grallon*, king of Cornouaille, who plays such an important part in the *Vita Winwaloei*.

Tref Carn, *Laith ti Teiliau* and *Menechi* are the only lands in this section mentioned in the list of Teilo estates just referred to, where they appear in the same order.[87] Our author tells us an interesting story about them. They were given to Teilo by *Aircol* in gratitude for his assistance in putting an end to drunken brawls among his soldiers and courtiers, which occurred nightly and always led to murders. "The king sent to S. Teliaus, who was then residing at his *podum* of Pennalun, asking him to come quickly to bless him and his court and to cause these constant murders to cease." Teilo came and gave his blessing and sent "his two disciples Iouil and Fidelis" to superintend the distribution of food and drink in the king's household. That night nobody was killed and the evil custom ceased. The king recognized that this was due to the prayers of S. Teilo and offered him the three estates *de propria hereditate sua*. Their bounds are given in Welsh. The clerical witnesses are *sanctus Teliaus testis, Iouil, fidelis discipulus suus*. Instead of the list of lay

---

[85] The death of *Morgetiud, rex Demetorum* is entered for the year 796 in the *Annales Cambriae*. He had a son called *Rein* (d. 808).

[86] In Harleian MS. 3859 he is the son of *Triphun map Clotri*, of the line of Constantius and Helen, and father of *Guortepir*, father of *Cincar*.

[87] BLD 124.

witnesses which usually follows that of the clerical witnesses, the words *testantibus rege Aircol cum suis principibus* are inserted before *De clericis*, etc. It is clear that the author of the *Liber Landavensis* added all this out of his own head.

The next story is an attempt to account for the name *Cil Tutuc*. It comes, we are told, from "a rich man named Tutuc", whose corn was ravaged by the pigs of a *Penn Alun* man. In a fury he killed with his lance "a certain infant named Typhei, the nephew of S. Teliaus". We have already pointed out the inconsistency of this legend with what is said about *Tyfhei* in the *Vita Teiliavi*, and have noted the fact that "Tyfei the martyr who lies in Pennalun" is found in the *Vita Oudocei*. *Tutuc*, we are told here, repented and asked Teilo's forgiveness, and by the advice of King *Aircol* he gave himself and his two *villae* of *Cil Tutuc* and *Penn Clecir* to Teilo and to the church of Llandaff. The clerical witnesses are again "Archbishop Teilo, with his disciples Iouguil and Fidelis". In this case the usual list of lay witnesses follows, beginning with King *Aircol*.

Finally, we have a long story to explain the origin of the name of an important Teilo church—Llanddowror, on the Taf near St. Clears in the west of Carmarthenshire. We are told that the *Dybrguyr . . . id est aquatici viri*, were the seven sons of a poor man of *Doucledif*[88] called *Cynguaiu*, born at one birth. The father in despair was pretending to drown them in the Taf at *Rytsinetic*, when (as he had foreseen) Teilo, at whose advice he had abstained from intercourse with his wife for seven years, happened to pass by. The saint rescued them and baptized them, and afterwards had them brought up "in his *podum* of Lanteliau, which by some is called after them Lanndyfrguyr [=The Monastery of the Watermen[89]] because they lived solely on seven fish taken out of the water and placed daily on a stone in the Taf called Lechmeneich [=The Monks' Stone], also because they were found in the water and escaped drowning in the water". On one occasion, when Teilo came to visit them, eight fish instead of seven were found on the stone. After a long

---

[88] *Cantref Dougledif*, now Daugleddyf in Pembrokeshire. (Index to BLD, p. 396).
[89] The place is called by both names on p. 254 of the BLD, *Lannteliau Lanndibrguir mainaur*.

sojourn in this place they lived for some time with blessed Dubricius, who sent them to their other place, which is called *Marthru*, in *Pepitiauc* [between Fishguard and St. David's], and there they are called "The Seven Saints of Mathru".[90] From whence they went to *Cenard Maur* [near Cardigan], where they lived for the rest of their lives. They bequeathed *Mathru* and *Cenarth Maur* to their holy patron and master *Teliavus* and to the church of Llandaff.

We have here a typical topographical legend. The author of the *Liber Landavensis* must have learnt it at Llanddowror. He has added some of his usual formulae to claim the churches mentioned for Llandaff. The real explanation of the name *Lanndyfrguyr*[91] may be that it was a daughter house of Mynyw, the monastery of 'David the Waterman'.[92] The mention of the stay of the seven Watermen "with blessed Dubricius" reminds us of the statement in one of the Dubrician charters (that of *Penn Alun*) that "Lan Maur on the bank of the Tyui with its two territories, where Teiliaus the *alumnus* and disciple of S. Dubricius lived, and the territory of the *Aquilentes* on the bank of the river Tam", was given to Dubricius by "Noe, son of Arthur", and the statement is repeated in the *Vita Oudocei*.[93] Our author must have found traditions of Dubricius surviving in the whole of this district.

It remains to examine the evidence afforded by Welsh and Breton topography.

The traces of the cult of S. Teilo are very widespread throughout South Wales. Few local saints have so many dedications. The industry of the late Dr. Fisher and other Welsh antiquaries has collected a very large number of them.[94] It is the most eloquent testimony to the real greatness of this

---

[90] The scribe spells the name in two different ways in the same sentence.
[91] There was another church of this name in Edeligion (Monmouthshire, the site is unknown), stated in the *Vita Cadoci* to have been given by that saint to S. *Doguuinnus* (c. 22). In the *Vita Kebii* (CBS 184; *VSBG 238]) it is said to have been given to *Kepius* by *Ethelic*. It may be *Capel* in Llangybi.
[92] It is to be observed that the name *Dubricius* is derived from *dwfr*='water'.
[93] BLD 133. *Also p. 217 of this volume.]
[94] See *Lives of the British Saints*, iv. 237-240. *Also Bowen, SCSW 56-58. Cf. also C. Lewis, *Llên Cymru* vii. 149, J. Conway Davies, EAWD i. 152-3.]

old-time leader of religion in Wales and to the extent of the
influence exercised by him, though, as we have seen, the true
story of his career and actions has perished.

There are twenty-one places called *Lann Teliau* in the
Book of Llandaff, besides several others containing his name with
some other prefix. It will be convenient to give these first,
printed in capitals, arranged according to the counties in which
they are situated, afterwards giving places in each county dedicated to Teilo which are not mentioned in the *Liber Landavensis*.

The centre of Teilo's evangelistic work was, as we have
seen, Llandeilo Fawr, on the river Tywi in Carmarthenshire.
LANN TELIAU MAUR is mentioned ten times in the *Book of Llandaff*,
the words *cum pertinentiis suis* or *cum duobus territoriis suis* being
frequently added. It is the place *ubi conversatus est Teiliaus
alumnus Sancti Dubricii et discipulus.*[95] It claimed his body at his
death *ob conversationem suam et solitariam vitam quam inibi duxit
per tempus super ripam Tyui, et quod ibi vitam gloriose finierat.*[96]
The bounds of the monastery land are given on p. 78. The
present parish church, standing on the site of his monastery, has
been rebuilt, except the tower. It contains the heads of two large
Celtic crosses. In the churchyard, east of the church, is the
ancient holy well called Ffynnon Deilo (now covered in), and
there are (or were) three other places in the parish called after
him; Carreg or Sedd Deilo (at Glynmeirch, on the edge of
Llandybie parish), Ynys Deilo and Maenor Deilo.

Somewhere in the valley of the Teifi was LANN TELIAU
BECHAN [=Little] IN DIFRIN TEIUI. LANN TELIAU MAINAUR
BRUNUS, now Llandeilo Rwnws, was on the Tywi between
Llandeilo Fawr and Carmarthen, in Llanegwad,—the stones of
the chapel have been used to build the modern farmhouse.
LANN TELIAU PIMPSEINT KAIR CAIAU, LANN TELIAU GARTH TEUIR
(now Capel Teilo in the parish of Talley, "on a farm called
Brondeilo, where, from under the hill hard by, gushes out
Pistyll Teilo"[97]) and LANN TELIAU NANT SERU were all on the
banks of the Cothi, a tributary of the Tywi from the north.[98]

---

95 BLD 77.
96 ib. p. 116.
97 LBS iv. 238.
98 *super ripam Cothi.* The reader will remark how often the writer notes that a
  Teilo church or estate is on the bank of a river.

LANN TELIAU LANNDIBRGUIR on the Taf and LANN TELIAU
APER COUIN on the Cywyn are in the south-west of Carmarthen-
shire—both rivers are the scenes of stories recorded in the
Liber Landavensis. LANN TELIAU PENN TYUINN is thought to be
Pendine, in the same neighbourhood, on the coast south of
Llanddowror.

S. Teilo is the patron of Brechfa[99] on the Cothi, and of
Trelech on the Cywyn. Llanpumsaint north of Carmarthen
is called, on Professor William Rees's map, *Llan Teilo Pumpsaint*,
and the Five Saints are the same as at the place of the same name
in Caeo already referred to.[100] Browne Willis mentions a
Llandeilo Welfrey in the deanery of Carmarthen, which may be
Castelldwyran under Cilymaenllwyd. There is a Capel Teilo in
Pen-bre, near Cydweli, of which the south wall still stands.[101]
Professor Rees's map shows a Ffynnon Deilo on a mountain
north-west of Llandeilo Fawr.

Pembrokeshire is full of places associated with S. Teilo.

First of all comes Penally, between Tenby and Caldy.
It was, after Llandeilo Fawr, the chief centre of his cult. Near it
was the traditional place of his birth.[102] It was the "place of
burial of his fathers", and he possessed hereditary rights there.[103]
The body of "the martyr Typhei", his nephew, "lay at Pennalun",[104] and the body of another saint, believed in the eleventh
century to be that of Teilo himself, was buried in its church.
A story related of him in the *Liber Landavensis* describes him as
"residing in his *podum* of Pennalun".[105] All round it were
estates asserted by the same authority to have been given him by
kings of Dyfed: such as LANN RATH HALANN CRONNGUERN
(i.e. Cronware, called in 1479 *Cornwere, alias dicta Landeylow*

---

[99] The author of *Lib. Land.* must have known of a place of this name, since he
inadvertently writes *Brecua* on p. 255 when he means *Brecheniauc*.

[100] We have an interesting parallel to this at Llan-gors, which contains a
Finnaun Doudec Seint and a *Lann i Doudec Seith*, while the parish is dedicated
to S. Paulinus, whose twelve disciples are mentioned several times in his *Life*.

[101] LBS iv. 239.

[102] BLD 124.

[103] ib. 116.

[104] ib. 130.

[105] ib. 126.

Gronewern)[106] "with the three territories of Amrath", in whose church he was said to have worked a miracle,[107] *Tref Carn*, LAITH TI TEILIAU and *Menechi*, LUIN TELIAU, which was "only a *villa*", and ECCLUIS GUNNIAU (*Luin Teliau* is Trefloyne near Penally, close to which is a field called Castle *Gwynne*).[108]   It is clear that there was once an important monastery at *Penn Alun*. Two charters in the *Liber Landavensis* purporting to grant land to S. Oudoceus are signed by an abbot of *Penn Alun* called *Guencat*, *princeps Aluni Capitis* (a latinization of *Penn Alun*), who signs after the abbots of the three chief monasteries of Glamorgan. There was a tradition that both Dubricius and Teilo had lived here, and the explanation of the story that Penally claimed to possess the body of Teilo may be that the body of an unknown saint was venerated in the church[109] and that the Teilo tradition was so strong there that an idea arose, and was finally accredited, that it was *his* body. For some reason, of which we are ignorant, the monastery of Penally ceased to flourish and finally disappeared, and with it the cult of S. Teilo at Penally. The dedication of the church is now unknown.

There was another very important centre of the cult of S. Teilo in Pembrokeshire—at LANN TELIAU LITGARTH IN DOUCLEDIF (=Daugleddyf). It is the fifth in the list of the "seven bishop-houses in Dyfed" in the Laws of Howel the Good, and one of the more important ones—"the abbot of Teilaw should be an ordained scholar". It is in the parish of Maenclochog. In 1898 the Cambrian Archaeological Association visited "the ruined chapel of Llandeilo, close by which is St. Teilo's well and a farmhouse, in which a skull—traditionally called *Penglog Teilo*—has been kept from time immemorial."[110]

---

[106] *Chronicon Monasterii S. Albani*, ii. 192.

[107] BLD 115, 116.

[108] For this, and for "the three territories of Amrath", see *Royal Commission on Ancient Monuments in Wales, Inventory of Pembrokeshire*, pp. 5, 6.

[109] We have an interesting parallel in the story of the body of the unknown saint in S. Iltut's cave at Llwynarth in Gower (*Vita Iltuti*, c. 22, Nennius, *Hist. Brit.* c. 71).

[110] "The family in whose possession the skull has remained (it may be for centuries) is named Melchior. It is of a dark colour, and polished by continual handling . . .   It is used as a cup for drinking water from St. Teilo's well . . . Mrs. Melchior remembered being taken to the well and made to drink water from it when, as a little girl, she suffered from whooping-cough. She said that many people used to come up there from

It is really the skull of a young person, and is "probably a pre-Reformation relic". There are two ancient inscribed stones in Llandeilo churchyard. After *Lann Teliau Litgarth* comes, in the list of churches and estates belonging to Teilo on p. 124 of the *Book of Llandaff*, LANN TELIAU CILRETIN IN EMLYN. This is Cilrhedyn, the most easterly parish in Pembrokeshire. Earlier in the list is mentioned LANN TELIAU LUIN GAIDAN, described as "a *villa* only, in Euelfre". These last words indicate the position of this estate. It must have been in the parish of Llanddewi Felffre, east of Narberth and near the Teilo church of Cronware, where there is a place called Henllan. It has been suggested[111] that LANN TELIAU TREF I CERNIU in the list I have referred to may have been in Crinow, near Narberth, the dedication of which is unknown. In the parish of Crinow is a holy well, called *Ffynnon Deilo* in the Tithe Schedule. It rises in the field "directly S. of Llwyn Gwathan farmstead, on the boundary line between this parish and that of Llanbedr Velfrey. Traditions of its healing powers are still current in the district, and a number of place-names testify to the former popularity of the spring".[112]

The *Liber Landavensis* contains references to four places in Glamorgan called after S. Teilo.

The list of churches in the bull of Calixtus II[113] mentions, first, SANCTI TEILIAUI DE MERTHIR MYUOR[114], now Merthyr Mawr, near Bridgend. The stepping-stones across the Ogmore here were called *Stepsau Teilo*. Next to it comes SANCTI TEILIAUI DE LANN MERGUALT, where there was a monastery of *S. Cinuur*.[115] It is now *Llandeilo Ferwallt* or Bishopston in Gower. The site of

---

Haverfordwest, and more distant places, on horseback." AC xv, 1898. It is to be observed that there are three inscribed stones in Llandysilio churchyard, south of Maenclochog, and the famous 'Votipore' stone was discovered in Castelldwyran churchyard (already mentioned), close to Llandysilio (cf. p. 24). The persons commemorated on these stones may have been contemporaries of Teilo.

[111] BLD 409.

[112] *Royal Commission on Ancient Monuments in Wales. Inventory of Pembrokeshire*, p. 84.

[113] BLD 90.

[114] For the name *Myuor* see Doble, *S. Gudwal*, p. 19.

[115] BLD 239. Such names as *Lann T. de Lann Mergualt* may indicate that the cult of S. Teilo has superseded an older cult.

LANN TEILIAU PORTULON seems to be Caswell Chapel in Bishop-.
ston,—it was therefore closely connected with the last-named
church.   LANN TELIAU TALYPONT was a *villa*, now Llandeilo
Tal-y-bont, on the river Llwchwr, north of Gower. At Llandaff
is a small Celtic cross (*Croes Deilo*), and a *Ffynnon Deilo* on the
steep hill near the cathedral. The legend of the butter washed
in this well and changed into a gilt bell which was preserved in
Llandaff cathedral in the Middle Ages, related by the author of
the *Liber Landavensis* and by him ascribed to S. Oudoceus, is
ascribed to S. Teilo in the Middle English metrical *Life* of
S. Teilo in the British Museum (Egerton MS. 2810)[116]

> a maide clene
>
> clansede her boter. bi a welles streme
> sein telyou her bed. him zuf drink anon
>
> ....
>
> & in forme of a belle. ye boter togader clonge
>
> ....
>
> in ye churche of landaf. thulk uessel is.

There is a figure of Teilo over the great west door of the cathedral.
'S. Teilo's Tomb' is on the south side of the presbytery; solemn
oaths were taken *super tumbam S. Theliawi*. Till the Reformation
his silver shrine was in the Lady Chapel, on which was a statue
of the saint.[117]

The three Teilo churches in Monmouthshire mentioned in
the *Liber Landavensis* have been dealt with already. They are
now respectively Llan-arth, Llantilio Pertholey and Llantilio
Crossenny (Llandeilo Bertholau, Llandeilo Gresynni). As the
second of these bore the alternative title of LANN MAUR, it must
have been the chief of the little group.

In Breconshire Llandeilo'r-Fân, on the site of *Lann Guruaet*,
has already been mentioned. Teilo is also, with David and
Llywel, the patron of the church of Llywel in the same county.

---

[116] This manuscript is "an early 14th century copy of the South English
Legendary (which is generally supposed to have been put together by monks
of Gloucester towards the end of the 13th century). It is the only copy
which contains the *Life* of S. Teilo. Gloucester held various churches in
S. Teilo's diocese." (Note kindly sent me by Mr. Robin Flower). There is
a Ffynnon Deilo in the parish of Pendeulwyn (Pendoylan), east of Cowbridge.
*Cf. also 'Saint Oudoceus', pp. 219-20 of this volume.]

[117] LBS iv. 241-2.

He is the eponym of Llandeilo Graban in Radnorshire, and the
patron of Llanfechan in Llanwennog in Cardiganshire.

The festival of S. Teilo is found on 9 February in the
kalendar in Vesp. A. xiv. and later Welsh kalendars, including
that of Tewkesbury abbey. A fair called 'Ffair Wyl Deilo' was
held at Llandaff and at Llandeilo Fawr on that day (it is still held
at the latter place on 20 February). On this day the treasurer of
Llandaff cathedral received the oblations made there.

The study of the cult of S. Teilo in Brittany is of special
interest, in view of the important place occupied in his *Life* by
the story of his visit to Dol.

Cornouaille is the district which has the greatest number of
churches dedicated to him and where his cult is most deeply
rooted.[118]

He is the eponym and patron saint of Landeleau (spelt in
the cartulary of Quimper *Ecclesia Sancti Deleui* in 1220 and
Landeleu in 1313, *Lanteleau* 1368), on the Aulne, east of
Chateauneuf-du-Faou. It is here that he is best remembered
by the people. Popular tradition explains the great size of the
parish by a story that the seigneur of Landeleau proposed to
S. Teilo that the boundaries should embrace all the land he
could go round between sunset and cockcrow. The saint chose a
stag as the swiftest mount on which to travel, and so covered a
considerable distance in the time, to the surprise of the seigneur,
who, however, kept his word.[119] Hence statues of the saint (such
as that in the évêché at Quimper) and the picture of him in
ancient stained glass at Plogonnec, represent him in cope and
mitre, carrying his staff and riding on a stag. A famous *troménie*
(procession) follows each year the course he took, starting at
7 a.m. and finishing at 5 p.m.[120] A halt is made at 'S. Elau's

---

[118] "Thélo, Edern and Herbot are the three great saints of the *Montagne* of
Cornouaille" (L. Le Guennec, *La Légende de Saint Edern*, in *Vieux souvenirs
bas-bretons*, 1938.)

[119] Duine in *Rev. des. trad. pop.*, 1905, pp. 283, 399.

[120] A very interesting article by a distinguished antiquary and scholar, the late
Canon Peyron of Quimper, entitled *La Légende de S. Theleau et la troménie
de Landeleau*, was printed in the *Mém. de l'association bretonne* (Congrès de
St-Brieuc) in 1906. Cf. also Anatole Le Braz, *Les Saints bretons d'après la
tradition populaire en Cornouaille*, 1937. c. 4. Duine was told "The Troménie

Tree', where a sermon is preached. There are several other places in the parish to which his name is attached : a dolmen is called 'Ty Sant Heleau', two fields are called respectively 'Parc Sant Elau bras' and 'bihan', and there is a 'Goarem Sant Elau'. In the church is a sarcophagus, formerly in the church-yard, with which a local legend about him was connected, referred to in the seventeenth century (though it must be much older) by Albert Le Grand, in his *Vie de S. Yves* [1253-1303]. He says :

> On one occasion, when, in the same chamber with a man named Maurice du Mont, he was sleeping in the bourg of *Land-Elleaw*, in Cornouaille, the latter was wakened by a voice which told him that the saint was lying on the cold stone, and finding Saint Yves was not in the room, he went out to the churchyard and found him there in the stone [coffin] in which Saint Elleaw had done his penance.

15 kilometres south-west of Landeleau is the parish of Leuhan, of which S. Théleau is patron, according to the 1935 *Ordo* of Quimper (p. 31).[121]

16 kilometres east of Landeleau, but still in Cornouaille, in the parish of Plévin, is a village called Landêliau, where there was a chapel, which fell into ruins about 1880. Now it is remarkable, in view of the confusion of S. Teilo with S. Turiau made, as we have seen, by the author of the *Liber Landavensis*, that the patron saint of this chapel was S. Turiau, whose aid was invoked against fever, and the pardon was on his festival, 13 July.[122] It is very significant that at Plogonnec, also in Cor-nouaille (north-west of Quimper), where the eponym is the Welsh saint Cynog[123], the parish church is dedicated to S. Turiau,

is so important that all the Saints attend it, though they are rarely seen. On one occasion a peasant who was on his way to market, instead of attending the Troménie, met S. Anne and S. Joachim and asked them where they were going. They replied, 'Why, to the Troménie of Landeleau, of course' ". A *gwerz* in honour of the saint is sung during the procession.

[121] The statements in *Lives of the British Saints*, iv. 234, that he is patron of Châteauneuf-du-Faou (where Baring-Gould says he has a statue) and of Lennon, seem incorrect. The diocesan *Ordo* gives St. Julien as the patron of the former place and says Lennon is dedicated to the Trinity. The information about the cult of Teilo in Brittany in LBS needs checking before it can be relied on.

[122] Duine, *Vie antique et inédite de S. Turiau*, Rennes, 1912, pp. 22 and 23.

[123] Llangynog adjoins Llandeilo Abercywyn in Carmarthenshire, cf. Doble, *S. Winnoc*, pp. 17, 18, 60. *Toquonocus* was one of the disciples of S. Paul (Paulinus) of Léon.

while there is a large and beautiful chapel of S. Teliau in the parish. Further, just south of Plogonnec is the parish of Guengat, in which is a granite 'Chair of St. Délo', in which fever patients are placed.[124]   Now it surely cannot be a mere coincidence that the *Liber Landavensis* shows us a *Guencat* abbot of Teilo's monastery of *Penn Alun* in the time of S. Oudoceus.[125] He may have been the founder of Guengat church, and have introduced the cult of St. Teilo in this part of Brittany.

Teilo is also patron of St.-Thélo (in 1181 *San Theliaut*) on the Oust, north-west of Loudéac. Not far away, in Noyal, there is (M. Couffon tells me) a place called St-Theleu. As Saint-Gerand is the next parish this dedication might be due to the influence of the *Vita Teliavi*. The name of Monterthelot (also on the Oust) may perhaps be derived from *Monasterium Teiliavi*.

M. Loth considers Saint-Hilio in Saint-Pabu (in Léon) to be dedicated to our saint.[126]

There is a Lande-de-Saint-Eliau in the parish of Bubry, (not far from Lorient, in the extreme west of the Dep. of the Morbihan), with a village of the same name.

Finally, there is the parish of Plédéliac[127] (*Pludeliau* 1219, 1234, *Pludelia* 1248, 1298, *Pledelia* 1286), west of Dinan, not far from St-Thélo. The next parish is Landébia. Again, it cannot be a mere coincidence that Llandybie adjoins Llandeilo Fawr in Carmarthenshire exactly as Landébia adjoins Plédéliac in Brittany. Our study of Breton place-names shows that there have certainly been emigrations from Wales to both Cornouaille and north-east Brittany. The author of the *Liber Landavensis* found the cult of S. Teilo firmly established in both districts in the twelfth century—he seems to have got the story of *Budic natus de Cornugallia*, with which he begins the *Vita Oudocei*, from the list of the counts of Cornouaille in the *Cartulary of*

---

[124] Diverres, *La commune de Guengat* in *Bull. de la soc. arch. de Finistère*, T. xviii, 1891.   The same *Bulletin* in 1900 described the Chapelle St. Théleau in Plogonnec.

[125] cf. p. 200. BLD 149.

[126] *Noms des ss. bretons*, p. 117.

[127] The final *c* is not sounded. The church is now dedicated to S. Malo. (Landébia, which possesses a holy well of S. David, was an enclave of Dol). Between Plédéliac and Pleneuf are two adjacent parishes dedicated to S. Alban and S. Aaron, whose cult must have been brought from Gwent.

Landévennec.[128]   It is possible that Teilo, like his master Paulinus (Paul) of Léon,[129] may have laboured in Brittany.   It is possible, too, that daughter establishments of his monasteries, and perhaps even whole communities surrounding them, forced for some reason to leave Wales, may have carried his cult to Brittany at a later (but still early) period.   Such communities may even have taken with them the names of the places from which they came and given them to their new homes.[130]   In any case the connection between Brittany and Carmarthenshire is evident.[131]

---

[128] In the line which follows the names *Budic et Maxenri, duo fratres*, comes an enigmatic entry, *Iahan Reith.   Huc rediens Marchel interfecit et paternum consulatum recuperavit.*

[129] *Paule* adjoins Plévin.   Cf. p. 204.

[130] Besides Landébia, we have interesting examples of Welsh place-names in Brittany at Langolen, Lanedern, etc.

[131] For *Llandyfân*, in the parish of Llandeilo Fawr, see Loth, *Noms*, pp. 31, 32, 131.   Rosenzweig, *Dict. Top.* and *Dép. du Morb.*, also Duhem's *Églises du Morbihan.   Merthyr Dyfan* in Glam. lies between Nantcarfan and *Cadox*ton, while Llan*dyfân* is near Llan*gadog.*   There is a *Llandefand* in *Llanmartin* in Monmouthshire, while the parish church of *Landevant* in Brittany (on the Sea of Etel, which contains the famous island monastery of *S. Cadoc*) is dedicated to *S. Martin.*   See LBS ii. 394. *Note *A Gazetteer of Welsh Place-names* (Cardiff, 1957), p. 58, where the name of the Monmouthshire parish appears as *Llandevaud.*   On *Merthyr Dyfan* see Pierce, *The Place-names of Dinas Powys Hundred* 133-5.]

SAINT OUDOCEUS[1]

A GREAT deal of the work which has been done in the realm of Celtic hagiography up to the present day has been of little value because the *Lives* of Saints which have come down to us have been taken as real biographies, containing narratives which, after eliminating passages that are obviously absurd and others in which the writers contradict each other (and often themselves), may be regarded as statements of fact. We are beginning to realize that to do so is pure waste of time. These *Lives* were written centuries after the period in which the saints lived, when the true story of what they did had been almost entirely forgotten. As they stand, they are not historical. But if we treat them primarily as literary problems and try to see how and why their writers put them together, we shall not be labouring in vain; we shall obtain some valuable evidence about the church and people in Celtic countries in the early Middle Ages, and we may even indirectly learn something about the Age of the Saints.

The *Vita Oudocei* (taken together with the charters appended to it), which follow the Teilo section in the *Liber Landavensis*, is a case in point. The famous 'Book of Llandaff', an anonymous compilation made by one of the clerks of the energetic Bishop Urban (d. 1133), is a great *plaidoyer* in favour of the claims put forward by the see of Llandaff as recently reorganized by the Normans. The author uses charters and other documents, which he cuts up, alters, and adds to, and supplements by local traditions he has found. And, like other authors of medieval cartularies, he prefixes to his collection *Lives* of the chief saints honoured in his church. Two of the greatest names in the ecclesiastical history of South Wales, Dubricius and Teilo, had already been claimed for the see of Llandaff, and in the *Lives*

---

[1] *Published in *The Journal of Theological Studies* xliii (1942), 204-16, xliv (1943), 59-67.]

he provides for them, consisting of local legends, with plagiarisms from *Lives* of other saints, and many fancies of his own, he enhances the prestige of the diocese by calling them 'Archbishops'. Not content with this, he adds one more saintly name he has found honoured with a cult in the diocese, and gives us a *Vita Beati Oudocei, Landavensis Archiepiscopi*, which will now be critically examined. I hope to show that the 'Saint Oudoceus' it presents to us is a creation of the author of the *Book of Llandaff*, in which legends about two or three different characters, and some documents about one of them, have been, not very skilfully, woven together. But these legends have thereby been preserved for us, and some of them are of considerable interest and charm.

The opening section of the *Vita Oudocei* is closely related to the pages which precede it in the *Liber Landavensis*, and contains, not only several characters we have already met with and incidents already recorded, but one whole passage copied word for word from the *Vita Teiliavi*.[2]

The writer plunges straight into his subject, as in the *Vita Dubricii*, without any kind of introduction whatever, and begins thus :

There was a certain man called Budic, the son of Cybrdan, born in Cornugallia, who came to the region of Demetia in the time of Aircol Lauhir, king of that realm, with his fleet, having been expelled from his own country. While he tarried in the land, he took as wife a woman named Anauued, daughter of Ensic[3] and her mother was Guenhaf the daughter of Liuonui. Of this Anaumed (sic) were born to him two sons, Ismael and Tyfei—the martyr who lies in Pennalun. While he tarried in the land, messengers were sent to him from his native country of Cornugallia, praying him to return without delay, with all his *familia*, and, with the help of the Britons, receive the kingdom of the Armorican nation. For, since their king was dead, they desired to have a scion of the royal line to rule over them. As the request was unanimous, he accepted the offer gladly, and, taking with him his wife, who was pregnant, and all his *familia*, he embarked, and,

---

[2] BLD 131 : *Flaua quidem* . . . *ad interitum*. It is copied from the *Vita Teiliavi* written by Geoffrey Stephen, brother of Bishop Urban.

[3] Teilo's father *Ensic* is called *Eussyllt* (which seems to be the Latin *Auxilius*) in the collection of pedigrees of the Welsh saints called *Bonhed Seint Kymry* (Peniarth MS. 45), written in the late thirteenth century. *See now Bartrum, EWGT 55.]

arriving in his own country, reigned over the whole land of Armorica, which then reached to the Alps. And his wife gave birth to a son, named Oudoceus, whom, as soon as he was old enough, he sent to study letters [we are not told exactly where], for he had previously, while in Britain, promised Saint Teilo that, if he had a son, he would give him to God, as he had already given his two brothers, of whom we made mention. And Saint Oudoceus began, while still a child, to be enriched with learning and eloquence, so that he excelled all his companions in goodness and holiness. And after a long time the Yellow Pestilence came and raged throughout Greater Britain.

Here the writer gives the description of the pestilence in the *Vita Teiliavi*. Then, after stating that "its violence was at last assuaged by the prayer of S. Teilo and of the saints of Britain", he tells us :

A divine voice came to Saint Teilo, bidding him go, with his clerks and people, to Cornugallia, which was afterwards called Cerniu Budic. And there he found his nephew Oudoceus, already famous, but humble and gentle, and learned in both the Old and New Law, *like a candle upon a stand*.[4] And after his stay there was ended, S. Teilo, the archbishop of the church of S. Peter the apostle of Llandaff, returned to his native soil,[5] accompanied by his nephew, who increased so greatly in piety and learning that he was finally chosen to succeed him in the bishopric of the church of Llandaff, by the election of the clergy, Mercguin and Elgoret and Gunnuin the master; and of the three abbots— Catgen, abbot of Ildut [now Llantwit Major], Concenn, abbot of Catmail [i.e. Llancarfan, founded by S. Cadog], Cetnig, abbot of Docguinn [now Llandough or Llandochau, near Cardiff]; and of the laity, viz. King Mouric and his sons Athruis and Idnerth, Guidgen and Cetiau, Brocmail, Gendoc, Louhonerd, Catgualatyr, and all the nobles (*principum*) of the whole diocese (*parrochia*).

We have already made the acquaintance of *Budic* in the long story added by the author of the *Book of Llandaff* to Geoffrey

[4] Matt. v. 15.
[5] It is worth observing that the phrase *rediit ad natale solum* is copied from Geoffrey Stephen's original account of Teilo's return from exile, not from the expanded version by the author of the *Book of Llandaff* (who has *repetivit sedem suam episcopalem*), which looks as if the latter wrote the *Vita Oudocei* before he added the story of Teilo's stay in Brittany to the *Vita Teiliavi*. In my study on 'S. Teilo' I have given the reasons which prove that the shorter *Life* of Teilo in Vesp. A. xiv, *a Magistro Galfrido* (*i. Stephano* interlined) *fratre Urbani Landavensis ecclesiae episcopo dictata*, must be regarded as the original, to which the author of the *Liber Landavensis* has made a great number of significant additions—one of immense length.

Stephen's original version of the *Vita Teiliavi*, but there he appears at Dol in the extreme east of Brittany, far from Cornouaille; he is described as *rex terrae, Budic nomine*, and Cornugallia is not mentioned. Here he is *natus de Cornugallia*, and Teilo emigrates to Cornouaille,[6] not to Dol. The first two pages of the *Vita Oudocei* are a proof of the existence of literary intercourse between Wales and Cornouaille in the twelfth century, but the inaccuracy of some of the statements made seems to indicate a very imperfect knowledge of Breton history. The writer apparently considers Cornouaille as identical with Brittany (later, on p. 181, he speaks of "the archbishop of Dol in Cornouaille"), instead of being only a part of the duchy, and he is of course quite mistaken in thinking that Armorica ever reached to the Alps. But he does seem to have had some knowledge, direct or indirect, of certain early traditions of Cornouaille. The story of *Budic*'s exile must be based on a story briefly referred to in the list of the counts of Cornouaille. This list is found, in slightly varying forms, in the cartularies of Landévennec,[7] Quimper,[8] and Quimperlé.[9] Three of the counts there enumerated bear the name of *Budic*, and of the first we read that "he returned and slew Marchel and recovered his father's dominion".[10] The third *Budic (Budic Bud Berhuc)* in the Landévennec list follows a count called *Diles Heirguor Chebre*.[11] Is it possible that our author's *Cybrdan* may be an imperfect reminiscence of this name ? In any case the *Vita Oudocei*, in making *Budic* a ruler of Cornouaille, is more accurate than the *Vita Teiliavi*. The assertion that Cornouaille was once called *Cerniu Budic* is of great interest. Although we have no other authority for this statement it may be based on an ancient tradition. Not only was *Budic* (as we have seen) a favourite

---

[6] *ut iret . . . Cornugalliam.*

[7] pp. 172-3 in La Borderie's printed edition (Rennes, 1888).

[8] Ed. by Peyron, Quimper, 1909, pp. 6 and 7.

[9] Ed. 1904, pp. 89-91.

[10] *paternum consulatum recuperavit.* In no version of the list, however, is Wales mentioned, and those of Quimper and Quimperlé state that it was *ab Alamannia* that *Budic* returned, with his brother, *Maxenri*. That of Landévennec says that *Budic*'s father was *Alamannis rex*. For some useful remarks on the Quimper list see La Touche, *Mélanges d'histoire de Cornouaille* (Paris, 1911), pp. 72-77.

[11] *Kembre* in the Quimper and Quimperlé lists.

name for the counts of Cornouaille, but it appears in a good many of the place-names of Cornouaille in the cartulary of the abbey of Landévennec. Charter No. XVII mentions *Budic* near Goezec; No. XIX the *Locus Sancti Uuingualoei in Buduc*; No. XLIII, granted by Diles, mentions *Buduc Les Buduc* (Nos. XXXVI, XLII, XLV, and XLVI are all grants by *Budic, comes Cornubiensis*).

Aircol Lauhir (='The Long-armed')[12] is another link between the Teilo and the Oudoceus sections of the *Liber Landavensis*. He is mentioned among "the kings who lived in the time of S. Teilo" in the appendix to the *Vita Teiliavi*; the charter on pp. 125, 126, dealing with places near Tenby and Penally, begins '*Regnante Aircol Lauhir, filio Tryfun, rege Demeticae regionis*'; and both the charters that follow refer to him. I have shown[13] that he is a legendary rather than an historical character, though there may have been a Demetian king of that name. *Ismael* and *Tyfei* also figure in the *Life of S. Teilo*[14] and in the charters which follow it, and in the topography of Carmarthenshire and Pembrokeshire. Our author, in all probability, found local traditions (of doubtful authenticity) stating that each of these saints was a 'nephew of S. Teilo'—the chief saint of the neighbourhood (the stories about them having a strong legendary flavour). We observe at the same time that, while there was certainly a cult of Ismael and Tyfei, there are no traces of any cult of Oudoceus in Demetia.

The sentence describing the election of Oudoceus to succeed S. Teilo leads to a new section of the writer's work, in which he skips several centuries. It is true that the first three names of *clerici* who elect the new bishop are taken from the list of 'disciples of S. Dubricius' in the *Vita Dubricii*,[15] where they appear in the same order, because our author wishes to connect Oudoceus, not only with Teilo, but also with Dubricius, as the three saints of the church of Llandaff. But with the names that follow we are transported to the diocese of Glamorgan as it

[12] *Aircol* is from the Latin *Agricola*. He is not found in the *Annales Cambriae*.
[13] *S. Teilo*, Lampeter, 1942. *See now pp. 193, 195-6 of this volume.]
[14] In the *Vita Teiliavi* they are 'disciples of S. Dubricius' who join Teilo after his return from Brittany.
[15] BLD 80.

began to take shape four hundred years later. 'The three abbots
of Llantwit, Llancarfan (properly Nantcarfan), and Llandochau,[16]
who are now to be so often mentioned in the *Book of Llandaff*,
here appear for the first time. Then follow the names of the
laity joining in the election, after which S. Oudoceus was sent,
with his clerks aforesaid—*Merchui* and *Elguoret* and *Gunnbiu*, and
with the delegates of the three abbots and of the king and the
nobles, to Canterbury,[17] to the blessed archbishop [whose name
is not given], where he was consecrated bishop of the church of
Llandaff founded in honour of S. Peter. On his return King
Mouric, with his two sons and his wife *Onbraus*, daughter of
Gurcant Magnus,[18] and the three abbots of the three monasteries
(*cenobitarum*), received him with joy. The king confirmed to
him the privilege granted before to S. Dubricius and S. Teilo,
and there was a solemn procession around the *confinium* [of
Llandaff], the king holding the Four Gospels in his hand,
preceded by the holy cross and the holy choir following, the
summus pastor intoning the psalms *Fiat pax* . . . *turribus tuis*,
Gloria et diuitiae.[19] The 'privilege given to S. Dubricius' and
the right of sanctuary at Llandaff are again referred to, and it is
stated that "as the Roman church exceeds the dignity of all the
churches of the Catholic faith, so the church of Llandaff by right
exceeds all the churches of the whole of South Britain in dignity
and privilege and excellence".

The story of the election and consecration of Oudoceus is
modelled on the procedure observed in the tenth century, when
the diocese of Glamorgan, not yet bearing the name of Llandaff
(except in the pages of the *Liber Landavensis*), had already become,
or was becoming, under the growing political influence of the
Saxon kings and ecclesiastical influence of Canterbury, a diocese

---

[16] The monastery of *Docguin* or *Dochou* (BLD 145) had a daughter house in
Cornwall, called *Docco*, mentioned in the *Vita Samsonis*. Much confusion
has been caused, even among scholars, by the element *doc* entering into the
names of several different saints—Docco, Cadoc, and Oudoceus. See Loth,
Saint Doccus et l'hagio-onomastique (*Mém. de la soc. d'hist. de Bret.*, 1929).
*Cf. further G. O. Pierce, *The Place-names of Dinas Powys Hundred*
111-5.]

[17] *Ad Doroberensem ciuitatem.*

[18] Like *Aircol Lauhir*, *Gurcant Maur* appears in the appendix to the *Vita
Teiliavi* among S. Teilo's contemporaries and benefactors (BLD 118).

[19] Ps. cxxii. 7 and cxii. 3.

of the normal type.[20] On p. 246 of the *Book of Llandaff* we find the consecration of *Gucaunus*, 'bishop of Llandaff', by Archbishop Dunstan at Canterbury in 982, and on p. 252 the election and consecration first of Bishop *Bledri*, and then of Bishop *Joseph*, described in almost the same terms as those used in the story of the election and consecration of S. Oudoceus.

Further, it is most significant that eight of the names of those who are said to have taken part in the election of Oudoceus are found in a charter in the *Vita Cadoci*[21] (c. 65), in which the first witness is *Eudoce, episcopus*. This leads us to the consideration of a most important fact, which promises to provide a remarkable clue to the problem of the composition of the *Liber Landavensis*. The coincidences between certain pages of the latter and some of the charters of the *Vita Cadoci* have been long ago remarked by scholars.[22] I do not think that many to-day will agree with Mr. Gwenogvryn Evans's dismissal of them as "very slight parallelisms".[23] Four at least of the charters with which the *Vita Cadoci* concludes have been reproduced or utilized in the *Book of Llandaff*. In c. 62 of the former we have a charter dealing with property on the river *Nadauan* (the Thaw), with a story about a courtier of King *Morcant* called *Guengarth*, who gave it to 'Saint Cadoc' (i.e. to St. Cadog's monastery of Nantcarfan). It seems to refer to land at Llansannor *ultra Nadauan* mentioned in a charter on p. 148 of the *Book of Llandaff* which is signed by *Guengarth*.

---

[20] The diocese of Llandaff was not a creation *de novo* of the Normans. It was a gradual growth, which can be traced to some extent in the *Book of Llandaff*. Urban still called himself 'bishop of Glamorgan' in 1107 and is not called 'bishop of Llandaff' till 1127. We have an interesting parallel in the case of Cornwall, where a Celtic kingdom possessing several abbey-bishoprics was gradually assimilated to the rest of England. In the middle of the ninth century Kenstec, 'Bishop in the monastery in Cornwall called Dinuurin' (probably Bodmin), submitted to the archbishop of Canterbury (Ceolnoth), and about eighty years later Athelstan made the whole country into a diocese. It was not, however, named after a see-city, as in the rest of England, but was called the bishopric of Cornwall (like the dioceses of Cornouaille and Léon in Brittany), and its bishops ruled sometimes at St. Germans and sometimes at Bodmin. The first bishop, Conan, bore a Celtic name and may have been abbot of St. Germans.

[21] Brit. Mus. MS. Vesp. A. xiv, printed by Rees, *Lives of the Cambro-British Saints*, 1853. It is one of the earliest of the *Lives* of Welsh saints by Norman clerks. *See VSBG 132.]

[22] Haddan and Stubbs, *Councils*, p. 147.

[23] BLD xxviii, note 49.

The next charter in the *Vita Cadoci* (c. 64) is also signed by *Guengarth*, whom the author of the *Liber Landavensis* has introduced several times into his compilation. Then comes the charter signed by *Eudoce* (c. 65), already referred to. That in c. 66 deals with land at *Lisdin Borrion*, granted by *Conbelin* to 'Saint Cadoc'. This has been imitated by the author of the *Book of Llandaff* in a charter (p. 210) in which *Cinuelin* grants *Din Birrion* to *Catguaret*, bishop of Llandaff. In c. 67 we have the charter of *Lann Catgualader* (Bishopston, south-east of Caerlleon, one of the chief manors of the bishops of Llandaff in the Middle Ages). It is stated to have been granted to 'Saint Cadoc' by King *Guoidnerth*, in penance for his murder of his brother *Merchiun*. The first witness is *Berthgwinus, episcopus,* and the third *Terchan*. Turning to the *Book of Llandaff* (pp. 180-3), we find the lengthy charter of *Lann Catgualatyr*, in which the same king grants the same land, for the same reason, but to *Berthguin*, bishop of Llandaff, successor of S. Oudoceus, instead of to Saint Cadog. The witness has thus become the recipient. *Torchan* also appears as a witness. The writer has greatly elaborated the story he found in the *Vita Cadoci* and introduced every name contained in it into his work.

The places referred to in chapters 62, 66, and 67[24] of the *Vita Cadoci* belonged to the see of Llandaff in the Middle Ages and were clearly in the possession of Llandaff when the *Liber Landavensis* was written. The three great monasteries of Glamorgan—Llanilltud, Nantcarfan, and Llandochau—were in a state of decline in the eleventh century (and perhaps had been for a considerable period). They finally died away and were absorbed into the parochial system,[25] their property being transferred to other churches. Tewkesbury abbey, which had been founded by Robert Fitz Hamon, the conqueror of Glamorgan, and S. Peter's, Gloucester, got the lion's share,[26] but Llandaff obtained some of the Nantcarfan lands. The compiler of the *Liber Landavensis* re-wrote the charters he found in

---

[24] C. 60 of the *Vita Cadoci* seems to have been utilized on p. 150 of the BLD.

[25] The process can be traced on pp. 258, 268, 271-4 of the BLD. Nantcarfan and Llantwit were collegiate in the eleventh century.

[26] Hence Bishop Urban's complaint (BLD 88) that his church had been *dispoliata . . . monachorum inuasione.*

the *Vita Cadoci* relating to this newly acquired property. He refers to the author of the *Life of S. Cadog*, Lifris, *filius episcopi, Archidiaconus Gulat Morcant, et Magister Sancti Catoci*, on pp. 271-4 of the *Book of Llandaff*. The problem of the connection between the two documents and the sources of the information they jointly contain is not an easy one. The *Vita Cadoci* belongs to the same class of literature as the *Liber Landavensis*. Their respective authors are both Norman clerks and both have 'faked' the Welsh originals they copied in the same way, inserting stories they have learned from local tradition, though the literary skill and inventive powers of the writer of the *Book of Llandaff* are greatly superior. It is to be observed that it is not only in the charters at the end of the *Vita Cadoci* that we find 'parallelisms' with the *Liber Landavensis*. A careful study of the latter will show the existence in several passages[27] of incidents and phrases plagiarized from the former, showing that its author was very familiar with Lifris's work.

I think we may safely conclude that the writer of the *Book of Llandaff* took the names of Bishops *Eudoce* and *Berthguin*, together with that of *Terchan* or *Trichan*, *Berthguin*'s successor, from the *Vita Cadoci* and added all three to his list of the bishops of Llandaff, identifying the first (as we shall see) with a local saint of east Monmouthshire, and attempting to link him with Dubricius and Teilo by making him a nephew of the latter. That there was a Glamorgan bishop called *Eudoce* we need not doubt, nor that he was the predecessor of *Berthguin*. The witnesses signing after *Berthguin* in c. 67 of the *Vita Cadoci* are contemporaries of *Eudoce* (as several of them appear in c. 65), and the author of the *Book of Llandaff* definitely states (on p. 181) that *Berthguin* succeeded Oudoceus (though afterwards he changed his mind and inserted ten Herefordshire bishops between them), while the witnesses to the *Eudoceus* and *Berthguin* charters which he gives are again in many cases the same persons. But perhaps *Eudoce* would never have become 'Saint

---

[27] C. 12 of the *Vita Cadoci* has suggested not only the details but the language of the *Maidoc* story in BLD 101-2. The curious expression *liquefactus est* in c. 40 has been copied on p. 116 of the BLD. The reference to Gildas living as a hermit on *Echni* (BLD 138-9) is borrowed from the *Vita Cadoci*, c. 34. *For references to more recent studies of this *Life*, see p. 12 n. 69 of this volume.]

Oudoceus' if he had not been identified with the eponym of Llandogo, who *was* regarded as a saint.

It seems impossible to date these three bishops. Apart from the possibility of the *Nobis* of the *Book of Llandaff* being the same person as the Bishop Nobis referred to in the *Annales Cambriae*, who *in Miniu regnavit* in 840 and died in 873, we have no means of dating any of the bishops of Glamorgan before the tenth century. The writer of the *Book of Llandaff* tells us that Bishop *Cimeilliauc migravit ad Dominum* in 927. We have independent evidence (from the *Anglo-Saxon Chronicle*) for the correctness of this date, and the dates which follow in the *Liber Landavensis* seem to be accurate. *Eudoce, Berthguin*, and *Torchan* probably belong to a slightly earlier period. The charters in the *Vita Cadoci* which contain their names are among the last in the series, and have a much more historical look than the earlier ones (some of which give lists of primitive Welsh saints as witnesses !).

We come finally to the very important question : Where did these bishops reside? The name 'Llandaff' has been inserted in the margin of c. 65 of the *Vita Cadoci* opposite the name *Eudoce*, but this must be an after-thought of the Brecon scribe who copied it at the end of the thirteenth century. It has been suggested that *Eudoce* and *Berthguin* were abbots of Llanilltud, because in the charters which they sign members of 'the *familia* of Eltut', but no abbot of the monastery, appear.[28] There is, however, no *evidence* for this; it is only an hypothesis. In c. 64 there are also witnesses *de familia Eltuti*, but no abbot, or bishop either : in fact no abbot of Llanilltud is there mentioned after c. 55. The *Vita Samsonis* clearly represents the monastery as *not* an abbey-bishopric. It is to be observed that the last of the charters said to be granted to Oudoceus (that of *Lann Menechi*) deals with the site of the present cathedral of Llandaff.

After describing Oudoceus's return from Canterbury, the writer proceeds to define the limits of his diocese, in almost the same words as in the *De primo statu Landavensis ecclesiae* on p. 69—*a Gungleis . . . infra Taf et Elei . . . a Mochros . . . usque ad insulam Teithi*. For some time Oudoceus held the whole of the diocese unchallenged, till one day King *Catguocaun* [of Demetia]

---

[28] A. W. Wade-Evans, *Welsh Christian Origins*, 120.

at the instigation of the devil wounded one of Oudoceus's clerks. The quarrel was not made up, and the king "determined to expel the holy man, with his *familia*, from the territory he had possessed beyond the Tyui. And S. Oudoceus departed, leaving the country under a curse, and from that time the Tyui divided the two bishoprics as it divided the two kingdoms—that of Mouric from that of Catgucaun. After an interval Catgucaun repented, asked pardon and restored to him the lands of the church of Llandaff, namely Pennalun and Lannteiliau Maur and Landyfuyrguyr, which had formerly, from the time of Nouy, son of Arthur, belonged to Archbishop Dubricius, and all the churches which had formerly been Teilo's, with their lands". He goes on to state, in a hurried and confused way, that in Oudoceus's time a Saxon invasion rent away the district of Anerging, in the north of the diocese, as well, and, leaving the sentence unfinished, adds incoherently a document in Welsh, headed *Haec est divisio*, which gives a detailed boundary (he does not say of what).[29]

We are next told that Oudoceus, *post tempus suae maturitatis*, visited Rome and obtained there a confirmation of the Privilege of SS. Dubricius and Teilo. Not content with this long journey, "desirous of visiting the places of the saints, he sought with devotion the *locus* of S. David, out of veneration for that saint and the daily remembrance he made of him in his prayers, and reverently took what he pleased of the relics there, and from his own *locus* of Lan Teliau Maur he took away some of the relics of the disciples of his uncle S. Teliau, and placed them all together in a suitable shrine (*arca*). As he was returning through his bishopric to Llandaff, he was attacked by some covetous and disaffected persons at Pennalt in Cetgueli" (Cydweli), who accused him of carrying off "the treasures of S. Deui and S. Teliau". They were struck blind, and their arms, brandishing spears, with which they were threatening the saint, became stiff, but on their repentance they were healed by his prayers.

We have in this section an account of two events of great

---

[29] The document he quotes was probably drawn up when the limits of the diocese of Llandaff were fixed.

historical interest, about which we should be very glad to have authentic information, the creation of the diocese of Llandaff in its present limits, and the transference of the cult of S. Teilo from Llandeilo Fawr in Carmarthenshire, which is here admitted to have been its original *locus*, to Llandaff.

Our author's statement that King *Catgucaun* considered that the boundary of the two dioceses should correspond to the political divisions of the country is his first reference to the existence of the diocese of Menevia. He is describing what we know must have happened when the diocesan system was introduced into South Wales. The reason for the decision where to fix the western boundary of the diocese of Llandaff, put into the mouth of King *Catgucaun* (a personage not otherwise known to history),[30] is quite likely to have been the real one.[31] Later on, in one of the charters appended to the *Vita Oudocei*, our author admits that the diocese had suffered further curtailment in this neighbourhood, losing the peninsula of Gower, which, all through the Middle Ages, formed part of the diocese of St. David's though (according to the *Liber Landavensis*) part of the *dominium Morgannuc*. On the north the boundary defined in the document headed *Haec est divisio* (which must have been among the Llandaff records in our author's time, together with the similar *carta* quoted on pp. 247-8 of the BLD) "is the same as the present boundary between the counties of Carmarthen and Glamorgan, and between Glamorgan and Brecknock as far as the head of the Rumney river".[32] Exactly when the fixing of these boundaries took place we do not know, though it is probable that it took place long after the times of 'Bishop Eudoce'. On the other hand, it need not have been so late as the Norman Conquest. Our author is careful to support Bishop Urban's claims for the restoration of the territory, the loss of which is here described, by saying that *Catgucaun* repented of his action.

The introduction of the normal diocesan system involved the abolition of the older system by which powerful episcopal

---

[30] On p. 118 our author (whose memory was erratic) mentions him among the benefactors of S. Teilo.

[31] Cf. BLD 247 : *Septem sunt cantref in dominio Morgannuc et in episcopatu suo.*

[32] BLD 367, note 4.

monasteries exercised jurisdiction over widely scattered daughter churches. Bishop Nobis, as we know from the marginal entries in the famous *Book of St. Chad*,[33] was 'bishop of Teilo', by which Llandeilo Fawr must be meant. The story of Oudoceus's adventure near Cydweli may be a reminiscence of the transference of the Teilo traditions and relics, together with much of the property, from Llandeilo to Glamorgan, and of the resentment which it naturally caused in Carmarthenshire.[34] In any case it is certain that, by the time of the Norman Conquest, the church of Llandaff had become, beyond dispute, the 'church of Teilo' and its bishop the 'bishop of S. Teilo'.[35]

Why our author describes a raid on the relics at St. David's at the same time it is not so easy to see, but presumably his object is to show the authority of the 'archbishop of Llandaff' over the rival see.

This section of the *Vita S. Oudocei* ends with a local Llandaff legend. There was a gilt bell preserved at the cathedral in the Middle Ages. We are here told that Oudoceus, on his return to Llandaff from the fatiguing journey just described, felt thirsty, and, proceeding to the holy well which still exists on the steep slope above the cathedral (it is accurately described by our author),[36] found some women washing butter there. Having no vessel from which to drink, he asked them to lend him one. They maliciously replied that they had none except the butter which they held in their hands. He took it, shaped it into the form of a bell, and drank from it. It was at once changed into the metal bell honoured in the church of Llandaff in memory of the blessed man. Its touch, they say, heals the sick. It is to be observed that this story reappears in the Middle English metrical *Life* of S. Teilo[37] in the British Museum (Egerton

---

[33] See BLD xlvi.

[34] The details *per viam Pennalt in Cetgueli* are so circumstantial that it looks as if the writer had heard a story of a skirmish near Cydweli, which may have happened not long before he wrote.

[35] BLD 119.

[36] *Fontem in valle Landaviae non multum ab ecclesia remotum.*

[37] Mr. Robin Flower tells me that this manuscript "is an early 14th century copy of one of the South English Legendary and is the only one of the copies of that collection to contain the Life of S. Teilo. The Legendary is generally supposed to have been put together by monks of Gloucester towards the end of the 13th century . . . Gloucester held various churches in S. Teilo's

MSS. 2810, f. 94-99). It is there told of S. Teilo, not of S. Oudoceus, and, as the holy well at Llandaff is called Ffynnon Deilo, it is possible that this represents the original tradition, and that, traditions about 'Saint Oudoceus' being non-existent at Llandaff, our author appropriated this Teilo legend for him.

The author next proceeds to tack on to what he has written in a most extraordinarily clumsy and incoherent way, a couple of local legends about a saint honoured at Llandogo, on the banks of the Wye. He evidently knew the place well and had found there a *Life*, written or oral, of the eponym.[38] *Lann Oudocei*, called *Villa Sancti Oudocei cum ecclesia* in the bulls of Honorius II and Calixtus II,[39] was also called *Lann Enniaun*[40] (we shall deal with the charter describing it later). The writer begins abruptly with a long story:

> Enniaun, king of Gleuissic, while hunting one day, as usual, among the woods and rocks of the river Guy, was greatly surprised to observe the course taken by the stag he was pursuing. Followed by his hounds, with sound of horn and shouts of huntsmen echoing through the valleys, the animal finally, guided by divine providence, took refuge on the cloak (*pallium*) of S. Oudoceus and lay there panting, the huntsmen not venturing to approach and the dogs looking on silent and stupefied. The cloak belonged to the blessed Oudoceus, a man of perfect age and moderate maturity,

diocese. It appears to be based on the Latin life as in the Book of Llandaff, except for the following incident;

hit bi uel upon a time.	that thorst him com opon
hii come bi a water.	wer a maide clene
clansede her boter.	bi a welles streme
sein telyou her bed.	him zuf drink anon
the maid nom the boter.	ne duelde zeo nozt longe
& in forme of a belle.	the boter togader clonge
in the churche of landaf.	thulk uessel is."

*Mentioned also in 'Saint Teilo', p. 202 of this volume.]

[38] It is inconceivable that anyone composing a biography of a real person, after writing seven pages about him, should describe him as *Oudocei, viri perfectae aetatis et moderatae maturitatis, servientis Deo prope flumen Guy, supra rivulum Caletan*, just as if he had never mentioned him before! It is obvious that the *Oudoceus . . . supra rivulum Caletan*, whose legend he now begins, is a different person from Oudoceus the bishop.

[39] BLD 31 and 43.

[40] One of the crosses at Margam is called the Cross of Enniaun, and has on it the inscription CRUX · XPI · + ENNIAUN ·–P ANIMA · GUORGORET · FECIT. *Cf. ECMW 146 : 'The Cross of Christ. Enniaun made (?erected) it for the soul of Guorgoret'.]

serving God by the brook called Caletan [now the Cledon], near
the river Guy. This cloak, upon which he was wont to sleep, he
had taken off, and the stag which had taken refuge with him lay
upon it; and (the saint) gazed upon the beast which the divine
power had tamed, and upon King Enniaun and his hunters, who
were kneeling, with hands uplifted to heaven, imploring pardon.
The king first gave him quiet possession of the stag, and then
granted to God and to Saints Dubricius, Teliavus and Bishop
Oudoceus . . . the whole of the territory he had traversed that
day—the course he had followed, by hill and stream and rock,
marking the limits of the church's land there for ever.   That
blessed saint, after the land, with its bounds, which took from its
donor the name of Lann Enniaun, had been given him, increased
in virtues, and founded there both a monastery (*locus*) and a chapel
(*oraculum*),[41] the place being pleasant and convenient, well supplied
with fish, and solitary; in which place he laboured, with his *familia*,
having abandoned the burden of the pastoral care of Llandaff
because he desired to serve God in the solitary life. And having
called the brethren to him he lived a holy life there with them in
community, assisting, as a kind father, all who came to seek his
counsel.

After a few commonplaces, our author adds that one day,

While he was engaged in prayer, one of the brethren came to him,
saying, 'Good father, come out and see [what has happened to]
the timber prepared for thy buildings', and as he looked, behold a
good and holy man, the historiographer of the whole of Britain,[42]
Gildas the Wise—as he is called in histories, who at that time was
living as a hermit on the island of Echni, passed by in a boat,
having carried off the logs, which he thought belonged to nobody,
seeing he had found them in such a lonely spot. When the blessed
Oudoceus saw this, he summoned his brother [Gildas] to restore the
logs he had taken, or [at any rate] to ask pardon for his unjusti-
fiable action, but no notice was taken and the boat continued on its
way. Oudoceus, filled with indignation, picked up an axe, not
indeed intending to strike his brother, but in order that the power
of God working through him might have a permanent memorial
there. The axe descended on a rock and smote it in two pieces,
and those rocks are still seen by everyone who passes along the
banks of the Guy

(apparently he refers to the stone called *Lech Oudoucui*, which,
as we learn later on, marked the bounds of the church land at

41 Cf. BLD 80, 81, 142, 194.
42 Gildas is thus described in Geoffrey's *Vita Teiliavi* (BLD 100).

Llandogo). The writer then complains of the scantiness of records about the saint (repeating, word for word, two phrases he had used in the *Vita Dubricii*,[43] where they are much more appropriate than they are here), and says that he had only been able to commit to writing a few of the miracles of that holy man, "who, having lived a holy and glorious life and acquired many lands for himself and his church of Llandaff, rested in the Lord on the 2nd of July".

The whole of this section is very carelessly written and is full of disjointed sentences and ungrammatical and obscure passages. It looks as if the writer had made a few hasty notes of stories he had heard during a hurried visit of Llandogo, jotted down anyhow, which he had not had time to work up into a straightforward narrative. The section is incorporated into the *Vita Oudocei* in a very inartistic way. He does not explain how Oudoceus comes to be living by himself on the banks of the Wye till the middle of p. 138, when he informs us, very awkwardly, that he had resigned the see of Llandaff—which flatly contradicts the story he gives us on p. 181, where Oudoceus dies in the midst of his episcopal duties and is succeeded by *Berthguin*.

It is clear that in Celtic times there was an important monastery at Llandogo. Its abbots are twice mentioned in the *Liber Landavensis* (*Guruarui* of *Lann Enniaun* signs a charter granting land to Bishop *Comeregius* on p. 166, and *Diuunguallaun*, *abbas Lann Enniaun*, *id est Lann Oudocui*, signs on p. 223 the charter granted by *Loumarch*, son of *Catguocaun*, after the synod held *apud Lann Oudocui*). The eponym seems to have had at one time a cult extending over the whole neighbourhood. A document of about 1190[44] mentions a *Fontem Sancti Eudaci* in the parish of Dixton farther up the Wye (a mile north of Monmouth). There were several legends about him at Llandogo in the twelfth century, of which our author gives us two. The theme of the stag taking refuge with a hermit is of course an exceedingly common one in hagiography generally (the best known example being in the legend of S. Giles). It also appears very frequently

---

[43] *Pauca miracula . . . antiquissimis scriptis litterarum, memoriae et scripto commendatum est.* Our author has also used this latter phrase on p. 115.

[44] *Lives of the British Saints*, iv. 36, note 1.

in Celtic hagiography,[45] as does that of the course followed
by a prince in a day's hunting becoming the boundary of church
lands.[46] Another story told about the eponym of Llandogo
explained why a stone in the parish looked as if it had been split
in half. It is a typical topographic legend, of the kind so common
in Brittany, in which the patron saint of the parish and that of an
adjacent parish appear in a comic light.[47] The writer had
learned about the residence of Gildas *in insula Echni* from the
Vita Cadoci (c. 34). He mentions *Echni* in the Welsh bounds on
p. 135, and on p. 142 he tells us that King *Teudiric* asked to be
buried there—*locum meum desiderabilem . . . Echni*. It does
not seem on the face of it likely that a hermit on the Flat Holme
needing timber would come all the way to Llandogo to get it,[48]
and perhaps the original story named some saint honoured in the
immediate neighbourhood.

The *Vita* ends most abruptly. The date of the saint's
festival is given, but nothing whatever is said about where, or
how, or when he died. As with innumerable other local Celtic
saints, the record of what he did had entirely perished, nothing
remained except his name, borne by the place where he had
lived and also by a remarkable rock there, and the date of his
annual commemoration.

The *Vita S. Oudocei* is followed by twenty-one charters, or
rather, records of gifts of land, asserted to have been made to the
see of Llandaff in the time of S. Oudoceus by eleven different
kings.[49] They are not in chronological order (this is also the
case with the *Berthguin* charters). They contain some
quotations from documents since lost, and interesting lists of
genuine Celtic names, but everything has been very much
doctored. Our author has inserted some stories of, and
references to, Oudoceus, which supplement the fancy picture he

---

[45] e.g. in the *Vita Petroci* and in the *Vita S. Neoti*.
[46] e.g. in the *Vita S. Kebii*.
[47] In Cornwall we have the story of S. Just purloining S. Keverne's chalice.
These tales were of course never intended originally to be taken seriously.
They were invented to amuse during the long winter *veillées*.
[48] Eighteenth-century prints show barges laden with timber on the Wye at
Llandogo, and this traffic may have suggested the detail in question.
[49] *Cf. J. Conway Davies, EAWD i. 156.]

has composed of 'Saint Oudoceus, archbishop of Llandaff' in the *Vita*. I will briefly note a few of the most interesting features of these so-called charters.

In many of them 'the three abbots' of Glamorgan sign among the clerical witnesses (sometimes as the only clerical witnesses). In others (particularly those not granted by kings of Glamorgan) they are not mentioned.

In the first, *Mouric*, king of Glamorgan, son of *Teudiric*, and his wife *Onbraust* (who in the *Vita* receive the bishop on his return from Canterbury) grant to Oudoceus land at *Cilciuhinn*, *Lann Gemei*, and *Lan Teliau Talypont* (north-west of Swansea). Oudoceus signs as *summus episcopus*—an interesting title, also used on pp. 145, 150 and 159, which looks as if it might possibly be explained by the multiplicity of bishops (many possessing no jurisdiction) in the Celtic Church. On p. 225 the words *sedes episcopi* SINGULARIS ET PERHENNIS *Landaviae* are used. I do not think that *summus episcopus* is merely a synonym for *archiepiscopus*: on p. 162 a Herefordshire dignitary is entitled *Deui*, SUMMUS SACERDOS, *filius Circan*. Six of the witnesses to this charter appear in c. 65 of the *Vita Cadoci* (the Llancarfan charter which is signed by *Eudoce, episcopus*).

Then follows the touching story of the death of *Mouric*'s father *Teudiric*, the patriot king who came forth from the hermitage at Tintern, to which he had retired, to save his country, and was killed at the battle of *Ryt Tindyrn*, and of his burial on *Echni*. It is one of the most beautiful tales in the whole of Celtic hagiography, and is related with exquisite taste and feeling. *Mouric* had an *oraculum* and *cimiterium* made on the spot where he died, and they were blessed by Bishop Oudoceus. He also gave the land (now called Matharn) to the church of Llandaff and its pastors for ever.[50] The Welsh bounds contain, among other interesting names, those of *Lech Lybiau* and *Otyn Lunbiu*. Both *Lybiau* and *Lunbiu* appear later in the *Book of Llandaff*, and *Lumbiu* appears in the *Vita Cadoci* (c. 67).

In the next charter (entitled *Ecclesia Gvrvid*) 'Saint Peter and the church of Llandaff' are mentioned; the three abbots

---

[50] The ancient palace of the bishops of Llandaff at Matharn near Chepstow still exists.

(who are the same as on p. 140) sign. The bounds include a place called *Sedes Cetiau*. *Cetiau* has already been mentioned in the *Vita* (p. 132).

Then follows a particularly interesting charter granting the *podum* and *cella* of *Lann Cingualan*, the *cella* of *Lann Arthbodu*, of *Lann Conuur* or *Congur* and *Lann Pencreic* in Gower. It begins with the cryptic statement that *Oudoceus episcopus suum proprium adquisivit agrum, id est podum Cyngualan, agrum quidem sancti Dubriccii in patria Guhyr*. It goes on to say that S. Oudoceus had lost this land "from the time of the mortality, that is, Y Dylyt Melen, up to the time of Athruis son of Mouric. But, after a great contention between Bishop Oudoceus and Biuon, the abbot of Ildut, who said it was his *ager*, it was finally adjudged to Bishop Oudoceus and to the altar of Llandaff for ever". *Biuon* must be the 'Biuon of the *familia* of Eltut', who is one of the witnesses to the *Eudoce* charter in c. 65 of the *Vita Cadoci*. *Jacob*, abbot of the altar of S. Cadog, also witnesses both charters. It is interesting to find the Yellow Pestilence here referred to by its name in the vernacular, but the statement about Oudoceus losing diocesan territory at that time is of course inconsistent with the *Vita Oudocei*. The *contentio magna* with the abbot of Ildut over this land in Gower is quite credible, for the celebrated cave of S. Iltut was close by—at Oystermouth.

In the charter headed *Lann Merguall* (Llandeilo Ferwallt or Bishopston in Gower) *Morcant*, son of *Athruis*, king of *Morcannhuc*, restores to Oudoceus, *summo pontifici*, together with *Merguald*, the *princeps* of that church under the bishop, on Christmas Day, "the church of Cyngur Trosgardi, which had formerly been Teilo's". The three abbots are witnesses, followed by *Guencat*, *princeps* of *Lann Cynuur*, who appears four pages later (in the *Liuhess* charter) as *princeps* of Penally (*Aluni Capitis*). I have shown elsewhere the significance of the abbot of this great focus of the cult of S. Teilo, which claimed to possess his body, bearing the same name as the eponym of Guengat near Quimper in Brittany, which is a centre of the cult of S. Teilo in that part of Cornouaille.[51] Perhaps Guengat was the channel

---

[51] In the *Liuhess* charter the lay witnesses are the same as in the *Lann Merguall* charter, but the three abbots are all different. The abbots of the *Lann Merguall* charter appear again in the grant of *Villa Conuc* to Bishop *Berthguin*

through which our author got his knowledge of Cornouaille traditions.

Next comes the charter of *Lann Cors*. It is to be observed that the patron saint of Llan-gors church is S. Paulinus, and that *Finnaun Doudecseint* referred to in this charter clearly commemorates the twelve disciples of S. Paul or Paulinus of Léon mentioned by Wrmonoc in his *Vita Pauli Aureliani*.[52] We have here yet another proof that Bishop Oudoceus belongs to a much later period, when a diocesan bishop inherits the property of ancient monasteries already derelict.

The next charter begins with a story of how King *Mouric* and *Cynuetu* made a solemn oath at Llandaff, on the relics of the saints, in the presence of Oudoceus, that they would keep the peace. *Mouric* eventually slew *Cynuetu* by guile at a place *ultra Nadauan*, and was excommunicated by Oudoceus. After an interdict lasting two years the king asked forgiveness. Oudoceus imposed a penance *coram tribus abbatibus*. The king gave the church of Llandaff four *villas* near Llansannor for the redemption of his soul and that of *Cynuetu*. Of these villas one was the place where *Cynuetu* was slain and a second was the scene of another royal crime (*ubi filius regis mechatus est*). Among the witnesses is *Guengarth*. (We have already called attention to this charter and its connection with the *Vita Cadoci*.) The charter which follows also refers to *Cynuetu*'s murder (the exact spot where *Mouric* killed him is mentioned), so that the property with which it deals (*Villa Guilbiu*) must be in the same neighbourhood. *Guengarth* is again a witness, and *Trycan* and *Berthguin* are among the clerical witnesses.

Liuhess [in Radnor] is granted to Bishop Oudoceus by King *Morcant*. Like *Lann Cors*, it was the site of a once famous monastery, mentioned in the *Vita Gildae* as having been founded by S. *Mailoc*, but now apparently derelict. *Guencat* appears as *princeps Aluni Capitis*, and another of the witnesses is *Saturn, princeps Taui urbis*. It has been thought that this means

---

(BLD 176). In the charter in c. 67 of the *Vita Cadoci* the grantor seems to be the same as the *Guednerth* who is a witness to the *Villa Conuc* charter, the abbots of Nantcarfan and Llandochau are the same, and Bishop *Berthguin* witnesses both charters.

[52] I have given the proof for this in my *S. Paul of Léon* 9, 26-30. *See now SC i. 15, 34; also pp. 139, 152, 199n. of this volume.]

Llandaff. It certainly cannot mean Llandochau, whose abbot (*Iudhurb, abbas Docunni*) signs at the same time. In the next charter *Bertguin* signs after Bishop Oudoceus.

On pp. 152-4 we have another story of a royal murder and perjury. *Morcant* and his uncle *Frioc* made a solemn oath to live on friendly terms with each other, at the *Podum S. Ilduti*, in the presence of 'Saint Oudoceus with his congregation' and the three abbots. *Morcant* kills *Frioc* and Oudoceus calls a synod at Nantcarfan (*ad podum Carbani Vallis*). The king comes *cum senioribus Morcannuc* and is absolved after promising to do penance, amend his life, and administer royal justice with mercy. As part of his penance he remits a tribute due to the king from the church of S. Ildut[53] and grants immunities to the three abbeys. Later (on p. 155) we find him granting *Lann Cyncyrill* to Oudoceus *pro anima Frioc*.

On p. 156 our author gives the charter of *Lann Oudocui*. But whereas in the *Vita* it is granted to S. Oudoceus by King *Enniaun*, here it is "restored to Bishop Oudoceus and SS. Dubricius and Teliavus and the church of Llandaff founded in honour of S. Peter" by *Morcant*, king of *Gleuissic*, with its sanctuary (*refugium*), *velut insulam*[54] *undique liberam positam in salo*. The 'Stone of Oudocui' (*Lech Oudoucui*) is one of the boundary marks, which shows that the eponym must have lived long before the time of Bishop Oudoceus. Another place marking the boundary was *Trylec* (='Three Stones'). The *Caletan* also formed a bound. Among the witnesses are the three abbots, with *Berthguin* and *Guengarth*.

The charter of *Ecclesia Elidon* (St. Lythan's, near Cardiff) begins with a story of how "King Iudhail was out riding one day in the land of Guocob, when his horse stumbled and threw him to the ground. He arose unhurt and gave thanks to God, and, looking at the church of Elidon, he said, with his hands raised to God, 'I give this church which I see in front of me, with all its

---

[53] *Utrem mellis et lebetem ferream, quae ecclesia sancti Ilduti regi debebat reddere, quietam rex Morcan clamavit.* This obviously genuine detail gives a curious glimpse into life in Wales in the Dark Ages. To the modern reader it seems very strange that a matter like this should be mentioned in connection with a penance for a murder.

[54] There is a similar expression in the *Vita Paterni* (Rees, *Lives of the Cambro-British Saints,* 194). King *Caradauc* grants to S. Padarn *sint ecclesiae tuae ceu insulae maris magni.* *Also VSGB 260.]

land, and the *villa* of Guocof, where I am standing, to Almighty
God, who has saved me from this danger'." The grant is made
to Bishop Oudoceus, in the presence of the three abbots, and the
first clerical witness is *Trychan*.

The last of the Oudoceus charters is the grant of *Lann
Menechi*. The name, which is the same as the Breton *minihy*,
implies that it had long been church property. It apparently
includes the site of what is now Llandaff. This charter therefore
marks an important step in the history of the diocese. The
grantor is *Brochmail filius Guidgentiuai*. *Guidgentiuai* appears in
our author's *Vita S. Dubricii* (BLD 82), though he must have
lived long after the time of Dubricius. *Guidgen* and *Brocmail*
are among the laymen who elect Oudoceus as bishop in the
Vita S. Oudocei. In this charter we are told that the land adjoins
*villa Giurgii . . . quam dederat Brochmail idem antea simili modo
Oudoceo episcopo*. When we turn back to the charter on p. 151
to which we are referred, we find that *Villa Greguri, quae
dicitur Coupalva* [Gabalfa, near Llandaff] *super ripam Taf* was
given to Bishop Oudoceus by *Guedgen*, son of *Brochmail*. He
must be the same person as the *Brochmail filius Guidgentiuai* of
the later charter. In c. 68 of the *Vita Cadoci* he signs a charter as
Guedgen [also called *Guodgen*] *filius Brocmail*. At least nine of
the persons mentioned in that charter also appear in c. 65—the
charter signed by *Eudoce episcopus*.

We have one more mention of S. Oudoceus in the *Book of
Llandaff*. In one of the *Berthguin* charters (that of *Lann Catgualatyr*,
on pp. 180-3, to which we have already referred), we are told :

> Know ye, most dear brethren, that in the time of Bishop Oudoceus,
> Guidnerth, at the suggestion of the devil, slew his brother
> Merchion . . . and was excommunicated by the blessed
> Oudoceus and by a synod of the whole diocese assembled
> at Llandaff. . . After three years he asked pardon from the blessed
> Oudoceus. The latter granted him pardon and sent him on a
> pilgrimage to the archbishopric of Dol in Cornouaille on account
> of the ancient friendship between the holy fathers his predecessors,
> viz. S. Teliau and S. Samson, first archbishop of the city of Dol,
> and also because Guidnerth and the Britons and the archbishop
> of that land were of one tongue and one race, though separated by
> living far from each other.

(our author repeats, almost in the same words, a sentence in the

story he had inserted in the *Vita Teiliavi*).[55] *Guidnerth*, we are
then told, returned from his exile before the appointed period of
penance was over.   In consequence Oudoceus refused to
absolve him, and he continued excommunicate.

> Before the end of the year [i.e. the year of penitential exile imposed
> upon the king—an interesting reference to this Celtic institution],
> Saint Oudoceus, bishop of Llandaff, *famosissimae vitae*, departed
> to the Lord, and was succeeded by Berthguin.[56]

By comparing this elaborate 'charter' with that in the *Vita
Cadoci* (c. 67) on which it is based, we shall have a very illuminating example of how our author has altered, added to, and
'improved on' older documents, to compose the *Book of Llandaff*.

To sum up, I think we are now in a position to explain a
circumstance that must strike every reader of the *Liber Landavensis*. S. Dubricius, with whom pp. 69-86 are concerned, is
the chief saint of Herefordshire and has a great many dedications
there. The *Life of St. Teilo* deals with a saint whose name is borne
by an exceedingly large number of places all over South Wales.
When we come to the *Life of S. Oudoceus*, we find that only one
place (Llandogo) bears his name (if we except the now forgotten
holy well in Dixton), and no other church is dedicated to him.
It seems clear that the third saint of Llandaff is a bishop who
probably never had any cult at all in early times and who has only
come to be regarded as a saint because the author of the *Book of
Llandaff* has identified him with the eponym of Llandogo.[57]

---

[55] BLD 109; cf. also p. 131 for the writer's fancy that Dol is in Cornouaille.

[56] I have already called attention to the fact that the author of the *Lib. Land.*
afterwards inserted ten bishops between Oudoceus and Berthguin. If the
reader will examine the charters said to have been granted to them, he will
find that they all deal with places in Herefordshire or adjoining districts,
and perhaps came from Mochros.

[57] The statement in *Lives of the British Saints*, iv. 35, that "S. Oudoceus has
found his way into many English kalendars" (the writers fancied that "this
liberal admission into the English kalendars was entirely due to the fable of
his having submitted to be consecrated at Canterbury") seems based on a
mistake. They have confused *S. Iudocus* (St. Josse), the well-known saint of
Ponthieu, who had a great cult at Winchester and whose name does appear
in a great many English kalendars, with *S. Oudoceus. Iudocus* is spelt *Eudocus*
in the *Pontificale Lanalatense* (ed. Henry Bradshaw Society, p. 104) and
Edoce in the kalendar of Salisbury cathedral (MS. 150).

ABBREVIATIONS

AB   *Analecta Bollandiana.*

AC   *Archaeologia Cambrensis.*

AMCA   An Inventory of the Ancient Monuments of Wales and Monmouthshire, vol. viii, *Anglesey* (London, 1937).

ASE   F. M. Stenton, *Anglo-Saxon England* (2nd ed. Oxford, 1947).

ASECC   N. K. Chadwick, *The Age of the Saints in the Early Celtic Church* (Oxford, 1961, reprinted 1963).

BBCS   *The Bulletin of the Board of Celtic Studies.*

BLD   J. G. Evans and J. Rhys, *The Book of Llan Dâv, Liber Landavensis* (Oxford, 1893)—often referred to as the *Book of Llandaff.* Reprinted Aberystwyth, 1979.

CB   M. W. Barley and R. P. C. Hanson, *Christianity in Britain 300-700* (Leicester, 1968).

CCL   D. L. Gougaud, *Christianity in Celtic Lands* (English ed., London, 1932).

CE   I. Ll. Foster and Leslie Alcock, *Culture and Environment. Essays in honour of Sir Cyril Fox* (London, 1963).

CEB   H. Williams, *Christianity in Early Britain* (Oxford, 1912).

CIIC   R. A. S. Macalister, *Corpus Inscriptionum Insularum Celticarum,* 2 vols. (Dublin, 1945, 1949).

Councils   A. W. Haddan and W. Stubbs, *Councils and Ecclesiastical Documents relating to Great Britain and Ireland* i. (Oxford, 1869, reprinted 1965).

Cymmr.   *Y Cymmrodor.*

EAWD   J. Conway Davies, *Episcopal Acts relating to Welsh Dioceses 1066-1272,* 2 vols. (Historical Society of the Church in Wales, 1946).

EC   *Études celtiques.*

ECMW   V. E. Nash-Williams, *The Early Christian Monuments of Wales* (Cardiff, 1950).

EWGT   P. C. Bartrum, *Early Welsh Genealogical Tracts* (Cardiff, 1966).

HW   J. E. Lloyd, *History of Wales*, 2 vols. (3rd ed. London, 1939).

JHSCW   *Journal of the Historical Society of the Church in Wales.*

JRS   *Journal of Roman Studies.*

JTS   *Journal of Theological Studies.*

LBS   S. Baring-Gould and J. Fisher, *The Lives of the British Saints*, 4 vols (London, 1907-1913).

LCBS   W. J. Rees, *Lives of the Cambro-British Saints* (London, 1853).

LHEB   K. H. Jackson, *Language and History in Early Britain* (Edinburgh, 1953).

LRB   A. R. Birley, *Life in Roman Britain* (London, 1964).

NLWJ   *The National Library of Wales Journal.*

PEW   I. Ll. Foster and G. E. Daniel, *Prehistoric and Early Wales* (London, 1965).

PL   Migne, *Patrologia Latina.*

PLECG   N. K. Chadwick, *Poetry and Letters in Early Christian Gaul* (London, 1955).

RBES   R. G. Collingwood and J. N. L. Myres, *Roman Britain and the English Settlements* (2nd ed. Oxford, 1937).

RC   *Revue celtique.*

RCAHM   Royal Commission on Ancient and Historical Monuments in Wales and Monmouthshire.

SC   G. H. Doble, *The Saints of Cornwall*, ed. D. Attwater, 5 vols. (Truro, 1962-70).

SCSW   E. G. Bowen, *The Settlements of the Celtic Saints in Wales* (Cardiff, 1956).

SEBC   N. K. Chadwick (ed.), *Studies in the Early British Church* (Cambridge, 1958).

SEBH   N. K. Chadwick (ed.), *Studies in Early British History* (Cambridge, 1954, reprinted 1959).

SHR   *Scottish Historical Review.*

SPOC   R. P. C. Hanson, *Saint Patrick : His Origins and Career* (Oxford, 1968).

SSSCL   E. G. Bowen, *Saints, Seaways and Settlements in the Celtic Lands* (Cardiff, 1969).

Trans. Cymmr.   The Transactions of the Honourable Society of Cymmrodorion.

TYP   R. Bromwich, *Trioedd Ynys Prydein* (Cardiff, 1961).

VSBG   A. W. Wade-Evans, *Vitae Sanctorum Britanniae et Genealogiae* (Cardiff, 1944).

VSH   C. Plummer, *Vitae Sanctorum Hiberniae*, 2 vols. (Oxford, 1910, reprinted 1968).

WHR   *Welsh History Review.*

ZCP   *Zeitshcrift für celtische Philologie.*

INDEX